The Basics Series

The Basics is a highly successful series of accessible guidebooks which provide an overview of the fundamental principles of a subject area in a jargon-free and undaunting format.

Intended for students approaching a subject for the first time, the books both introduce the essentials of a subject and provide an ideal springboard for further study. With over 50 titles spanning subjects from artificial intelligence (AI) to women's studies, *The Basics* are an ideal starting point for students seeking to understand a subject area.

Each text comes with recommendations for further study and gradually introduces the complexities and nuances within a subject.

ARCHAEOLOGY (SECOND EDITION)
CLIVE GAMBLE

ART HISTORY
GRANT POOKE AND DIANA NEWALL

ARTIFICIAL INTELLIGENCE
KEVIN WARWICK

ATTACHMENT THEORY
RUTH O'SHAUGHNESSY, KATHERINE BERRY, RUDI DALLOS AND KAREN BATESON

BEHAVIORAL ECONOMICS (SECOND EDITION)
PHILIP CORR AND ANKE PLAGNOL

THE BIBLE
JOHN BARTON

THE BIBLE AND LITERATURE
NORMAN W. JONES

BIOETHICS
ALASTAIR V. CAMPBELL

MINDFULNESS
SOPHIE SANSOM, DAVID SHANNON, AND TARAVAJRA

For more information about this series, please visit: www.routledge.com/The-Basics/book-series/B

MINDFULNESS

Mindfulness: The Basics provides a comprehensive introduction to what mindfulness is, how and why it's useful, and guidance for practice.

Mindfulness practice can help reduce anxiety, stress, and low mood, giving way to creativity, happiness, and tranquillity. It also offers us a way in which to acknowledge the limitations and challenges inherent in the human condition. This book covers a brief history of mindfulness, its applications, and a review of the current evidence base, as well as some key debates in the field. Divided into three broad sections, this book explores understanding mindfulness, practicing mindfulness, and future directions. Chapters particularly emphasise the role mindfulness can play in addressing the major environmental, social, and political challenges of our time. The book also contains a glossary of key terms, chapter summaries, diagrams, and an e-resource of audio-guided practices. This book is essential for anyone interested in learning more about practising mindfulness.

Students of mindfulness as well as those in healthcare training programmes (such as nursing, medicine, psychology, and psychotherapy) will find this an invaluable guide.

Sophie Sansom is Co-Director of the Centre for Mindfulness Research and Practice (CMRP) at Bangor University where she teaches on the master's programme. She sits on the International Panel of Acknowledgement (IPA) for the European Association of Mindfulness-Based Approaches and is chair of the British Association of Mindfulness-Based Approaches (BAMBA).

David Shannon is Senior Psychologist at St. Luke's Radiation-Oncology Hospital, Dublin, with a special interest in the application of mindfulness in oncology and palliative care. He previously taught on and led the master's programme at the Centre for Mindfulness Research and Practice (CMRP) at Bangor University.

Taravajra lives in Sussex and has a master's degree in mindfulness from Bangor University. He trains teachers in the English and Spanish-speaking worlds, locally with the Sussex Mindfulness Centre and internationally with the Mindfulness Network. He also guides mindfulness retreats. He is currently the UK member of the International Integrity Network (IMI).

MINDFULNESS
THE BASICS

Sophie Sansom, David Shannon, and Taravajra

Routledge
Taylor & Francis Group

NEW YORK AND LONDON

Designed cover image: Getty Images © peter bocklandt

First published 2026
by Routledge
605 Third Avenue, New York, NY 10158

and by Routledge
4 Park Square, Milton Park, Abingdon, Oxon, OX14 4RN

Routledge is an imprint of the Taylor & Francis Group, an informa business

© 2026 Sophie Sansom, David Shannon, and Taravajra

ISBN: 978-1-032-59214-5 (hbk)
ISBN: 978-1-032-58643-4 (pbk)
ISBN: 978-1-003-45359-8 (ebk)

DOI: 10.4324/9781003453598

Typeset in Bembo
by Deanta Global Publishing Services, Chennai, India

Access the Support Material: https://resourcecentre.routledge.com/
books/9781032586434

"To all our students and teachers."

KEY TO THE ONLINE SUPPORT MATERIAL

Throughout this book a headphone symbol can be found in the margins to reference one of the online audio-guided practices. For example:

Please refer to the audio-guided Intentions Practice.

All support material can be found here: https://resourcecentre. routledge.com/books/9781032586434

CONTENTS

ACKNOWLEDGEMENTS

The authors would like to thank their colleagues at the Centre for Mindfulness Research and Practice (CMRP) and the Mindfulness Network (MN), U.K.

Particular thanks to Prof. Rebecca Crane, Karunavira, Ciaran Saunders (Ruchiraketu), Dr Gemma Griffith, Trish Bartley, Dr Bridgette O'Neill, and Prof. Willem Kuyken (Oxford Mindfulness Centre).

We also wish to thank Prof. Mark Williams and Prof. Paul Gilbert for permission to reproduce their work.

Our thanks too to Routledge and in particular to Ellie Broadhurst, Sarah Rae, and Pragati Sharma.

Sophie extends heartfelt thanks to David and Taravajra for their wisdom and joyful collaboration on this project. Deep appreciation also goes to her colleagues at the Centre for Mindfulness, Bangor University, and the Mindfulness Network for the invaluable learning and growth gained through working alongside them. Finally, she expresses profound gratitude to her family – especially her parents and children – whose guidance and presence continually reinforce the essential role of mindfulness in her daily life.

David would like to thank his co-writers, Sophie and Taravajra, for their support, openness, and sharing in the writing process. Thanks too to David Rynick and my colleagues at St. Luke's Radiation Oncology Network (Rathgar, Dublin), especially Dr

Nicola Elmer for her support and understanding. Finally, my love and thanks to my family and to Siobhán Healy for reading an early draft.

Taravajra would like to thank Sophie and David for their good humour and dedicated work in creating this book. Much gratitude, also, to my colleagues and students in the English and Spanish-speaking worlds who have taught me so much over the years. And of course my love and thanks to my wife Tessa for all her kind support.

INTRODUCTION

Mindfulness has emerged as a key capacity in contemporary discussions about health and well-being, human flourishing, and the challenges of modern living. With its roots embedded in ancient contemplative traditions, mindfulness has transcended cultural boundaries to become a global phenomenon, influencing disciplines as diverse as psychology, education, healthcare, and leadership. This book offers a comprehensive overview of mindfulness, from its origins and mechanisms to its practice and applications.

Structured into three sections, the book aims to provide a nuanced understanding of mindfulness as both an ancient contemplative practice and a contemporary tool for navigating the complexities of life. Section I establishes the foundational concepts of mindfulness. Chapter 1 begins by addressing the question, "What is mindfulness?", offering a clear definition and exploring its multidimensional nature. It considers mindfulness as both a state of awareness and a practice, highlighting its relevance in cultivating presence, reducing stress, and enhancing emotional resilience.

Chapter 2 traces the origins of mindfulness, situating it within ancient traditions (particularly Buddhism) while examining its adaptation and secularisation in modern contexts. The chapter invites readers to appreciate the rich historical and philosophical

DOI: 10.4324/9781003453598-1

underpinnings that inform contemporary mindfulness practices. Chapter 3 focuses on several mechanisms and conceptual models of mindfulness, drawing on neuroscientific, psychological, and pedagogical insights to help explain its effects. As the evidence base and neuroscientific insights continue to grow, this offers a flavour of what happens both objectively and subjectively as people develop a mindfulness practice over time. (The impacts on a socio-cultural level are explored further in Section III.) Chapter 4, "Why practice mindfulness?", synthesises evidence from research and lived experiences, emphasising its potential to foster well-being, improve relationships, and promote personal growth. Together, these chapters provide a robust theoretical framework for understanding mindfulness and its significance in addressing the challenges of twenty-first-century living.

Section II shifts focus to "practice," offering a detailed guide to specific mindfulness practices and their benefits. Chapter 5 discusses the importance of clarifying intention and managing expectations when embarking on a mindfulness journey. It underscores the need for patience, commitment, and self-compassion as individuals start to explore mindfulness. Chapters 6–9 introduce core mindfulness practices. Beginning with the body scan in Chapter 6, this practice cultivates awareness of bodily sensations and acts as the foundation of being present. Chapter 7 explores mindful movement, integrating physical activity with mindfulness to further promote embodied awareness. Chapter 8 delves into formal sitting practice, offering insights into posture, breath awareness, and different ways to structure this type of practice. Chapter 9 highlights short practices for weaving mindfulness into daily life, as well as providing practical tips for those with limited time. The chapters in this section offer a roadmap for developing a sustainable mindfulness practice tailored to individual needs and lifestyles. They also attempt to anticipate some of the common pitfalls and misconceptions that can hamper the development of mindfulness in its early stages.

Finally, Section III expands the scope of mindfulness, exploring its role in broader socio-cultural and existential contexts. Chapter 10 examines the mainstreaming of mindfulness, critically reflecting on its integration in various sectors (e.g., healthcare, education) and the tensions between its traditional roots and contemporary applications. Chapter 11 addresses the "meta-crisis," situating mindfulness within the context of global, human-made challenges such as climate change, social inequality, and technological proliferation. It considers how mindfulness can contribute to collective resilience and systemic transformation. Chapter 12 concludes the book by reflecting on mindfulness as a way of embracing the fullness of human experience, fostering connection, and cultivating wisdom in an increasingly fragmented world. Crucially, this recognises that "being human" means we take our place as a part of nature and not as the rulers of it.

This book invites readers to embark on a journey of exploration, discovery, and transformation. Whether you are new to mindfulness or seeking to deepen your understanding, it offers a comprehensive guide to integrating mindfulness into your life and engaging with its profound implications for humanity.

AUTHORS' NOTE

The authors note their location in the U.K. and Ireland, where the standardised eight-week programmes of Mindfulness-Based Stress Reduction (MBSR) and Mindfulness-Based Cognitive Therapy (MBCT) have had a significant and far-reaching impact. These programmes, as will be discussed, were instrumental in establishing much of the foundational evidence base for the application of mindfulness in healthcare and broader societal contexts worldwide. Additionally, all three authors have contributed as educators on the master's programme offered by the Centre for Mindfulness Research and Practice (CMRP) at Bangor University, North Wales, a programme that is rooted in the principles and practices of MBSR and MBCT.

WHO IS THIS BOOK FOR?

This book is designed to serve a wide and diverse audience, reflecting the multifaceted nature of mindfulness itself. Its structured approach, encompassing foundational concepts, practical applications, and broader societal implications, ensures that readers from various backgrounds and levels of familiarity with mindfulness can find value and relevance in its content. We next provide an overview of the primary audiences for whom this book is intended.

THOSE NEW TO MINDFULNESS PRACTICE

This book provides an accessible introduction to the concept, its origins, and its benefits. Section I lays the groundwork by addressing foundational questions such as "What is mindfulness?" and "Why practice mindfulness?" These chapters demystify mindfulness, making it approachable for individuals who may feel overwhelmed by the breadth of information available. Beginners will benefit from the clear explanations and evidence-based insights that make mindfulness both understandable and relatable.

EXPERIENCED PRACTITIONERS LOOKING TO DEEPEN THEIR PRACTICE

For readers with an established mindfulness practice, this book offers opportunities for deeper engagement and refinement. Section II presents a comprehensive guide to specific mindfulness techniques, including the body scan, mindful movement, and sitting practice. These chapters delve into the nuances of each practice, providing detailed instructions and addressing common challenges. Experienced practitioners will also find value in the discussion of "Clarifying intention," which encourages reflection on the purpose and direction of their mindfulness journey.

EDUCATORS, THERAPISTS, AND HEALTHCARE PROFESSIONALS

As mindfulness becomes increasingly integrated into educational, therapeutic, and healthcare settings, professionals in these fields will find this book to be a practical and theoretical resource. The detailed exploration of practices in Section II equips them with tools to guide clients, patients, or students in adopting mindfulness strategies. Discussion on how mindfulness works in Section I and its historical roots provide a robust framework for understanding its mainstream applications (detailed in Chapter 10) and potential benefits in professional contexts.

SCHOLARS AND RESEARCHERS

This book also caters to academics and researchers interested in the interdisciplinary study of mindfulness. The evidence-based discussions in Section I, combined with the critique of its mainstreaming in Chapter 10, offer a rich foundation for scholarly inquiry. Furthermore, the exploration of mindfulness in relation to global challenges in Chapter 11 provides fertile ground for interdisciplinary research at the intersection of mindfulness, social science, and environmental studies.

INDIVIDUALS SEEKING PERSONAL GROWTH OR COPING STRATEGIES

Mindfulness is often sought as a tool for personal transformation and managing life's challenges. For those seeking to improve their emotional well-being, build resilience, or navigate stress, this book offers practical techniques and inspiring insights. Chapters provide approachable ways to integrate mindfulness into even the busiest lifestyles, while Chapter 12 in Section III invites readers to reflect on mindfulness as a pathway to authenticity, connection, and fulfilment.

SOCIAL AND CULTURAL CHANGE AGENTS

Finally, this book speaks to individuals and organisations striving to address broader societal issues. Chapter 10 examines the role of mindfulness in mainstream culture, exploring both opportunities and pitfalls, while Chapter 11 situates mindfulness within the context of urgent global challenges. These discussions encourage leaders, activists, and policymakers to consider how mindfulness can contribute to collective well-being and systemic change.

By addressing diverse needs and perspectives, this book offers something for a wide range of readers, whether they seek personal insight, professional tools, or a deeper understanding of mindfulness in the context of human and societal flourishing. Its blend of theory, practice, and critical reflection ensures it remains a valuable resource for readers at any stage of their mindfulness journey.

HOW TO USE THIS BOOK

This book is designed as both a theoretical guide and practical resource for cultivating mindfulness. To maximise its benefits, readers are encouraged to approach the content sequentially, beginning with Section I, which lays a solid foundation by exploring the history, mechanisms, and benefits of mindfulness. This context will enrich your understanding as you progress to Section II, which focuses on specific mindfulness practices. These chapters are accompanied by guided meditation audio files, which provide step-by-step instructions to help you experience and refine techniques such as the body scan, mindful movement, and sitting practice. Integrating these practices into your daily life is further supported by the chapter on short practices, offering tools for mindfulness even in brief moments. Section III invites deeper reflection on mindfulness within broader societal and existential contexts, making it ideal for readers interested in the wider implications of their practice. Whether you read cover to cover or focus on particular chapters, this book encourages an experiential approach – you are invited to engage with the practices, reflect on your insights, and revisit sections as your understanding of mindfulness deepens and evolves.

SECTION I
Background

WHAT IS MINDFULNESS?

Beginning a book by defining mindfulness is not as straight forward as it may seem. Although it is no doubt helpful to ensure that reader and writer are both on the same page, as it were, when it comes to the topic of discussion, the inherently experiential nature of mindfulness renders it challenging to describe within the confines of language. Genuine understanding requires direct personal experience, and we have attempted to intersperse such opportunities throughout.

> We invite you to take a moment to look around you. What colours can you see? What shapes? On closing your eyes, what are you able to hear – either from inside the room or outside the building? Now take a moment to notice what sensations are present in your body – warmth, coolness, tension, softness, stillness, movement, the flow in and out of the breath? Simply noticing whatever is there without trying to relax or change anything forms the basis of the experience of mindfulness.

The term "mindfulness" functions as an overarching descriptor and can be used to refer to a type of meditation practice, a particular mode of mind, a way of being, and a trait disposition. Despite the challenge of arriving at an agreed definition, a shared understanding of the term is needed for the integrity of research aimed at evaluating its effectiveness and outlining its potential to influence the human condition.

DOI: 10.4324/9781003453598-3

In 2015, Ladybird published the *Ladybird Book of Mindfulness*, which playfully highlighted common misconceptions and infused lightness and humour into the academic discourse on mindfulness. Receiving three copies of this publication as Christmas gifts prompted the realisation that presentation of evidence needs to be balanced with concepts that resonate with individuals and their everyday lives.

This chapter firstly explores the nature of mindfulness through the identification of prevalent misconceptions and an examination of popular notions and beliefs. Illuminating what mindfulness *is not* serves as a foundational step, allowing us to touch into some indications as to what mindfulness might be. Subsequently, we offer an overview of widely accepted definitions and thus outline some of the conceptual disagreements regarding its fundamental nature.

WHAT MINDFULNESS IS NOT

● **Not simply a way to relax**

"Why not practice mindfulness ... it helps you relax!"

One of the prevailing misconceptions about mindfulness is that its objective is solely relaxation. While altering our relationship with experience by adopting an observational stance can sometimes foster a sense of ease, actively pursuing a distinct state of calm or relaxation is not the primary goal. When we turn our awareness to our mind, body, and emotions, we can often notice that we are far being in a relaxed state. Tensions, frustrations, boredom, and restlessness, along with a diverse array of thoughts, feelings, and emotional states, may come to the forefront. This is normal.

The absence of immediate relaxation does not indicate a failure in the practice. On the contrary, valuable insights and understanding can emerge by acknowledging and exploring such experiences. Approaching these moments with an attitude of curiosity and kindness enriches our exploration of whatever is present for us.

● **Not a way to clear the mind**

"I've tried to meditate but I can't do it … I can't stop myself from thinking."

If the primary aim of mindfulness were to achieve an absence of thoughts, individuals might quickly encounter frustration and discontinue their practice. The human mind inherently operates dynamically, often involved in activities such as planning, reviewing, and analysing. It consistently displays a range of thoughts and emotions, along with memories, concerns, and daydreams.

Even when momentarily experiencing a state of stillness and spaciousness within the mind, it is helpful to acknowledge that this state is transient, with the inevitable resurgence of thoughts on the horizon. The essence of mindfulness does not lie in the eradication of thoughts. Anyone earnestly attempting to "clear their mind" can attest to the near impossibility of this task.

Instead, mindfulness involves redirecting our attention to the present moment, focusing, for instance, on the breath. When our attention strays, as it invariably does, the practice encourages us to gently guide our focus back, repeatedly. This iterative process serves as a training ground for our attentional faculties, thereby enhancing our capacity to choose when to engage in and disengage from the thought process.

Contemporary mindfulness practice does not seek to transition the mind from a state of chaos to one of serenity; rather, it encourages us to acknowledge the chaos, allowing it to exist without interference. In this way, we learn to step back, assuming the role of spectators, observing any internal tumult from a disidentified vantage point, rather than being caught up in the whirlwind.

● **Not just about being happy**

"I practice mindfulness, but I still experience low mood."

Many individuals find themselves contending with unhappiness, physical and/or emotional pain, stress, addiction, or various forms of suffering, and they turn to mindfulness with the expectation of alleviating their distress. Others embark on this path with the purpose of enhancing the quality of their lives, aiming to cultivate a heightened awareness of the often-over-looked moments of pleasure in their pursuit of happiness and inner peace. Irrespective of the initial motivation, sustained engagement in a mindfulness practice has the potential to foster more frequent experiences of contentment, equanimity, and joy in the long run. However, mindfulness practice does not actively seek to induce any specific emotional state. The vicissitudes of life, replete with unwanted events, are an intrinsic facet of the human experience and will invariably persist in some form or another. By observing our lived experiences without judgement and permitting them to exist as they naturally do, we can begin the process of liberating ourselves from the deeply ingrained patterns of thought and emotion that tend to ensnare us. Following this approach, mindfulness can serve as a catalyst for breaking free from cycles of stress, anxiety, and depression.

If possible, inviting you to take a moment now to stop what you are doing and closing the eyes or lowering the gaze. Directing your attention to notice sensations in your feet. Registering perhaps the sensations of contact between the feet and the floor, with socks or shoes, points of pressure or numbness. When you choose, coming to notice the contact between the body and whatever is supporting you. Feel the weight of your body, supported by the ground beneath. Taking a moment now to notice your state of mind; perhaps your mind is busy, full of thoughts, maybe planning or worrying. Or maybe it is quite calm and spacious. Perhaps there is strong emotion around like frustration, anxiety, or fear, or maybe you feel excited or relaxed. Maybe tiredness is here for you right now. As much as possible, simply noticing what is here in the body, heart, and mind. No need to change a thing. Just noticing. Now whenever you are ready, returning your attention to the sensations of contact, wherever the body is being supported. Widening the focus of attention to include, once again, an awareness of the room or place you're in and opening your eyes if they've been closed.

• Not only practiced within religious traditions

"I already have a religion, and it feels like a conflict."

Engaging in mindfulness does not necessitate adherence to a specific belief system or lifestyle. It is fundamentally the act of cultivating a conscious connection to our immediate experiential reality. The insights derived from this practice, whether pertaining to self-understanding, interpersonal dynamics, or our perception of the world at large, can potentially alter our perspective and guide us toward lifestyles that promote not only personal well-being but also that of our broader interconnected world.

While it is true that classical mindfulness finds its historical roots within religious contexts, most notably as a constituent of the Buddhist "Eightfold Path," and many of its insights may have been articulated by adherents of contemplative and religious traditions, it is crucial to recognise that the practice is essentially an exploration of the human condition. Mindfulness has relevance to us all, irrespective of religious or philosophical convictions, offering a pathway to gain deeper insights into our shared human experience.

• Not synonymous with meditation

"Aren't mindfulness and meditation exactly the same thing?"

Mindfulness is a mode of being that can spontaneously emerge or be intentionally cultivated at any moment, such as when observing a beautiful sunset or reading stories to children. It encompasses both a state of experience and a trait disposition, with regular mindfulness meditation practice likely to enhance both. Perhaps taking a mindful moment just now? Pausing and feeling the contact of your feet on the floor or body, wherever it is resting. Allowing your experience of the body in this moment to be as it is.

It is true that mindfulness can be nurtured through meditation, and the term is often associated with a specific type of meditative practice. However, it's important to note that a variety of meditation techniques exist. For example, some meditation practices emphasise the visualisation of certain images or the recitation of specific prayers or mantras, making the two terms non-interchangeable. In this way, the terms do not always mean the same thing.

CLASSICAL DEFINITIONS OF MINDFULNESS

Classical definitions of mindfulness are rooted in the rich philosophical and contemplative traditions of Buddhism. Mindfulness, known as "Sati" in Pali and "Smrti" in Sanskrit, holds a central place in Buddhist teachings (Anālayo, 2019). Key aspects of Buddhist definitions of mindfulness are outlined here.

Present moment awareness (Pali: "Sati"): Mindfulness in Buddhism involves being fully present and aware of each moment. It is about cultivating a deep and clear awareness of one's thoughts, feelings, bodily sensations, and the surrounding environment without being consumed by them.

Non-judgemental awareness: Mindfulness encourages an open and non-judgemental observation of one's experiences. Practitioners are urged to observe thoughts and emotions without attachment or aversion, fostering a balanced and impartial awareness.

Observing impermanence (Pali: "Anicca"): Buddhism emphasises the impermanent nature of all phenomena. Mindfulness involves recognising the transitory nature of thoughts, feelings, and sensations, understanding that they arise and pass away.

Cultivating equanimity (Pali: "Uppekha"): Mindfulness aims to cultivate a sense of equanimity or mental balance. This involves not getting overly attached to pleasant experiences or averse to unpleasant ones but rather maintaining a calm and steady awareness.

Awareness of the breath (Pali: "Anapanasati"): Mindfulness meditation often involves focusing on the breath. The breath serves to connect to and return (when the mind wanders) to the present moment. The breath is also used as a focal point to cultivate concentration and mindfulness.

Mindful action (Pali: "Samma Sati"): In the context of the Noble Eightfold Path, which outlines the path to the cessation of suffering, "Right Mindfulness" (Samma Sati) is a crucial aspect. It involves being mindful and ethical in one's actions, speech, and livelihood.

Four ways of establishing mindfulness (Pali: "Satipatthana"): The Buddha outlined four foundations of mindfulness – mindfulness of the body, feelings, mind, and mental objects. Practitioners systematically explore these aspects of experience to deepen their awareness and understanding of the nature of existence.

Mindful loving-kindness (Pali: "Metta"): Mindfulness is not only about self-awareness but also extends to cultivating compassion and loving-kindness toward oneself and others. This is an integral part of Buddhist practice.

Clear comprehension (Pali: "Sampajañña"): Mindfulness is often accompanied by clear comprehension, which involves an awareness of one's actions, their purpose and suitability, and the impact they have on oneself and others.

Buddhist definitions of mindfulness are interconnected with the broader teachings of Buddhism, emphasising the path to liberation from suffering through understanding the nature of the mind and reality. Different Buddhist traditions contain nuances in interpretation, but the core principles of present-moment awareness, non-judgemental observation, and cultivating a balanced mind remain central.

CONTEMPORARY DEFINITIONS OF MINDFULNESS

In modern times, efforts to define mindfulness in a way that captures its full complexity have been anything but straightforward. The classical understandings, rich in nuance and depth, resist being neatly packaged into a single, universally agreed-upon definition (Chiesa & Malinowski, 2011). To date, there has been no clear consensus on what mindfulness really means or what its core components are (Van Dam et al., 2018). Over the last four decades, researchers have worked hard to dissect, analyse, and explore the essence and relevance of mindfulness. This discussion will spotlight some of the most rigorously studied definitions in the field.

In one study, a group of seasoned meditators (326 participants) shared their interpretations of mindfulness, revealing seven key themes:

1. Attention and awareness – seeing mindfulness as a heightened sense of being present.
2. A non-judgemental attitude – approaching experiences without criticism or evaluation.

3. A strategic approach – using mindfulness as a practical tool in life.
4. Theoretical interpretations – deriving mindfulness from conceptual frameworks.
5. A psycho-affective-spiritual state – connecting mindfulness to emotional, psychological, and spiritual well-being.
6. A path to personal growth – viewing mindfulness as integral to self-development.
7. Uncertainty about its meaning – some admitted they didn't fully grasp it.

Interestingly, these definitions seemed to align more closely with the scientific and academic view of mindfulness than with its roots in Buddhist traditions (Alvear et al., 2022). Next, we explore a few contemporary takes on mindfulness that have emerged from this evolving conversation.

OPERATIONAL DEFINITIONS OF MINDFULNESS

- "Mindfulness means paying attention in a particular way: on purpose, in the present moment, and non-judgmentally" (Kabat-Zinn, 1994, p. 4).
- Ellen Langer describes mindfulness as a flexible state of mind in which we are actively engaged in the present, noticing new things, and sensitive to context and perspective. This is contrasted with mindlessness, described as rigid and automatic behaviour driven by pre-established categories or assumptions. (Langer, 1989).
- Mindfulness, in the context of dialectical behaviour therapy (DBT), is described as a core skill in emotion regulation and distress tolerance (Linehan, 2014).
- "Mindfulness is proposed to involve two components. The first component involves the self-regulation of attention so that it is maintained on immediate experience, thereby allowing for increased recognition of mental events in the present moment. The second component involves adopting a particular

orientation toward one's experiences in the present moment, an orientation that is characterized by curiosity, openness, and acceptance" (Bishop et al., 2004, p. 232).

- Mindfulness is measured across five facets – observing, describing, acting with awareness, non-judging of inner experience, and non-reactivity to inner experience (Baer et al., 2008).
- Mindfulness is operationalised as the presence or absence of attention and awareness in daily experiences (Brown & Ryan, 2003).
- Mindfulness involves the awareness and acceptance of one's thoughts and feelings without attachment or judgement (Feldman et al., 2007).

MINDFULNESS AS A TRAIT DISPOSITION

Mindfulness isn't just something you dip into during a meditation session or a moment of focus – it can also be a personality trait. Think of it as two sides of the same coin: on one side, mindfulness is a temporary state that might come and go depending on the moment; on the other, it can be a more permanent trait – a natural tendency to be mindful throughout your everyday life.

This means that some people might be naturally more mindful, even if they've never done a single mindfulness practice. They're the ones who tend to be more present, aware, and non-judgemental as they go about their day-to-day lives. For those with high trait mindfulness, this quality shows up consistently – whether they're working, spending time with loved ones, or just relaxing. It's like mindfulness is built into their personality, giving them a stable ability to stay grounded and attentive no matter the situation.

PRACTISING MINDFULNESS

Although in many ways the capacity to become mindful is mystical and unfathomable, in other ways it is mundane and straightforward; to know the true nature of mindfulness, it is essential to have an experiential, first-person account of the process. Section II of this book gives a comprehensive overview of the main mindfulness practices. If new to mindfulness, consider using guided meditations, such as those included with this book. There are also many mindfulness apps and online resources that offer guided practice sessions led by experienced meditation instructors. These can help to structure your practice sessions and provide valuable insights. Consistency is key. Set aside time for mindfulness each day, integrating it into your routine. Regular practice enhances the benefits and gradually deepens your mindfulness skills. Remember, mindfulness is a skill that develops over time with practice. Be patient with yourself and approach each session with a sense of openness and curiosity. As you integrate mindfulness into your daily life, you may find it contributing to increased clarity, reduced stress, and a greater sense of well-being.

MINDFULNESS AS A HEALTH AND WELL-BEING INTERVENTION

Mindfulness has been extensively applied and researched in health settings as a mind–body intervention, integrating insights from psychology and stress physiology. Within therapeutic contexts, the aim is to cultivate a heightened awareness of the present moment, serving to highlight automatic tendencies of thinking, feeling, sensing, and behaving. This approach leverages insights gained from an objective observation of thoughts and emotions, allowing individuals to see and acknowledge them, resulting often in being less driven by them.

MINDFULNESS-BASED STRESS REDUCTION (MBSR)

Mindfulness-Based Stress Reduction (MBSR), initially developed by Jon Kabat-Zinn (1990, 2013) to address chronic pain and other chronic health conditions, fosters a renewed sense of the preciousness of present-moment experience, leading to a changed perspective on one's thoughts, emotions, and bodily sensations. Central to MBSR is the cultivation of acceptance of the present moment and recognising habitual tendencies towards avoidance or suppression.

Structured as an eight-week intensive immersion in mindful meditation training, the MBSR curriculum entails weekly two-and-a-half to three-hour classes. Additionally, participants engage in a (predominantly silent) seven-and-a-half-hour intensive retreat session, between weeks six and seven. Its group-based delivery and highly immersive, experiential format facilitated by trained instructors/teachers are notable features. Throughout classes and assigned homework, participants engage in both formal and informal meditation techniques, aimed at enhancing awareness and insight. Regular class discussions provide a forum for participants to share experiences and explore challenges.

In MBSR, non-judgemental awareness of the present moment is a pivotal factor in fostering acceptance and mitigating chronic conditions, as well as addressing the psychological effects these conditions entail. MBSR offers course participants a renewed connection to life beyond the confines of whatever health condition or living situation the person finds themselves trapped within. Students are encouraged to sense the "wholeness" that is part of being human, whatever challenges are being faced.

MINDFULNESS-BASED COGNITIVE THERAPY (MBCT)

Mindfulness-Based Cognitive Therapy (MBCT), developed by Zindel Segal et al. (2002, 2013), is a programme based on MBSR, combining exercises and insights from cognitive behavioural therapy (CBT; Beck, 1979). MBCT was specifically designed to support individuals who were in remission from major depressive disorder (MDD) to prevent future episodes by adopting a kindlier relationship to experience – particularly those thoughts, feelings, and physical sensations that can act as a trigger to future depression. The programme imparts skills that empower patients to disengage from automatic and habitual cognitive processing. Also delivered over eight weeks, MBCT comprises weekly two-hour group-training sessions and a one-day silent retreat. In addition, participants are assigned meditation practices and exercises designed to transfer acquired mindfulness skills into daily life as part of their home practice.

At the core of MBCT is the notion that increased awareness facilitates early identification of signs indicative of depressive relapse. Furthermore, it encourages active disengagement from the ruminative thought patterns typically associated with the depressive cycle (Teasdale et al., 2000). Teasdale and Barnard's (1993) initial research is grounded in an information processing framework. Depression, often triggered by life events, is theorised to establish a connection between the dysphoric, low feeling state and repetitive, ruminative thought patterns. This association reinforces subsequent unhelpful thinking and feeling, heightening vulnerability to relapse. This cycle often happens automatically in a "mindless" state. The concept of "awareness" is posited to integrate cognitive sub-systems and facilitate control over information processing. In response to the dysphoric state, the framework suggests that dysfunctional schemas (ways of thinking and feeling) can be replaced by more adaptive patterns (Teasdale & Barnard, 1993).

THE STRUCTURE OF MINDFULNESS-BASED PROGRAMMES

THE "WARP" FEATURES OF MINDFULNESS-BASED PROGRAMMES

In the context of mindfulness-based programmes, the "warp" features, as outlined by Crane et al. (2017) refer to the common threads or essential elements that define these programmes. These features serve as the foundational principles that weave together the fabric of mindfulness interventions. The "warp" features are integral components that contribute to the effectiveness and consistency of mindfulness-based programmes (MBPs).

INTENTIONALITY AND ATTENTION

Mindfulness programmes typically emphasise the cultivation of intentional, non-judgemental attention to present-moment experience. Practitioners are encouraged to direct their awareness to the unfolding of each moment, fostering a heightened sense of presence and awareness.

ATTITUDINAL FOUNDATIONS

The cultivation of specific attitudes, such as non-judgement, acceptance, patience, and compassion, is a central aspect of mindfulness practice. These attitudes contribute to a more open and receptive approach to experience.

SYSTEMATIC TRAINING

Mindfulness-based programmes often involve a structured and systematic training process. Participants gradually develop their mindfulness skills through guided practices, exercises, and progressive learning experiences.

EDUCATIONAL COMPONENTS

Mindfulness-based programmes frequently incorporate educational elements that provide participants with a conceptual understanding of the principles behind mindfulness. This includes insights into the nature of thoughts, emotions, and the potential for cultivating a mindful way of life.

INTEGRATION INTO DAILY LIFE

The application of mindfulness beyond formal practice sessions is emphasised. Mindfulness-based programmes encourage participants to integrate mindfulness into their daily lives, fostering a continuous awareness that extends beyond the structured sessions.

GROUP LEARNING AND PRACTICE

Mindfulness interventions often involve group settings where participants can share their experiences, challenges, and insights. Group dynamics and collective learning contribute to the effectiveness of these programmes.

THE "WEFT" FEATURES OF MINDFULNESS-BASED PROGRAMMES

In the context of mindfulness-based programmes, the "weft" features, as outlined by Crane et al., (2017) refer to the contextual and variable elements that can be adapted and woven into the overall structure of mindfulness interventions. Unlike the "warp" features that are considered essential and foundational, the "weft" features allow for flexibility and customisation based on the specific context and population.

TAILORING TO POPULATION CHARACTERISTICS

Mindfulness-based programmes can be adapted to suit the characteristics, needs, and preferences of participants. This includes considerations for cultural and neurodiversity, age groups, and specific populations such as clinical or non-clinical settings.

PROGRAMME FLEXIBILITY

The "weft" features acknowledge the adaptability of mindfulness-based programmes. They can be modified to accommodate variations in programme length, intensity, and format based on the goals of the participants and constraints of the setting.

Since the development of MBSR and MBCT, a diverse array of mindfulness-based approaches to emotional health and well-being have emerged, finding application in various settings. One example is Mindfulness-Based Relapse Prevention (MBRP; Bowen et al., 2009a) which has evolved through the integration of cognitive behavioural relapse prevention (Marlatt & Gordon, 1985) and mindfulness practices. MBRP is designed as a six-week course specifically tailored to assist individuals in remission in overcoming addiction challenges. The approach seeks to elevate unconscious automatic triggers of addictive behaviour into conscious awareness, thereby facilitating conscious control. Targeting negative mood and cravings, the therapy aims to diminish the risk of substance-use relapse.

In more recent times, novel and inventive programmes, such as the BAM! (Boxing and Mindfulness) programme in the U.K. have emerged with the aim of expanding the scope and application of mindfulness, as well as enhancing its accessibility. Noteworthy initiatives include mindfulness-based inclusion training (MBIT; Francis & Francis, 2021), designed to cultivate inclusivity; and Inner Change Works, developed at Bangor University, which harnesses mindfulness, compassion, and other meditative practices to promote pro-social and environmental behaviours and support change makers with eco anxiety and burn out, commonly associated with social justice and environmental recovery. Mindfulness is also a core component of other therapeutic interventions, collectively known as third wave therapies. These include acceptance commitment therapy and dialectical behaviour therapy, outlined next.

ACCEPTANCE AND COMMITMENT THERAPY (ACT)

Acceptance and commitment therapy (ACT; Hayes et al., 2001), rooted in relational frame theory (RFT; Hayes, 1991), posits that the potency of thoughts, emotions, and physical sensations is derived from the verbal evaluation of the context in which they arise. The theory delineates six key elements: "acceptance" of unpleasant thoughts and feelings; "defusion," involving the dis-identification of cognition and emotion; 'contact with the present moment'; the conception of the "self as a context" (a transitory process), and a commitment to engaging in adaptive and functional "values" and "actions." The overarching objective of ACT is to foster the acceptance of unwanted thoughts and emotions while discouraging "avoidance" behaviours. This approach aligns with the fundamental principles of relational frame theory, emphasising the transformative potential of altering one's relationship with internal experiences through acceptance and committed action.

DIALECTICAL BEHAVIOUR THERAPY (DBT)

Dialectical behaviour therapy (DBT), developed by Marsha Linehan in 1993, is specifically tailored for the treatment of borderline personality disorder (sometimes called emotionally unstable personality disorder (EUPD)), postulated to stem from an "invalidating" developmental environment. This therapeutic approach encompasses weekly sessions customised to individual needs. The treatment structure incorporates four categories of group skills training, namely, inter-personal effectiveness skills, emotion modulation skills, distress tolerance skills, and core mindfulness meditation skills. The primary focus of DBT is to enhance awareness of dysfunctional thought patterns and emotions. Through targeted skill development in interpersonal effectiveness, emotion regulation, distress tolerance, and mindfulness, the therapy seeks to empower individuals to navigate and manage their internal experiences more effectively.

MINDFULNESS AS A PSYCHOLOGICAL RESEARCH METHOD

Mindfulness has become a go-to tool in therapy, mainly used to improve health and well-being. While this is undoubtedly valuable, focusing solely on mindfulness as a health intervention risks overlooking its broader potential. Stanley et al. (2015) caution that squeezing mindfulness into the framework of traditional scientific methods could dilute its deeper significance as a unique way of exploring the mind.

Often described as a kind of "interior empiricism" (Williams, 2011), mindfulness offers a first-person method for investigating mental processes. It's not just about fixing problems but about deeply understanding the workings of the mind. William James (1890), often hailed as the father of American psychology, shared a similar vision. He argued that objects and subjective experiences aren't separate but deeply intertwined – an idea that aligns closely with Buddhist teachings on the interconnectedness of mind and world (Wallace, 2002).

Stanley et al. (2015) delved into how mindfulness and introspection compare as tools for psychological inquiry. Both involve turning inward, observing thoughts and emotions, and investigating the present mental state. Buddhism's view of the mind as interdependent and constantly shifting has clear parallels with James' concept of the "stream of consciousness." But there's a key difference: introspection focuses on observing and analysing thoughts, while mindfulness emphasises awareness and direct experience.

This shift from thinking to experiencing makes mindful awareness a potentially more objective way to study the mind. It echoes Einstein's assertion that true understanding doesn't come from pure logic alone but starts and ends with experience (Einstein, 1954). Mindfulness, in this sense, isn't just a therapeutic tool; it's a powerful means of exploring what it means to think, feel, and exist.

THE WORK OF ELLEN LANGER

Ellen Langer is an American social psychologist who developed a Western form of mindfulness distinct from the Eastern, meditation-based practices (Langer, 2014). Her approach emphasises novelty seeking, creativity, flexibility, and engagement. In her work, mindfulness is defined as the everyday capacity to notice new things, fostering awareness of variability, and actively drawing distinctions. Langer's perspective emerged independently of Buddhist influences and is grounded in Western scientific frameworks, prioritising adaptability and practical engagement over meditative discipline. Her work provides an alternative lens for investigating mindfulness, encouraging exploration and a responsiveness to one's environment.

THE CHALLENGES OF MEASURING MINDFULNESS

As we have seen, the term *mindfulness* refers to a diverse array of practices, processes, and attributes. This makes measuring mindfulness challenging, and research often relies upon self-report scales that examine a range of related qualities. A few examples of the most widely used tools in measuring mindfulness include:

The Mindful Attention Awareness Scale (MAAS; Brown & Ryan, 2003)
The Freiburg Mindfulness Inventory (FMI; Buchheld et al., 2001)
The Cognitive and Affective Mindfulness Scale (CAMS) Revised (Feldman et al., 2007)
The Southampton Mindfulness Questionnaire (SMQ; Chadwick et al., 2008)
The Five Facet Mindfulness Questionnaire (FFMQ; Baer, 2008)
The Toronto Mindfulness Scale (TMS; Lau et al., 2006)

Grossman (2008) raises some important – and thought-provoking – questions about how we measure mindfulness, shining a light on issues that are often overlooked. The following is a breakdown of some key concerns:

Conceptual confusion: Different researchers often understand and apply the concept of mindfulness in vastly different ways, leading to inconsistencies.

Buddhist roots overlooked: Many psychometric tools for measuring mindfulness are developed by individuals with limited knowledge of Buddhist philosophy, even though mindfulness is deeply rooted in these traditions.

Misinterpretation of scale items: Respondents may interpret mindfulness questionnaire items in very different ways, often influenced by their own experiences and practices.

Perceived vs. actual mindfulness: There's often a gap between how mindful someone thinks they are and their actual mindfulness levels.

Experience bias: People with long-term meditation experience might view and answer mindfulness scales differently from those new to brief programs like MBSR or MBCT.

Another layer to this discussion is the growing reliance on neuroscience to validate mindfulness. While the neuroscientific evidence base has gained popularity in recent years, it's worth asking whether this trend addresses – or perhaps amplifies – some of the conceptual and methodological issues Grossman highlighted back in 2008. It's a reminder that while measuring mindfulness is valuable, it's far from straightforward.

CONCLUSION

In conclusion, this chapter has attempted to provide a comprehensive exploration of mindfulness, a construct that has evolved significantly across classical, contemporary, and operational definitions. By delineating what mindfulness is and is not, it has established the conceptual boundaries necessary for both theoretical clarity and practical application. The examination of mindfulness as a trait disposition has highlighted its innate and enduring qualities, while its role as a health and well-being intervention has underscored its transformative potential in mitigating psychological distress. Furthermore, positioning mindfulness as a psychological research method has revealed its utility in advancing empirical inquiry and understanding human cognition and behaviour. Nevertheless, the chapter also addressed the inherent challenges in measuring mindfulness, including issues of construct validity, methodological consistency, and cultural considerations. These challenges underscore the necessity for continued critical engagement and methodological innovation within the field. As mindfulness continues to permeate diverse domains, an interdisciplinary and reflective approach remains vital to ensuring its integrity, efficacy, and applicability across contexts. This chapter may serve as a framework for navigating the complexities and promise of mindfulness, in answering the foundational question, "What is mindfulness?"

CHAPTER SUMMARY

- Mindfulness, originally rooted in Buddhist philosophy, has evolved to encompass various dimensions, including meditation, experiential awareness, and a way of life.
- This chapter has outlined several misconceptions surrounding mindfulness, highlighting what it does not entail.
- Classical, contemporary, and operational definitions of mindfulness were offered.
- Beyond its traditional role as a religious practice, mindfulness has found contemporary application in diverse psychological interventions aimed at enhancing health and well-being.
- Subsequent chapters will outline key research underpinning the efficacy of mindfulness.
- Important conceptual and methodological disparities in the study of mindfulness were highlighted. Establishing consensus on the nature of mindfulness is a prerequisite for accurate measurement and developing research in this area.

WHERE DOES MINDFULNESS COME FROM?

As we saw in the previous chapter, there are diverse understandings and a myriad of approaches that include the word *mindfulness*. A simple internet search will show us that it is possible to find "mindful running," "mindful knitting," "mindful chef," "mindful tango," and many other applications. In this chapter, we will explore mindfulness as it is understood in contemporary psychological interventions as described in Chapter 1.

It could be argued that as mindfulness is synonymous with awareness, it does not "come from" anywhere but is rather an inherent human capacity that is available for each of us to develop. Indeed, people have been practising mindfulness for thousands of years, whether on its own or as part of a larger tradition. As Jon Kabat-Zinn points out, we do not call gravity "British" because it was "discovered" by Isaac Newton (Boyce, 2011). It is a universal quality. In an interview with Vox (2023), Kabat-Zinn stated: "in the case of mindfulness, it's something that has very ancient roots in humanity and is, I would say, universal in its availability to us as human beings. So, although it is, formally speaking, the heart of Buddhist meditation practice, it really is universal, as most of the Buddha's core teachings have to do with the nature of mind and the nature of reality and not being part of a particular kind of clique or subset or religious group."

The question of the origins of mindfulness can be explored from at least two perspectives: firstly, by peering into the dim and distant mists of long, long ago; and, secondly, by looking at more modern approaches and identifying the main influences on the development of these.

DOI: 10.4324/9781003453598-4

A COMPARISON WITH THE ROOTS OF MODERN APPROACHES TO YOGA

The practice of mindful movement, rooted in hatha yoga postures, has always played a key role in Mindfulness–Based Stress Reduction (MBSR) and, to a lesser extent, Mindfulness–Based Cognitive Therapy (MBCT). This is because Jon Kabat-Zinn, the founder of MBSR, was both a yoga practitioner and teacher. Since yoga is a globally recognised practice, it may be useful to explore its origins first before examining the development of modern mindfulness. One intriguing question is whether ancient texts or images, especially from India, reveal recognisable yoga postures (asanas).

It's believed that early meditators, dealing with aches from long hours of sitting, began observing the movements of nearby animals and realised the benefits of stretching (Stahl & Goldstein, 2010). This discovery is thought to have given rise to yoga, with its origins traced back over 5,000 years to northern India. The term *yoga* first appeared in the Rig Veda, a sacred text written in Sanskrit, where it referred to the harmonising of body and mind. The Vedas, a collection of four ancient texts, remain foundational to Indian spiritual traditions.

However, modern researchers like Singleton (2010) argue that many of the yoga postures practiced today are far more recent. Singleton's surprising thesis suggests that contemporary yoga, rather than being a direct continuation of ancient traditions, owes much to the influence of Indian nationalism and even early twentieth-century European bodybuilding and women's gymnastics. According to this view, most popular yoga postures date back only to the 1930s, particularly under the guidance of the teacher Krishnamacharya.

LOOKING BACK INTO THE DISTANT PAST FOR MINDFULNESS

We can identify mindfulness in many ancient traditions and religions. Certainly, Buddhism, Hinduism, Christianity, Islam, and Judaism all have meditative traditions although these may have different methods and intended outcomes. For example, practising the Presence of God (Christianity) or having a continuous awareness of Allah (Islam) may be examples of comparable mindful practices. Can we accurately discover these practices and principles in ancient writings? When we investigate different traditions, what precisely is being compared?

CAN WE TRACE ANY ROOTS OF MINDFULNESS IN HINDUISM?

It is possible that mindfulness can be traced back to the yogic practices of the Hindu people, which date from around 2300–1500 BCE in the Indus Valley, near modern-day Pakistan. Hindu scriptures contain numerous references to meditation, silence, and acceptance, all of which are key elements of modern mindfulness.

One such practice is "Dhyāna," which in Hinduism means contemplation. It is practiced during yoga exercises and involves attaining "samadhi," a state of meditative consciousness where the mind becomes very still and merges with the object of attention. In this state, one observes internal processes without becoming entangled in them. Mindfulness is a preparatory practice for *raja yoga*, which leads to the advanced attainment of higher states of consciousness and, ultimately, union with the Divine as the omnipresent and loving consciousness within us (*Hinduism Today*, 2019).

MINDFUL PRACTICES IN OTHER RELIGIOUS TRADITIONS

Mindfulness practices are not exclusive to Eastern religions; they may also be found in Judaism, Christianity, and Islam (Trousselard et al., 2014). There are Jewish mindfulness teachers who draw on the approaches of Jewish spiritual teachers going back thousands of years (e.g., Epstein, 2019; Feiner, 2021). In Christianity, mindfulness is reflected in several teachings and practices. For example, Jesus speaks of the innermost "I Am" referring to the essence of every individual's identity and life. Another example is Brother Lawrence, who emphasised being aware of the "Holy Spirit" in his work "Practising the Presence of God" (Lawrence, 1999).

Several Christian authors have explored the concept of mindfulness from a Christian perspective. Irene Kraegel's *The Mindful*

Christian (2020) and David Harper's *A to Z of Mindfulness for Christians* (2023) are notable works in this area.

However, there is also opposition to mindfulness within the Christian community. Some argue that mindfulness has pagan roots and contradicts Christian teachings. They believe that true spiritual growth comes from uniting with Christ and the Holy Spirit, not from finding one's own divinity. The Spanish bishops' conference, for example, stated that mindfulness and other Eastern meditation techniques are not properly Christian practices of prayer and warned Catholics that engaging in such practices risks "effectively abandoning the faith" (*Catholic Herald*, 2019; *Christian News Journal*, 2020).

In Islam, mindfulness may be compared to the practice of "Muraqabah," which means maintaining continuous awareness that Allah is always watching. The concept of mindfulness in Islam is rooted in the idea of "Fitrah," the pure core within everyone that is present from birth, regardless of caste, creed, or religion (My, 2020).

Islamic mindfulness practices aim to retrieve this purity from the layers of life's experiences, lifting the heart, mind, and body into wellness, peace, and happiness. There is debate within the Muslim community about the compatibility of mindfulness with Islamic teachings. Some Muslims argue that mindfulness is un-Islamic or *haram* because of its origins in Buddhism and its potential to carry Buddhist ideas. Others, however, contend that mindfulness is fundamental to Islam and can enhance an Islamic way of life.

In conclusion, while mindfulness practices have the clearest historical roots in Eastern religions, they also may have significant expressions in Judaism, Christianity, and Islam. These practices are both embraced and contested within these traditions, reflecting a diverse range of perspectives on the integration of mindfulness with spiritual practice.

LOOKING AT THE MORE RECENT PAST

The second way of exploring these questions is to look at the primary influences on the main forms of mindfulness that most people in the twenty-first century will encounter (as we did with yoga, earlier in this chapter). In the modern world, (and increasingly around the world) people encounter mindfulness through the various mindfulness-based programmes that have been developed since the 1980s. MBSR and MBCT are perhaps the best known. Originally taught in an eight-week "in person" format, a range of different mindfulness courses can now be accessed online, as well as via podcasts, a multitude of apps (e.g. Headspace, Calm), and, of course, the ever-growing literature on the subject.

As we have seen, many religions have their own form of meditation practice or understanding of mindfulness conceptually. However, the primary form of mindfulness practiced today originated from the Buddhist tradition. As the developer of MBSR, Jon Kabat-Zinn, has pointed out, perhaps the best "articulation" of mindfulness comes from within the Buddhist tradition, as mindfulness has been playing a key role in being healthier, happier and less stressed within Buddhism for over two and a half thousand years.

In fact, many modern commentators (e.g. Gethin in Williams & Kabat-Zinn, 2011) consider that the word *mindfulness* is a translation of the Buddhist concept of *Sati*. This understanding is derived from the work of Victorian translators of Indian Buddhist texts such as T. W. Rhys David (1995). Sati, "moment to moment awareness of present events," or "remembering to be aware of something" is the first factor of the Seven Factors of Enlightenment (Anālayo, 2003), so it is easy to see how mindfulness is viewed as being at the core of Buddhism. The origins of modern mindfulness approaches like MBSR and MBCT are deeply rooted in classical Buddhist teachings, particularly the *Noble (or Ennobling) Eightfold Path* and the *Satipatthana Sutta*.

NOBLE EIGHTFOLD PATH

The Noble Eightfold Path, a foundational teaching of Buddhism, emphasises ethical conduct, mental discipline, and wisdom. Modern mindfulness practices draw upon several elements of this framework: Right Mindfulness (Samma Sati) and Right Intention (Samma Sankappa) are two of the eight limbs (Gethin 1998).

THE SATIPATTHANA SUTTA

The Satipatthana Sutta (*sutta*, literally a thread, means a teaching of the Buddha) outlines the four ways of establishing mindfulness, which directly inform both traditional meditation and modern mindfulness programmes (Anālayo, 2003).

1. Mindfulness of the Body (Kaya):

Buddhist teachings emphasise observing physical sensations, breath, and postures. In MBSR, the body scan meditation aligns closely with this practice, helping participants develop awareness of bodily sensations and physical tension (Kabat-Zinn, 2013).

2. Mindfulness of Feeling tone (Vedana):

The Sutta highlights observing pleasant, unpleasant, and neutral sensations. Both MBSR and MBCT programmes include pleasant and unpleasant event calendars.

MBCT incorporates this into training participants to notice emotional states and their transience, reducing reactivity to negative emotions (Segal et al., 2013).

3. Mindfulness of Mind states (Citta):

Buddhist practice involves recognising mental states (e.g., anger, joy).

Modern mindfulness helps participants identify and relate differently to mental events, fostering cognitive flexibility and emotional balance (Shapiro et al., 2006).

4. Mindfulness of Phenomena (Dhamma):

Observing the impermanence and interdependence of experiences is central in Buddhism. In contemporary mindfulness, this is reflected in exercises that encourage participants to observe thoughts and sensations as transient, reducing identification with distressing thoughts.

Given this clear background in Buddhist teachings, can we say that mindfulness is, in essence, a form of Buddhism? Is it stealth

Buddhism (as is sometimes asserted)? Can you practise mindfulness if you are a Christian, Muslim, atheist, Druid, or Rastafarian? Is it secular, non-religious? Certainly, it has always been the avowed intention of mindfulness teachers that the benefits of mindfulness practice be made available to anyone who wanted to give it a try (Vox, 2023). Perhaps a helpful approach is to acknowledge and honour the traditional roots of mindfulness and, at the same time, be open to other expressions of present moment awareness in other religions and traditions, for example, Ubuntu in the African tradition ("I am only because you are") (Ngomane, 2019). The theme of creating a more inclusive approach to MBSR teaching is explored in the important paper "Mindfulness-Based Stress Reduction for Our Time: A Curriculum that is up to the Task" (Crane et al., 2023).

And it is clear that the main "secular" forms of modern mindfulness (e.g. MBSR, MBCT) are available to all and taught in university Masters courses and offered as an evidence-based psychological treatment for recurrent depression within the UK National Health Service (Nice Guidance, 2022).

Now we will examine the cultural influences which shaped Jon Kabat-Zinn, the founder of MBSR. Matt Nisbet (2017) paints a vivid picture of the era in which Kabat-Zinn was immersed. During the 1960s, changes to US immigration policies opened the door for many Buddhist teachers from Asia to move to America. This wave of immigration included prominent Tibetan and Japanese Zen teachers who established Buddhist centres and visited college campuses, sparking a growing interest in Eastern philosophies. Their presence led to the creation of university courses on Buddhism, attracting students eager to explore counter-cultural alternatives to dominant Western ideologies. Some of these students, along with other spiritual seekers, travelled to South Asia to study Buddhism firsthand or encountered meditation practices through programs like the Peace Corps (Wilson, 2014).

By 1976, a pivotal moment in the spread of Buddhist-inspired practices in the West occurred. Joseph Goldstein, Jack Kornfield, and Sharon Salzberg – each having studied Buddhist meditation in Asia – founded the Insight Meditation Center in Barre, Massachusetts. Their goal was to bring their transformative experiences to the United States, but in a way that transcended the traditional monastic context. Their teachings and writings blended insights from Buddhist meditation with Western psychology and psychotherapy, stripping away elements like chanting, ceremonial practices, and Buddhist cosmology to make the practices more accessible and relatable to Western audiences (Wilson, 2014).

This rich cultural context of East meeting West, coupled with the blending of spiritual practices and scientific inquiry, set the stage for Kabat-Zinn to develop MBSR – a program rooted in mindfulness but designed for a secular, therapeutic setting.

Another significant influence on the rise of mindfulness in America was the Buddhist monk Thich Nhat Hanh. Exiled from Vietnam, he became well-known in the 1960s as a speaker and anti-war activist. By the mid-1970s, he had begun focusing on promoting mindfulness and meditation, writing *The Miracle of Mindfulness* (1991) and over 100 other books. Alongside the Dalai Lama, Thay (as his students called him) was one of the world's most well-known Buddhists, frequently appearing on Oprah Winfrey's talk show and touring the United States annually (Wilson, 2014).

THE ARISING OF MBSR

MBSR was developed by Dr Jon Kabat-Zinn in the late 1970s at the University of Massachusetts Medical School. Kabat-Zinn, a molecular biologist turned yoga and meditation teacher, drew upon various influences to create MBSR, which has since become one of the most widely used mindfulness programmes in the world. This section outlines some of the key influences and the development of MBSR.

Kabat-Zinn himself was heavily influenced by Buddhist meditation practices, particularly Vipassana and Zen traditions. He adapted these traditional practices into a secular form suitable for a Western audience, stripping away the religious and cultural elements to focus solely on mindfulness techniques. "I bent over backwards to structure it and find ways to speak about it that avoided as much as possible the risk of it being seen as Buddhist, new age, eastern mysticism or just plain flakey" (*The Guardian*, 2017).

Kabat-Zinn was also influenced by the burgeoning field of mind–body medicine, which emphasises the connection between mental and physical health. He recognised the potential of mindfulness meditation as a tool for managing stress and promoting overall well-being. He emphasised the notion of wholeness. Kabat-Zinn integrated principles from Western psychology, including stress physiology and behaviour modification techniques, into the MBSR programme. This incorporation helped to frame mindfulness practices in a language and context familiar to Western audiences and made them more accessible to a much broader range of people.

MBSR was initially developed as a programme for patients suffering from chronic pain at the University of Massachusetts Medical Center. Drawing from his experiences working with these patients, Kabat-Zinn tailored the programme to address their specific needs and challenges, such as managing pain-related stress and improving quality of life. Yoga played a significant role in the development of MBSR. As a practitioner and teacher of hatha yoga, Kabat-Zinn was well equipped to incorporate gentle yoga exercises into the programme to promote physical relaxation and embodiment, complementing the other mindfulness meditation practices.

His work has significantly contributed to the integration of mindfulness into clinical settings, transforming it from a spiritual practice to a secular, evidence-based intervention. Kabat-Zinn's key innovation, as noted by Wilson (2014), was to transform the traditional week-long meditation retreat, which was often inaccessible to those with busy lives, into a more flexible format. He offered participants classes once a week for two months, with each course typically accommodating between thirty-five and forty participants. These participants were assigned guided meditation recordings to use at home for 45 minutes each day throughout the course. Additionally, they were instructed on how to maintain mindfulness of their breath during daily activities, thereby integrating meditative awareness into all aspects of their lives (Kabat-Zinn, 2013).

Kabat-Zinn recognised that healthcare settings were ideal for the application of mindfulness because they are places where people seek relief from suffering. By positioning MBSR as a complement to medical treatment, he facilitated its acceptance in clinical contexts (Harrington & Dunne, 2015). By promoting mindfulness, he argued that meditation could help patients manage the suffering associated with illness by fostering greater acceptance of their experiences. This acceptance could, in turn, lessen pain, anxiety, and depression. While traditional medical treatment would still be necessary for most, meditation could expedite recovery and better prepare patients for future challenges (Harrington & Dunne, 2015).

To ensure the quality and fidelity of MBSR programmes, Kabat-Zinn established rigorous training and certification processes for instructors. Many instructors hold advanced degrees in mental health professions and are required to engage in ongoing training (Santorelli & Kabat-Zinn, 2013). By transforming meditation into a clinical intervention, its effects on a range of mental, physical, and behavioural outcomes could be systematically evaluated and published in peer-reviewed literature (Wilson, 2014). From the beginning, Kabat-Zinn's approach emphasised the importance of empirical research to validate the efficacy of mindfulness interventions. Numerous studies have since demonstrated the benefits of MBSR for a range of mental and physical health conditions (Baer, 2003, Grossman et al., 2004).

By publishing in peer-reviewed journals and presenting at scientific conferences, Kabat-Zinn helped establish mindfulness as a credible and effective intervention within the medical and psychological communities (Kabat-Zinn et al., 1992). Kabat-Zinn successfully transformed meditation from a practice rooted in Buddhism into a scientifically based form of health promotion. Meditation became the "property of psychologists, doctors, scientists, and diet counsellors and to be engaged in by clients rather than believers, who are not expected to take refuge, read scriptures, believe in karma or rebirth, or to become Buddhist" (Wilson, 2014; quoted in Nisbet, 2017). Kabat-Zinn's work paved the way for the adaptation of mindfulness practices to various settings, including education, business, and correctional facilities. These will be discussed in greater depth in Chapter 10.

THE DEVELOPMENT OF MBCT

As mentioned in the previous chapter, MBCT was developed by Zindel Segal, Mark Williams, and John Teasdale in the late 1990s as a relapse prevention treatment for individuals with recurrent depression. MBCT integrates elements of cognitive therapy with mindfulness practices and draws upon several key influences in its development. Segal et al. (2002, 2013) adapted the structure and techniques of MBSR to specifically target depression and prevent relapse. They incorporated mindfulness practices such as sitting meditation, body scans, and mindful movement into MBCT, building upon the foundation laid by Kabat-Zinn.

As cognitive researchers and therapists, the work of Segal et al. (2002, 2013) was also heavily influenced by cognitive therapy, which is based on the idea that thoughts and beliefs play a central role in shaping emotions and behaviours. They integrated cognitive exercises into MBCT to help individuals recognise and challenge patterns of negative thinking that contribute to depression. Like Kabat-Zinn, the developers of MBCT recognised the connection between the mind and body in influencing mental health. By incorporating mindfulness practices into therapy, they aimed to help individuals develop greater awareness of the patterns of thoughts, feelings, and bodily sensations which can lead to depression.

The acceptance of MBCT was greatly aided by research demonstrating its effectiveness in reducing the risk of depressive relapse in those most prone to it. A landmark randomised controlled trial (Teasdale et al., 2000) comparing MBCT to treatment as usual found that MBCT was most effective in preventing relapse among individuals who had experienced three or more previous episodes. Significantly also, Willem Kuyken and colleagues (Kuyken et al., 2016) compared MBCT with anti-depressant medication and found that MBCT was as effective as anti-depressants in preventing relapse.

As outlined in their publications, Segal et al. (2002, 2013) collaborated closely throughout the development of MBCT, drawing upon their collective expertise in clinical psychology, mindfulness, and cognitive therapy. Their collaboration facilitated the integration of mindfulness practices with cognitive therapy techniques, resulting in its adoption by NICE (the body responsible for recommending evidence-based interventions in healthcare) in the U.K. in 2004.

CHAPTER SUMMARY

- Mindfulness meditation, as popularised by evidence-based pro-grammes such as MBSR and MBCT, is rooted in the Buddhist tradition.
- We can also trace meditation practices in other traditions and religions.
- Jon Kabat-Zinn, the developer of MBSR, integrated mindful-ness with hatha yoga and group educational methods to support patients living with chronic health conditions.
- The developers of MBCT combined mindful meditation with cognitive and behavioural therapy (CBT) to help recovered depressed patients reduce the risk of relapse.

3

HOW DOES MINDFULNESS WORK?

When thinking about how mindfulness "works," it can be helpful to acknowledge again two main streams of learning – one from the contemplative traditions, the other from modern science. The structure of eight week secular MBPs, such as Mindfulness-Based Stress Reduction (MBSR) and Mindfulness-based Cognitive Therapy (MBCT), reflects traditional ways of establishing mindfulness. The early weeks (weeks 1–3) of the programme emphasise (re-)establishing a connection to the body and its changing physical sensations, moment by moment. Practices such as the body scan, mindful movement, and mindful eating can be deliberate opportunities to (re-)connect to the body and the range of sensations (touch, taste, sight, sounds, and smell). The middle part of the programme (weeks 4–6) builds on the early weeks in continuing to establish mindfulness of the body, while also learning about stress (MBSR) or depression (MBCT) through didactic input and group exercises. Participants are encouraged to apply this learning both during formal mindfulness practice and in everyday situations, such as difficult communications (MBSR) or when noticing triggers towards depressive rumination (MBCT). This is done with a view to developing familiarity towards common ways of relating – both to ourselves and others. The final weeks of these programmes (weeks 7 and 8) are designed to further apply the learning and insights gained beyond course completion.

As well as these well-articulated streams of learning (the contemplative and scientific), there is also each person's own subjective, first-person experience of mindfulness. Indeed, the Buddha

DOI: 10.4324/9781003453598-5

emphasised the importance of trusting one's own inner experience of the practice, over and above any blind acceptance (see Kalama Sutta, translated by Thanissaro, 1994) of how our mind works or understanding why we suffer. The ability to articulate how mindfulness *works* from this first-person perspective is more difficult to capture, as it reflects our ongoing relationship to the present moment. Language can only attempt to get close to this level of experience and, given its direct first-person nature, is unique to each person. These offer an insight into what is happening within the person who is engaged in mindfulness practice. This level of knowing and description is deeply personal. Helpfully, *qualitative research methods* that help to get closer to and clarify the subtleties of subjective experience are being developed and applied in mindfulness research (e.g. Stanley et al., 2015).

An early model that attempted to summarise how mindfulness works was offered by Shauna Shapiro and colleagues (Shapiro et al., 2006). This model recognises three fundamental building blocks or "axioms" of mindfulness – intention, attention, and attitude. Mindfulness is cultivated through *intentionally* focusing or directing *attention*, moment by moment, on a specific "object" or aspect of experience (e.g., sounds or sensations of the breath, or on the entire attentional field). This is practiced purposefully, with supportive *attitudes* such as kindness, patience, and curiosity, especially when noticing "mind wandering." (Jon Kabat-Zinn (2006, 2013) has published extensively on the "attitudinal qualities" of mindfulness.)

Another way to understand mindfulness is that it is the active cultivation of qualities of heart, or "heartfulness." Qualities of "heart" are integral to mindfulness practice, as without them the mind may get caught up in frustration, self-judgement, and impatience. These reactions could make practising mindfulness completely self-defeating. Indeed, this is one of the main reasons why people say they are "not good" at mindfulness, or "not able" to meditate. Seeing mindfulness as cultivating heartfulness from the outset directly addresses this tendency for the practice to be undermined by self-criticism and judgement.

The attitudinal qualities of mindfulness invite us to see the practice as a nourishing time, a time to restore and replenish

– especially when faced with stressors such as living with chronic pain, care-giving commitments, or work-related stress (we will say more about this in relation to practising mindfulness in Chapter 5). Connecting with these attitudinal qualities as part of our over-riding intention sets an important tone when practising mindfulness. Another way of seeing this is that mindfulness practice is as an act of kindness, care, and compassion. It is a real act of sanity to foster this in ourselves. If for whatever reason(s) we believe we cannot, we can practice bringing kindness to our *resistance* to prac-tising mindfulness. In this way, however we are and whatever we notice (including resistance) becomes part of the practice.

As well as the three "axioms" of mindfulness mentioned above, Shapiro et al. (2006) also proposed "reperceiving" as a meta-mechanism of mindfulness. Reperceiving is the term given to a fundamental shift in perspective, or what Kabat-Zinn (2013) has termed a "rotation in consciousness." This shift in perspec-tive allows us to disentangle our knowing of experience from being lost in and completely identified with it. This has also been called decentring, or detachment (Teasdale, 2022; Segal et al., 2013). This state of non-attachment, of reperceiving, is proposed to reveal four mechanisms of mindfulness – self-regulation, val-ues clarification, cognitive behavioural flexibility, and exposure (Shapiro et al., 2006). We will return to these mechanisms when we come to two additional models, later in this chapter.

HOW DOES MINDFULNESS WORK? A NEUROSCIENTIFIC PERSPECTIVE

One of the most exciting revelations from neuroscience in recent decades is just how flexible and adaptable the brain really is. Gone are the days of believing we're stuck with solely the abilities we're born with. Instead, studies show that we can actually reshape and train our brains – a concept often called *neuroplasticity*. And the results are amazing. Research using electro-encephalography (EEG) and functional magnetic resonance imaging (fMRI) scans has found measurable changes in brain activity after just eight weeks of mindfulness practice.

Take MBSR, for instance. It's been shown to boost connectivity between key brain areas like the posterior cingulate cortex (PCC) and the dorsolateral prefrontal cortex (DLPFC) (Kral et al., 2019). Even beginners to mindfulness have demonstrated brain changes, which makes it all the more remarkable to consider the results seen in advanced meditators – those with over 10,000 hours of practice. Their brain activity has been described as "off the charts" compared to typical expectations (Kral et al., 2018).

Interestingly, different styles of meditation seem to affect the brain in unique ways. A meta-review (Fox, 2016) identified distinct patterns of brain activity associated with focused attention, mantra recitation, open monitoring, and compassion or loving-kindness practices.

One groundbreaking early study by Norman Farb and colleagues (Farb et al., 2007) showed that mindfulness training leads to two distinct patterns of brain activity: one linked to mindful awareness and the other to what's known as the "default mode network" (Raichle et al., 2001; reviewed in Menon, 2023). The default mode network, active during mind-wandering or "default" thinking, contrasts with the focus and presence cultivated through mindfulness, offering a powerful glimpse into how mindfulness can transform how we experience the world.

Mindfulness has the power to change just about every facet of how we experience the world and ourselves. From changes in perception (i.e. how we "see" and experience our world) to changes in behaviour (i.e. how we act and behave), perhaps the most astonishing changes mindfulness can bring about are in relation to changes in the brain itself. Professor Richie Davidson from Madison, Wisconsin has pioneered research into mapping brain changes associated with different meditation practices (Davidson et al., 2003; Goleman & Davidson, 2017). EEG (involving electrodes placed on the surface of the scalp) measures the electromagnetic potential of different brain regions, that is, which areas of the brain are activated in any given moment.

The recording of both fMRI and EEG allows researchers to map brain activation through correlating regions of brain activity with different tasks given to research participants. For example, Davidson et al. (2003) identified the "down-regulation" (lowered activation) of the amygdala (the brain's alarm system) following just eight weeks of mindfulness training. This represents the external, observable manifestation of an internal, intentional process to attend to difficult or unwanted experience in a mindful way. The brain regions that act together to coordinate the stress response include the hypothalamic-pituitary-adrenal (HPA) axis. Given that the HPA axis is likely to have become dysregulated and overly sensitised to threat in those who have experienced previous trauma, this is a highly significant finding.

Two models from neuroscience helpfully build on the I-A-A model of Shapiro et al. (2006). Britta Hölzel and colleagues (2011b) presented the first integrated model that combined theory with observations from neuroscience and outcomes research. This model identified four key mechanisms that seem central to how mindfulness works. These are i) attention regulation, ii) body awareness, iii) emotion regulation, and iv) a change in self-perspective (Hölzel et al., 2011b). Emotion regulation was further delineated as comprising two aspects – (a) *exposure* leading to *reappraisal* and (b) *extinction* leading to *reconsolidation*.

A year later, a more detailed framework was published (Vago & Silbersweig, 2012). This model, abbreviated to S-ART (Self-Awareness, Self-Regulation, Self-Transcendence), reflected many elements of Hölzel et al.'s (2011b) paper and expanded it to include a total of six neurobiological mechanisms. These components are (i) intention and motivation, (ii) attention regulation, (iii) emotion regulation, (iv) memory extinction and reconsolidation, (v) prosociality, and (vi) non-attachment. The authors operationalise mindfulness as a skillset that underlies the maintenance of a healthy mind as well as an ongoing attentional capacity (Vago & Silbersweig, 2012).

As both Hölzel et al.'s (2011b) model and Vago and Silbersweig's (2012) model share many overlapping features (including detailed studies outlining the neural correlates of these mechanisms), commonalities between the two models are set out next.

ATTENTION REGULATION

Mindfulness involves training attention in a kindly way. Given the human preponderance to think about the past and future, one of the first things people tend to notice when practising mindfulness is just how difficult it is to keep attention where we want it to be. William James (widely regarded as the father of American psychology) wrote: *"The faculty of voluntarily bringing back a wandering attention, over and over again, is the very root of judgment, character, and will. No one is compos sui [master of oneself] if he have it not. An education which should improve this faculty would be the education par excellence. But it is easier to define this ideal than to give practical directions for bringing it about"* (James, 1890, p. 424). Although it seems from this quote that James was not aware of mindfulness meditation, he is said to have pre-empted the rise of Western interest in mindfulness following a talk by a visiting Buddhist monk to one of his lectures. After swapping places with the monk, he is said to have remarked, *"This is the psychology everybody will be studying twenty-five years from now"* (adapted from Sangharakshita, 1952, p. 78; cited in Stanley, 2012).

The neuroscientific study of attention has revealed that what we commonly call "attention" is in fact comprised of distinct abilities – alerting attention, orienting attention, sustaining attention, and switching attention. These different facets of attention appear to have their own unique neural signature when studied by fMRI. Depending on the type of mindfulness practice engaged in, each can be trained. For example, focused attention practice (e.g. attending to the breath) trains both the capacity to sustain attention on a single object, that is, the breath, as well as the ability to notice and shift attention back to the breath when attention has wandered. Given the number of demands on our attention in modern life, not least in the form of screens vying for our attention, it is perhaps no surprise that choosing to focus on just one thing might be experienced as an act of self-care.

EMOTION REGULATION

The term *emotion regulation*, a key component of self-regulation, is the ability to manage one's emotional responses, particularly when stressed or when excess demands are placed on us. As Hölzel et al. (2011b) have identified, emotion regulation is made up of discrete abilities such as the ability to reappraise or look again at the situation or context we find ourselves in with openness and acceptance. The effects of relating to difficult emotions in this way allows them (over time) to become more familiar and less scary, requiring less avoidance and other forms of escape. This can then lead to extinction and reconsolidation – learning that difficult emotions can be tolerated less personally, as just another part of the rich tapestry of human experience. The extent to which we are susceptible to "emotional hijack" likely reflects the extent to which the amygdala is activated. Reduced activation in the amygdala and enhanced activation in the prefrontal cortex appear to reflect greater ability to regulate emotion (e.g., Davidson et al., 2000).

CHANGE IN SELF-PERSPECTIVE

Perhaps at the most profound level, mindfulness practice can lead to a fundamental change in how we view ourselves. Given that shifts in attention and emotion regulation are likely to directly influence how we think about ourselves, it is perhaps no surprise that who we thought we were will be subject to change. Both the Hölzel et al. (2011b) model and Vago and Silbersweig's (2012) S-ART model present changes in how we view the self as later developments of the practice. Much as Shapiro et al. (2006) see reperceiving as a meta-mechanism of mindfulness, changes in how the self is viewed are likely to come about only through sustained engagement with the practice over time. We discuss how much time is sufficient to bring about such changes below.

There is growing interest in how different mechanisms of mindfulness (e.g. attention training or emotion regulation) may be more relevant in understanding its effects with some people (e.g. in addiction or depression or ADHD) over others (Webb et al., 2024).

HOW DOES MINDFULNESS WORK? PROPOSED MECHANISMS
FROM A WESTERN PSYCHOLOGY PERSPECTIVE

John Teasdale's book *What Happens in Mindfulness?* (2022) offers a fascinating exploration of two contrasting modes of mind that underpin how mindfulness works. Drawing on insights from cognitive psychology, neuroscience, and evolutionary systems thinking, Teasdale identifies two "shapes of mind" that influence our experiences.

First, there's the conceptual mode, which shines when tackling explicit tasks like solving problems or achieving goals. In this mode, attention narrows, focusing sharply on fixing issues or reaching desired outcomes. While this can be highly effective, it has its limits – particularly when dealing with life's inevitable challenges, such as emotional distress or grief, which cannot simply be "fixed."

Enter the holistic-intuitive mode, which allows for a broader perspective. Instead of zeroing in on solutions, this mode enables us to sit with difficulties as they are, without the compulsion to fix or resolve them. For experiences like grief or emotional struggles, shifting from the problem-solving conceptual mode to this accepting, intuitive mode can be a profoundly compassionate and wise act of self-care (Teasdale, 2022).

Teasdale and Chaskalson (2013a, 2013b) describe mindfulness as a tool for transforming suffering in three key ways:

- What the mind processes: redirecting attention to different aspects of experience.
- How the mind processes it: shifting from judgement and avoidance to openness and acceptance.
- The view in which suffering is held: reframing distress within a broader, more compassionate perspective.

Through mindfulness, we can intentionally reshape our mental approach, moving from avoidance to an approach mode of mind. This shift aligns with neuroscience findings, which show how mindfulness fosters patterns of approach-oriented brain activity (Davidson et al., 2003). Ultimately, mindfulness becomes a way to embrace life's difficulties with greater wisdom and resilience.

MBCT offers a powerful way to address key drivers of depression, such as persistent rumination and avoidance (Segal et al., 2013). Over an eight-week course, participants are guided to bring gentle, curious awareness to all aspects of their experience – thoughts, feelings, bodily sensations, behaviours, and impulses.

One of the most transformative insights from MBCT is learning to see "thoughts as just thoughts." This shift can be a game-changer when it comes to recognising and breaking free from the triggers that lead to depressive rumination. A special focus is also placed on redirecting attention into the body, moving away from overthinking and toward simple, grounded awareness of physical sensations.

Why does this matter? When the mind defaults into cycles of rumination (overthinking) or avoidance (distracting behaviours), it often reinforces the very problems it's trying to escape, such as depression or anxiety. Shifting attention to the body – perhaps noticing the sensation of the breath or the feeling of feet on the floor – offers an alternative. This practice not only changes what the mind focuses on but also how it attends. Approaching experiences with curiosity and kindness can disrupt long-standing patterns of self-criticism, blame, or shame.

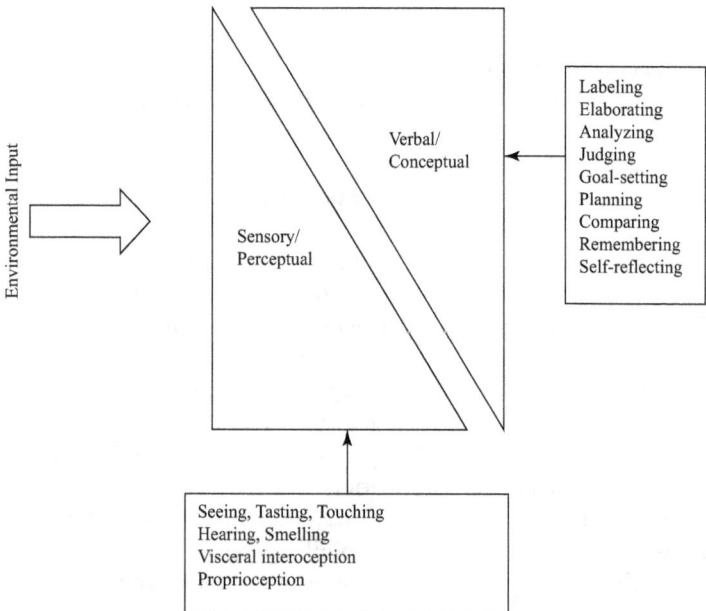

Figure 3.1 Modes of Mind (from Williams, 2010; with permission)

As illustrated in Figure 3.1, shifting from a conceptual "thinking mode" to a more grounded "sensing mode" is key to breaking cycles of brooding and worry. This shift lays the foundation for holding all aspects of experience – both sensory and conceptual – in a compassionate and balanced way, creating space for healing and growth.

A crucial aspect of developing mindfulness is the development of meta-awareness or the ability to see the contents of consciousness for what they are – thoughts, feelings, body sensations, and impulses to act. Without an awareness practice, opportunities to step back and "see" experience from this more "decentred" perspective are likely to happen only occasionally and by chance. Mindfulness offers a reliable way to connect with experience that fosters curiosity and compassion to whatever we may be experiencing. Over time, this can allow us to see patterns of reactivity less personally and develop greater perspective and understanding. This is changing "the view" as outlined by Teasdale and Chaskalson (2013b).

Another way of conceptualising how mindfulness works is through understanding Paul Gilbert's model of the three functions of emotion (Gilbert, 2010; see Figure 3.2). The three emotion

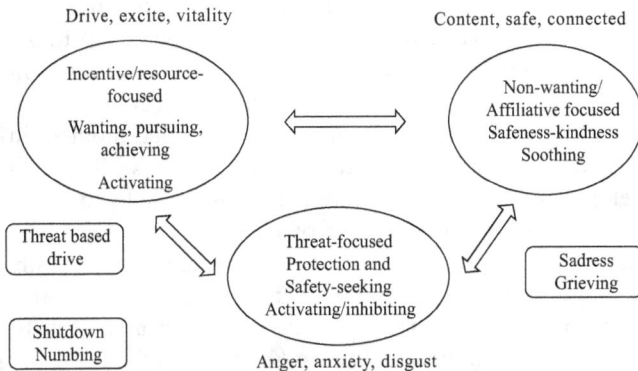

Figure 3.2 The Three Functions of Emotion, from Gilbert and Simos (2022). Compassion focused therapy: clinical practice and applications with permission from Routledge. Adapted from Gilbert (2010) The Compassionate Mind (Constable). © P. Gilbert

systems of "drive," "threat," and "soothing" (each with their own characteristic hormonal signature) underpin much of human feeling, motivation, and behaviour. Given that we spend much of our time in one of these three systems (e.g., in the "drive" system if pursuing a valued goal; in the "threat" system if seriously ill or socially excluded; in the "soothing" system if connecting with loved ones), mindfulness can become a way to consciously access the restorative body-mind benefits of the "soothing" system. It can also help us to recognise unhelpful patterns associated with both threat and drive systems and to navigate these with greater awareness and kindness. Frequently, competing demands and pressures can lead to spending much of our time unconsciously moving between the "drive" and "threat" systems. It is perhaps only during periods of sleep or rest at evenings or weekends that we may finally get an opportunity to restore and replenish – if we're lucky! As a result, we may need to be very deliberate about protecting some time each day to access, dwell in, and benefit from the "soothing" system, thereby rebalancing the three systems.

HOW DOES MINDFULNESS WORK? A BUDDHIST PSYCHOLOGY PERSPECTIVE

An important development in the teaching of secular mindfulness in recent years has been a focus on "feeling tone" or the tonality of experience (Williams & Penman, 2023). Feeling tone refers to the immediate, pre-conscious sense of whether one's present moment experience is "pleasant," "unpleasant," or neutral," Feeling tone is important to recognise, as it is deemed to be a pivotal moment in the perceptual process that mediates the stress response. Through the development of mindful awareness, it is possible to bring (greater) awareness to the tonality of experience in any given moment, thereby allowing us to identify our reactions more easily (e.g. the desire to hold on to things that are pleasant; to dismiss, avoid, or push away things that are unpleasant; or tune out, drift, and feel boredom about neutral things) (see Figure 3.3).

These reactions are immediate and often unconscious. However, we *can* become more aware of them. For example, we may suddenly have a thought that is unsettling in some way – perhaps a memory of a task we have been avoiding, or an interaction with

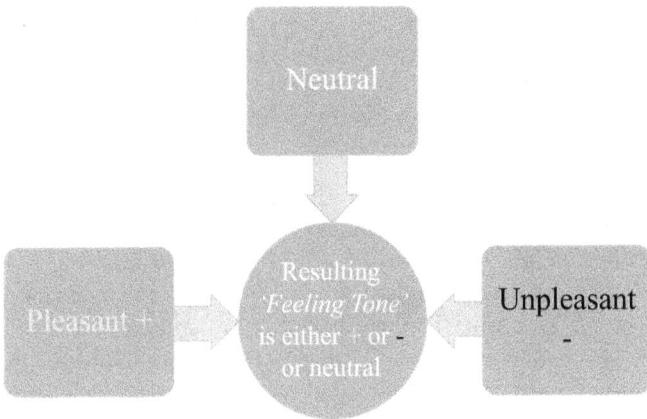

Figure 3.3 Map of the 'Feeling Tone' of Experience

a friend or colleague that didn't go so well. The "feeling tone" in the moment of remembering (quite understandably) may be "unpleasant." It is what happens next, however, that can make all the difference. So instead of getting lost in thoughts and judgement about the incident, or ignoring it, we might instead choose to acknowledge the memory – noticing the range of thoughts, images, feelings, and body sensations it gives rise to. From this place of greater awareness, we might then choose to continue with our day in a way that includes the memory – rather than running away from or being (unconsciously) driven by it.

A key teaching of the Buddha that goes to the heart of how mindfulness works is that of the Sallatha Sutta (see text box). This simple (and profound) teaching explains the way we tend to compound our suffering, making it worse than it already is.

The Two Arrows or Sallatha Sutta

The Blessed One said, "When touched with a feeling of pain, the uninstructed run-of-the-mill person sorrows, grieves, and laments, beats his breast, becomes distraught. So he feels two pains, physical and mental. Just as if they were to shoot a man with an arrow and, right afterward, were to shoot him with another one, so that he would feel the pains of two arrows; in the same way, when touched with a feeling of pain, the uninstructed run-of-the-mill person sorrows, grieves, and laments, beats his breast, becomes distraught. So he feels two pains, physical and mental" (translated by Thanissaro, 1997).

There may be little we can do about the first arrow (e.g., physical pain or grief), but we have a lot of say over how much and to what extent we perpetuate it. This 2,500-year-old teaching has tremendous resonance with the role of rumination and avoidance in maintaining despair. Rather than directly address the fears, worries, and concerns we may have, our mood can tend toward depression. When depressed, rumination can serve to lock a person into a fixed view of self, the world, and the future. Attempts to free oneself from despair can serve to act only as a reminder of where one finds oneself (depressed) and where one wishes to be (not depressed), further consolidating the feeling of being trapped (Williams et al., 2024).

HOW DOES MINDFULNESS WORK? MINDFULNESS AND STRESS PHYSIOLOGY

One of the most immediate and powerful effects of mindfulness training is its ability to reduce the body's stress response, particularly the fight/flight/freeze reaction. Stress is physically taxing, often triggered by the sympathetic nervous system, and the resulting changes in the body – mediated by stress hormones like epinephrine (in the short term) and cortisol (in the long term) – are profound. These include increased heart rate and breathing, muscle tension, higher blood pressure, digestive issues, irritability, and poor sleep (Kabat-Zinn, 2013). It's often our reaction to these stress responses – our desire to avoid or push through them – that can actually make stress worse and prolong its effects.

Much like Herbert Benson's relaxation response (1975), mindfulness helps activate the parasympathetic nervous system, which calms the body and counteracts stress. What makes mindfulness so powerful is the attitudinal qualities of curiosity and openness it fosters. These attitudes not only help us better understand how we experience stress, but they can also reduce its harmful effects (McGonigal, 2015).

A fascinating study on the physical benefits of mindfulness involved people with psoriasis, a skin condition aggravated by stress that causes dry, flaky patches of skin. Both groups in the study received UV light therapy, but one group listened to a mindfulness recording during their treatment. Remarkably, the group practising mindfulness experienced faster skin clearing, highlighting the mind–body connection in healing (Kabat-Zinn et al., 1998).

Recent research has continued to explore how mindfulness impacts physical health, particularly immune function and cell ageing. For example, mindfulness practitioners showed enhanced immune responses following a flu shot (Davidson et al., 2003), and other studies have explored how mindfulness may buffer telomere shortening – the protective caps at the ends of chromosomes that indicate ageing and cell degradation (e.g., Epel et al., 2009). In another study, blood markers of immune health were significantly improved in experienced meditators after a day of intensive meditation, compared to non-meditators who spent the day relaxing (Chaix et al., 2020). These findings provide compelling evidence that mindfulness training has real, measurable effects on the body's ability to cope with stress and promote healing.

HOW DOES MINDFULNESS WORK? THE ROLE OF THE GROUP

The influence of practising mindfulness with others in a secular context is only beginning to be understood (Bartley & Griffith, 2022). The most robust evidence base for mindfulness comes from RCTs (randomised controlled trials) of MBSR and MBCT. As group-based interventions, it is likely the group plays an important role in normalising the experience of stress and/or depression and deepening a sense of common humanity among participants. The willingness to explore what it means to be human – its joys and challenges – in the supportive context of a group practising mindfulness is a unique opportunity.

The exploration of the territory of stress (MBSR) or depression (MBCT) within a group learning environment requires significant attention to be paid to all aspects of group development – forming, storming, norming, performing and mourning (see Tuckman, 1965; Bartley & Griffith, 2022). For example, the "forming" stage relies on the ability of the teacher to create a context of safety for the work of the group. This relies on establishing good boundaries and a warm and welcoming environment where confidentiality and privacy can be established. Clarity and agreement around time and attendance boundaries allow the group to settle and build trust – all of which are fundamental to group forming. When effective, "forming" tasks (e.g., boundary-setting, establishing the goals of the group, getting to know one another, welcoming different perspectives) allow for the next stage, "storming" (e.g., challenges within the group and how the teacher responds to these) to occur. Such attentiveness to group development forms one specific domain of the MBI:TAC (see Domain 6 on the Mindfulness-Based Interventions Teaching Assessment Criteria; Crane et al., 2013).

Mindfulness is often referred to as "a solitary practice, best practiced in groups!" This points to the paradoxical nature of mindfulness practice in groups, where the support of others (often in silence) can foster a quality of attention that can allow participants to be more fully present to their own individual experience. There is a subtle power in knowing that each person in the group is engaged in their own inner work. This can lend a quality of stillness, quiet, and depth to the practice that may be difficult to replicate outside of a group learning context.

More recent advances in how mindfulness can support changes in attitudes and awareness towards the environment and climate change, as well as social changes in awareness of bias, prejudice, inclusion, and discriminatory practice, can be enhanced through group dialogue and exploration of these themes. For example, using mindfulness as a method to contain discussions around racism and prejudice (e.g., Saad, 2020) can foster qualities of openness and non-judgement when recognising and exploring our own biases.

HOW DOES MINDFULNESS WORK? FREQUENCY AND DURATION OF MINDFULNESS PRACTICE

The question of how long one needs to practice before noticing beneficial changes is not a straightforward one. Benefits can occur from simply taking a few mindful breaths. More long-lasting changes in the brain have been documented after just eight weeks of regular practice. Typically, mindfulness-based programmes such as MBSR and MBCT include a home practice requirement of up to an hour per day for the duration of the programme, that is, eight weeks. A recent study suggests that the *quality* of mindfulness practice might act as a mechanism that links the amount of practice time and outcomes in MBSR (Goldberg et al., 2020). Although home practice rates vary, evidence suggests that more frequent practice (as little as 12 minutes per day) results in greater mindfulness (Jha, 2021). A 2025 longitudinal study (Bowles and Van Dam, 2025) found that 35–65 minutes daily was correlated with improved wellbeing and 50–80 minutes with improved mental health. There is now little doubt that greater mindfulness results in a host of beneficial effects, from immune response to increased positive mood states and decreased stress.

Given that it is quite possible to spend large periods of time on "autopilot," even while meditating (especially while meditating!), the argument for the quality of time spent practising is a convincing one. Allied to this are different kinds of mindfulness practice, for example, focused-attention practice, open awareness/choiceless awareness practice, and compassion-focused or metta practice. As we have seen earlier, each practice is likely to train a different aspect of the attentional/perceptual system and foreground certain attitudinal qualities within the attending (e.g., kindness towards self and others within compassion-focused practices).

HOW DOES MINDFULNESS WORK? THE ROLE OF THE MINDFULNESS TEACHER IN GROUP-BASED COURSES

It is said that mindfulness is "caught" not "taught." This recognises the crucial role of the mindfulness teacher to embody mindfulness when relating to group members. This form of experiential learning happens not only when the mindfulness teacher is guiding mindfulness practices, but also in discussions immediately following mindfulness practice, in what is known as the "inquiry" process. At its best, "inquiry" allows the attitudinal qualities of mindfulness to be conveyed in a way that is immediate, genuine, and heartfelt, through sensitive dialogue with the teacher. It may also be understood as a form of compassionate dialogue. Although a similar process happens within psychotherapy, the awareness that gives rise to personal change within mindfulness tends to be self-guided and arises from periods of formal/informal mindfulness practice.

In inquiry, the teacher models ("embodies") a way of being with experience (e.g. painful physical sensations, troubling thoughts/ memories, negative feelings/emotions) by inviting participants to bring a sense of openness, curiosity, and kindness towards whatever is being noticed. This "turning towards" difficult or unwanted experience requires sensitive attuning and pacing, particularly where there may be potential to re-live or re-experience past trauma. This is one of the reasons why it is essential for mindfulness teachers to have a well-established personal practice and thorough training before teaching others. This is essential to ensuring that what is communicated or "caught" is mindfulness and not something else. The curiosity shown by a skilled mindfulness teacher to inquire of another person's experience, without agenda (e.g. a need to "fix" the person or problem/issue), seems to be key to facilitating participants' deeper understanding of themselves. Without the support of an experienced mindfulness teacher, the possibility for insight is likely to be much reduced. The role of the teacher in mindfulness is captured across several key features and domains on the MBI:TAC (Mindfulness-Based Interventions Teaching Assessment Criteria; Crane et al., 2013).

Given the territory being explored within mindfulness-based groups, that is, human vulnerability and resilience to stress and depression, the potential for high levels of distress even within public groups is likely. For example, a WHO study conducted on rates of trauma and PTSD (Kessler et al., 2017) found lifetime rates of 70% with an average rate of three events per capita. This translates into nearly thirteen episodes per 100 people. This means that in a group of ten people, trauma may be present in an active way for at least one person and in a historic sense for many more. Hence the need for those teaching mindfulness to do their own work first and to allow their ongoing relationship to the practice to inform their teaching and holding of the group learning environment.

CHAPTER SUMMARY

- Mindfulness can be viewed as a paradoxical approach to suffering. How mindfulness works is often counter-intuitive and the opposite of what one might first expect.

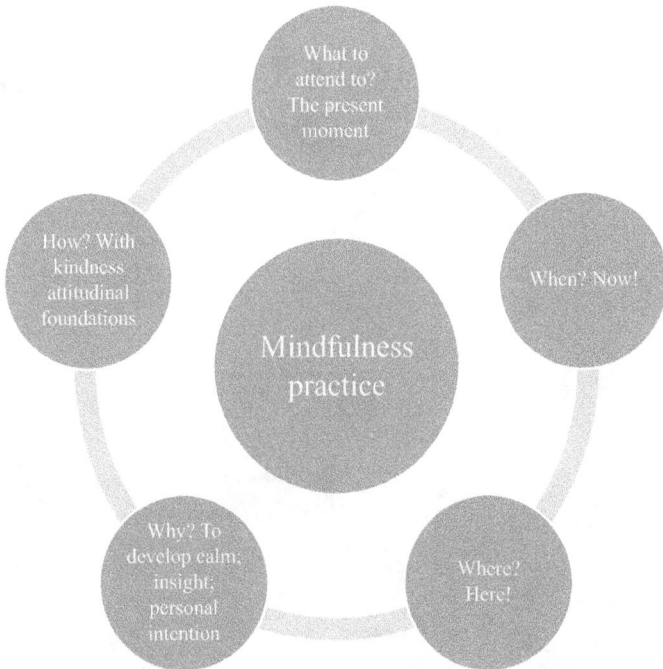

Figure 3.4 Summary Diagram of Mindfulness Practice

- At its core, mindfulness is about choice. Making wise, compassionate, and skilful choices about *what* aspects of present moment experience to relate to and *how* to be in relation to them, informed by the understanding that we can often compound and add layers of suffering to experience.

- This can be summarised in the format of: [*diagram*] *what* (we pay attention to; some reliable, accessible aspect(s) of present moment experience); *how* (attitudinal qualities of mindfulness such as kindness, patience, allowing); *why* (a wandering mind is an unhappy mind; we often add layers to suffering); *when* (now, present moment or whenever we remember that we can come back and inhabit the present moment); *where* (here – standing, sitting, lying down, while moving) (Figure 3.4).

4

WHY PRACTICE MINDFULNESS?

Mindfulness has become a global phenomenon in today's world. A-list celebrities and professional athletes are embracing the technique as a tool to manage performance anxiety, achieve a state of "flow," and navigate the pressures of modern-day fame. In healthcare, mindfulness interventions are supporting patients in managing a spectrum of physical conditions and mental health challenges, while in the general population, mindfulness provides a sanctuary for individuals to rest and reset.

The practice of mindfulness demands courage, sustained effort, and a significant level of commitment. But is it all worth it? This chapter delves into common motivations behind why people engage in mindfulness practice and then summarises key research on the topic. The recent surge in the popularity of mindfulness in Western culture has primarily revolved around individual health and well-being. However, contemporary developments are hinting at broader applications such as supporting social justice and environmental sustainability. This ongoing intersection of mindfulness with the challenges of our time may realise (make real) its much-needed potential in our world at a crucial juncture in human history.

WHAT WILL I GET OUT OF IT?

When embarking on a mindfulness practice, it is important to be aware of the underlying intentions that drive your journey. In today's fast-paced world, mindfulness has found its place in a wide array of contexts, some of which may have value systems that diverge from the original contemplative traditions that gave rise to

DOI: 10.4324/9781003453598-6

this practice. One criticism of contemporary mindfulness-based approaches is that they have become primarily outcome focused, which conflicts with the very nature of mindfulness itself.

In classical traditions, all experience, including emotions, thoughts, and actions, were believed to "rest upon the tip of intention." The teachings of the Buddha on Right Intention provide a guiding light for individuals looking to cultivate a mindful life. Right Intention, often referred to as "Samma Sankappa" in Pali, encompasses three core components: renunciation, loving kindness, and harmlessness. Renunciation encourages the intention to let go of attachments and desires for sensual pleasures and material possessions, fostering a mindset of contentment. Loving-kindness promotes the cultivation of goodwill (Metta) and compassion towards all living beings, involving the intention of empathy and a genuine desire for the well-being and happiness of others. Right Intention places a strong emphasis on harmlessness or non-violence (Ahimsa), which entails refraining from causing harm or suffering to oneself or others, be it through physical, verbal, or mental actions.

Research has shed light on the link between specific intentions in mindfulness practice and perceived outcomes. For instance, Brown and Ryan (2003) discovered that participants driven by personal growth and self-discovery reported heightened self-awareness, increased clarity of purpose, and greater life satisfaction. In clinical settings, individuals with chronic pain who engaged in mindfulness-based programmes with the intention of alleviating pain-related suffering reported reductions in pain intensity and improvements in pain-related outcomes (Veehof et al., 2016).

Therefore, the reasons underpinning our desire to practice mindfulness hold a pivotal role, and it is imperative to be conscious of the driving force behind our commitment to practice. This chapter provides an overview of the most frequently reported research outcomes associated with contemporary mindfulness-based approaches, outcomes that have significantly shaped the integration of mindfulness into health and therapeutic contexts. But before delving into a chapter titled "Why practice mindfulness?", it may be helpful to take a moment to reflect on what fuels your own personal interest, either by following the guided practice accompanying this book titled "Intentions practice" or following the guidance given next. *Please refer to the audio-guided Intentions Practice.*

Take a moment to close your eyes or lower your gaze and notice the sensations coming from the body. Perhaps having a sense of the weight and shape of the body. If it's comfortable for you, sensing the flow of the breath. Spending a few moments resting attention on the flow of the in-breath and out-breath. Now drop a question in to the practice. "What is my intention for reading this book? Why am I interested in mindfulness?" Notice if you go into thinking about answers to these questions. See if it is possible to simply note any ripples or resonance in the body or mind as you ask the question "what fuels my interest in mindfulness?" When you feel ready, returning attention to the breath, noticing the weight of the body once more, and opening your eyes.

IMPROVED MENTAL HEALTH

Mindfulness has firmly established itself in the field of mental health and well-being over the past three decades. It has become a key intervention in clinical settings, including those within the National Health Service (NHS) in the U.K., schools, workplaces, and veterans' care. Mindfulness-Based Cognitive Therapy (MBCT) is even recommended in the U.K.'s National Institute for Health and Care Excellence (NICE) guidelines for recurrent depression, underscoring its widespread impact.

As we saw in Chapter 2, "Where does mindfulness come from?", the roots of mindfulness in clinical research date back to 1992, when Kabat-Zinn et al. (1992) conducted one of the first trials assessing mindfulness for anxiety and panic disorders. Their study showed a small yet significant reduction in symptoms following participation in a Mindfulness-Based Stress Reduction (MBSR) program. This pioneering research laid the foundation for mindfulness to be integrated into clinical interventions.

Following this, Teasdale et al. (2000) introduced MBCT, which has since been shown to help individuals with recurrent depression maintain remission, particularly those who have experienced multiple depressive episodes. These early studies established mindfulness as an effective tool for addressing clinical anxiety and depression, opening the door for its broader application in mental health treatment.

As the evidence base has expanded, mindfulness-based therapies have been consistently shown to be effective in reducing symptoms of depression and anxiety in clinical populations. Studies often demonstrate that mindfulness approaches compare favourably to standard treatment options or waiting list controls.

A meta-analysis by Goldberg et al. (2018) confirmed the clinical benefits of mindfulness-based programs (MBPs), revealing moderate to large effect sizes for conditions such as depression, anxiety, post-traumatic stress disorder (PTSD), and borderline personality disorder. These findings suggest that mindfulness is an effective treatment for a broad spectrum of psychiatric disorders.

In addition to mood disorders, mindfulness-based interventions have shown promise in treating other behavioural conditions. For example, MBSR and Dialectical Behaviour Therapy (DBT) have been shown to reduce binge eating frequency and improve eating behaviours (Telch, Agras & Linehan, 2001). Mindfulness-Based Relapse Prevention (MBRP) has proven effective in reducing substance misuse and relapse, lowering cravings, and increasing mindful awareness (Witkiewitz & Bowen, 2010). Similarly, MBRP has shown potential in promoting smoking cessation (Bowen & Marlatt, 2009a).

While the body of research highlights the significant mental health benefits of mindfulness, it is essential to recognise that mindfulness may not be suitable for everyone. Mental health professionals should assess individual circumstances and potential contraindications before recommending mindfulness practices, ensuring it aligns with the needs and readiness of each person (see the section "Is mindfulness really for me?" for further guidance).

ENHANCED PHYSICAL HEALTH

Mindfulness programmes may also yield positive effects on physical health within medical populations. MBSR has demonstrated its efficacy as an intervention for individuals suffering from fibromyalgia (Adler-Neal & Zeidan, 2017), an increasingly prevalent clinical concern. In comparison to a waiting list control (WLC) group, MBSR significantly improved overall quality of life in fibromyalgia patients, particularly in coping strategies and the alleviation of sleeping difficulties and pain symptoms.

Additionally, MBSR has exhibited promising results in patients with psoriasis. Kabat-Zinn et al. (1998) originally observed that skin clearing rates substantially increased in a group receiving mindfulness as an adjunct to light therapy, compared to those receiving light therapy alone. A more recent systematic review has shown this finding to be robust across five randomised controlled trials (Bartholomew et al., 2022).

Furthermore, in a study involving individuals with type two diabetes, including 81 participants from a low-income community centre, a combination of Acceptance and Commitment Therapy (ACT) and education proved superior to education alone. After a one-day workshop on diabetes management, those who received ACT as an adjunct to education demonstrated improved coping strategies and reported enhanced self-care. Notably, ACT completers achieved glycated haemoglobin values within the target range (Gregg et al., 2007).

Mindfulness is becoming increasingly prevalent in diverse facets of cancer care. Its utilisation is yielding notable benefits in mitigating the adverse effects of treatment, alleviating symptoms stemming from cancer progression, and demonstrating cost-effectiveness when compared to conventional management approaches (Mehta et al., 2019).

Therapeutic outcomes in oncology predominantly centre on improvements in mood disturbance, reduced stress levels, enhanced quality of life, and improved sleep quality (number of hours of sleep per night). However, it is worth noting that no significant changes were observed in the number of lymphocytes or cell subsets, which are physiological markers associated with a shift from a depressed to a normal profile (Carlson et al., 2003).

Although meta-analytic reviews have shown moderately robust effect sizes for mindfulness-based therapies in addressing anxiety and mood disorders, as well as clinical and medical disorders, the breadth of psychological and physical disorders where mindfulness therapies may be effective remains a topic of debate. Overall, there is robust evidence that mindfulness-based programmes are very effective. More research is needed to understand the nuances in some populations.

Dysfunction in cognitive processing is a common feature in various conditions, such as chronic fatigue syndrome, fibromyalgia, and long COVID. It is also a prevalent complaint during hormonal changes associated with pregnancy and menopause. Enhanced cognitive processing capacity, including aspects like attention, memory, and decision-making, holds significant advantages in both professional and personal life settings.

Jha et al. (2007) conducted a fascinating study using functional magnetic resonance imaging (fMRI) to explore the effects of mindfulness practice on attention. Their research focused on 17 meditation practitioners who had just completed a month-long mindfulness retreat. The results highlighted three distinct sub-categories of attention, each tied to different brain functions. "Alerting" refers to the brain's ability to maintain a state of readiness, "orienting" involves directing and limiting attention to specific stimuli, while "conflict monitoring" helps prioritise tasks and resolve competing demands. When compared to both an eight-week MBSR group and a control group with no meditation experience, the retreat participants showed enhanced conflict monitoring, increased alerting, and better orientation of attention after the retreat.

In a related study, Van den Hurk and colleagues (2010) investigated 20 expert meditators and compared them to 20 age- and gender-matched controls. The meditators showed superior attentional processing, with improvements in both orienting and executive attention. This was reflected in faster reaction times, greater accuracy, and fewer errors in tasks requiring sustained focus, suggesting that long-term mindfulness practice can refine cognitive performance. While this study didn't randomise participants, it used meaningful controls, reinforcing the idea that long-term meditators may experience significant attentional benefits.

Research into the neuropsychological effects of long-term meditation has revealed notable differences in the brains of experienced meditators. Lazar et al. (2005) found that participants who practiced meditation for 40 minutes daily had increased cortical thickness compared to non-meditators. These changes were linked to the amount of meditation experience and affected areas of the prefrontal cortex, which are involved in attention and sensory processing. Remarkably, meditators showed a slower rate of age-related grey-matter thinning, suggesting that meditation might help protect the brain from the effects of aging.

Further supporting these findings, Moore and Malinowski (2009) found that mindfulness and meditation experience were associated with better performance on tasks measuring attentional functions and cognitive flexibility. In their fMRI study, mindfulness practitioners performed better than meditation-naive controls on tasks like the Stroop interference test, which assesses the ability to suppress irrelevant information and focus attention.

Taren et al. (2015) used neuroimaging to show that mindfulness meditation leads to structural changes in the brain, particularly in areas related to stress response. These changes point to the possibility that mindfulness practice can induce neuroplasticity, reshaping the brain's response to fight-or-flight triggers. As a result, meditators demonstrated superior selective attention, concentration, and flexibility in shifting perspectives, further supporting the idea that mindfulness cultivates a more efficient and adaptable brain.

Slagter et al. (2007) examined the effects of a 3-month mindfulness retreat on information processing. They found that retreat participants were quicker at detecting a second stimulus in an attentional blink task, showing improved processing capacity compared to a control group. This suggests that long-term mindfulness practice enhances the ability to attend to and process information more efficiently, highlighting another key cognitive benefit of regular meditation practice.

Acceptance of emotions has been shown to lead to efficient heart rate habituation and recovery following stress (Low et al., 2008). Eighty-one participants were randomly assigned to write about a stressful experience while either evaluating their emotional response, attending to their emotions in an accepting way, or describing the emotions (control condition). The acceptance condition displayed the most efficient recovery from stressful situations, with evaluative processing prolonging the stress response.

As explored in Chapter 3, "How does mindfulness work," mindfulness practice has been shown to boost positive emotions through improved emotional regulation, particularly by enhancing working memory capacity. Working memory is key in managing cognitive demands and regulating emotions, and mindfulness training has been found to increase working memory, especially in high-stress environments. For example, during pre-deployment periods, military personnel who participated in mindfulness training demonstrated better working memory capacity, while their non-trained counterparts showed a decline. Those with more out-of-class mindfulness practice reported not only higher working memory capacity but also lower levels of negative emotions and increased positive emotions (Jha et al., 2010).

Further support for mindfulness as an emotional regulation tool comes from Goldin and Gross (2010), who investigated how mindfulness training influences emotional reactivity and regulation in patients with social anxiety disorder. In their study, participants underwent fMRI scans while reacting to negative self-beliefs in either a breath-focused or distraction-focused condition. After completing an MBSR program, participants in the breath-focused task showed significant reductions in anxiety and depression, alongside improved self-esteem. Neuroimaging revealed that these improvements were accompanied by decreased negative emotional experiences and reduced amygdala activity, a key brain region involved in emotional responses. This suggests that mindfulness enhances emotion regulation by reducing emotional reactivity.

Emotional intelligence (EI) – the ability to accurately perceive, understand, and regulate emotions – has also been linked to mindfulness. Research by Baer et al. (2006) found that individuals with higher dispositional mindfulness, as measured by the Mindful Attention Awareness Scale (MAAS), exhibited better emotional regulation, less reactivity to emotionally threatening stimuli, and lower amygdala activation, as shown in fMRI studies. These individuals also showed stronger activation in the prefrontal cortex, which is associated with improved executive functioning and emotional regulation.

Studies on meditation and emotional intelligence have yielded both cross-sectional and experimental evidence of the benefits of mindfulness practice. In a cross-sectional study of 351 full-time working adults, those with more meditation experience demonstrated higher emotional intelligence, less perceived stress and better mental health. Similarly, in an experimental study involving ten participants who completed eight weeks of daily 20-minute meditation sessions, those practising meditation reported higher emotional intelligence, lower stress, and improved mental health, including reduced social dysfunction. Additionally, advanced meditation practice may enhance one's ability to read and understand the emotions of others, further highlighting the role of mindfulness in developing emotional awareness (Nielsen & Kaszniak, 2006).

SOCIETAL FUNCTIONING

The impact of mindfulness on relationship functioning has the potential to enhance various aspects of interpersonal dynamics, including relationship satisfaction, communication, conflict resolution, and attachment security. Numerous studies have delved into the role of mindfulness in relationship satisfaction. Barnes et al. (2007) demonstrated that individuals with higher levels of mindfulness reported greater relationship satisfaction.

Effective communication and conflict resolution are pivotal components of healthy relationships. Mindfulness techniques, such as active listening and non-reactive communication, have been shown to mitigate conflict escalation and increase emotional attunement within couples. Programmes like Mindfulness-Based Relationship Enhancement (MBRE; Carson & Carson, 2004) have been shown to reduce relationship distress and enhance relationship satisfaction (Carson et al., 2017).

Findings by Birnie et al. (2010) suggest that mindfulness may promote secure attachment styles, which are linked to more stable and satisfying relationships. Mindfulness-based interventions have emerged as promising tools for improving relationship quality. However, ongoing research is necessary to comprehend better the underlying mechanisms and address methodological challenges.

The intersection of mindfulness and pro-social behaviour explores how mindfulness practice may influence individuals' tendencies to engage in actions that benefit others and society.

Negative emotions, such as anger and hostility, can impede pro-social behaviour. Research by Hölzel et al. (2011b) indicates that mindfulness interventions can lead to a reduction in negative emotions. By mitigating these hindrances, mindfulness may create a more conducive psychological environment for pro-social tendencies to thrive.

Empathy, the capacity to understand and share the feelings of others, is a fundamental component of pro-social behaviour. Research by Condon et al. (2013) suggests that mindfulness meditation can enhance empathy by promoting emotional regulation and reducing ego-centered responses. Consequently, individuals with higher levels of mindfulness may exhibit greater empathic concern for others.

Significant increases in compassion were observed in graduate students following participation in an MBSR programme (Shapiro et al., 2007). An empathetic response to stimuli may be conducive to mental health and well-being. Arch and Craske (2006) examined the emotional effects of 15 minutes of focused breathing compared to unfocused attention and worrying in a sample of undergraduate students. The focused breathing condition reported a more positive affective response to neutral slides post-intervention compared to the control group.

Mindfulness involves the intentional cultivation of self- and other-focused compassion and non-judgement (Neff & Germer, 2013). Compassion is a foundation for altruistic actions such as volunteering or helping those in need. Self-compassion and empathy were assessed in a community sample following participation in an MBSR programme (Birnie et al., 2010). Reductions in stress and mood disturbance were observed, along with increases in mindfulness, spirituality, and self-compassion. However, no significant change occurred in empathetic concern. Mediation analysis showed that changes in self-compassion were predicted by changes in mindfulness. Emotional response to affective film clips was assessed following a brief laboratory-induced mindfulness session (Erisman & Roemer, 2010). There were no differences between the mindful and control conditions following the distressing film clip, but the mindfulness group displayed greater positivity in affective response.

Leiberg et al. (2011) investigated how mindfulness affects decision-making in pro-social contexts. Findings indicate that mindfulness may lead individuals to make more equitable and fair decisions in resource-sharing scenarios, highlighting its potential to promote fairness and cooperation. Mindfulness, characterised by non-judgemental awareness of the present moment, has the potential to mitigate stereotyping – the cognitive process of categorising and generalising about individuals or groups based on perceived characteristics.

Mindfulness practices encourage individuals to become more aware of their thoughts and reactions. Research by Lueke and Gibson (2014) suggests that mindfulness may weaken the automatic activation of stereotypes by promoting more deliberate and considered responses to social cues. Implicit biases are automatic associations and attitudes that individuals hold unconsciously. These biases can contribute to stereotyping. Research by Kang et al. (2013) suggests that mindfulness interventions may reduce implicit racial biases, highlighting the potential for mindfulness to counteract stereotypical thinking. Measuring the effects of mindfulness on stereotyping can be complex, as it involves both conscious and unconscious processes. Additionally, the generalisability of findings across different social contexts and diverse populations remains a topic for continued investigation.

Mindfulness practices often emphasise developing empathy and understanding for oneself and others. These practices can enhance perspective-taking – the ability to see situations from others' viewpoints. Enhanced empathy and perspective-taking may lead to reduced discriminatory behaviour by fostering a greater appreciation for the experiences and struggles of individuals from diverse backgrounds (Creswell, 2017).

There is a growing recognition that research to date has been overly focused on individual health and well-being, placing mindfulness within a Western medical model. While this trajectory has firmly established mindfulness within mainstream systems and institutions such as schools, the workplace, and healthcare services, it has also contributed to maintaining the status quo, shifting the responsibility for individual well-being onto the individual and overlooking the social causes of suffering.

We look further in to mainstream applications of mindfulness in Chapter 10. One critique is the possibility that workplaces might use mindfulness to increase productivity and help employees cope with heavier burdens of stress. Equally, there are concerns that some schools might employ "tick box" measures to meet well-being quotas and implement vague behavioural control methods. At its best, mindfulness fosters an inner awakening, aligning mind and body with healthy functioning and encouraging a growing recognition that we are inherent parts of a system rather than independent entities. Through this perspective, concerns such as social justice and climate recovery can take on a more direct significance for each of us.

ENVIRONMENTAL SUSTAINABILITY

Mindfulness practices have the potential to deepen one's connection with the natural world. Mindfulness encourages individuals to be fully present in their experiences, which can lead to a profound sense of connection with nature and a greater appreciation of its wonders. The relationship between humans and the natural world can be examined through the lens of ecological systems theory and complex systems thinking. This perspective views the natural world and human society as interconnected systems, with each influencing and being influenced by the other. The popularisation of mindfulness in Western culture may not be separate from the coinciding recognition of our direct connection with the natural world and the growing destabilisation we are experiencing because of climate breakdown.

Buddhism teaches the concept of interdependence or inter connectedness (known as "pratityasamutpada"). This principle emphasises that all things, including humans, are interconnected and interdependent. This interconnectedness extends to the natural world, highlighting that humans are not separate from nature but are an integral part of it. Actions in one part of the ecosystem can have consequences throughout the entire system. Buddhism places a strong emphasis on non-harming and compassion towards all sentient beings, not just humans. This includes animals, plants, and the environment. The First Precept in Buddhism is typically expressed as "Do not harm or kill any living being," reflecting this deep respect for life in all its forms. While Buddhism acknowledges the interconnectedness of all life, it also places a responsibility on humans to be good stewards of the natural world. This means taking care of the environment and not exploiting it recklessly. The concept of "right livelihood" in Buddhism encourages individuals to choose professions and livelihoods that do not harm the environment or other beings.

In recent research, the impact of mindfulness on individuals' attitudes, behaviours, and decision-making processes has been explored, revealing its potential to significantly contribute to sustainable consumption and environmental awareness. Bernal et al. (2018) emphasise the role of mindfulness in promoting sustainability by nurturing and reinforcing individuals' core values. They underscore the interconnectedness of mindfulness, personal values, and eco-conscious behaviours, highlighting their collective importance in addressing environmental challenges and fostering sustainable practices.

A comprehensive literature review conducted by Fischer et al. (2017) identified four key mechanisms in the relationship between mindfulness and sustainable consumption. These mechanisms include the disruption of routine, the alignment of attitudes and behaviour, the cultivation of non-materialistic values, and the enhancement of pro-social behaviour. Mindfulness, by reducing habitual tendencies, sheds light on routine behaviours that may hinder the adoption of a pro-environmental lifestyle.

Notably, there exists a recognised disparity between individuals' attitudes and their actual engagement in healthy behaviours, with this incongruence often attributed to inattention (Chatzisarantis & Hagger, 2007). The heightened awareness cultivated through mindfulness in daily life holds the potential to bridge this gap, increasing the likelihood of aligning actions with intentions and thereby supporting more sustainable patterns of consumption. The association between material consumption and a sense of lack and dissatisfaction is well documented. The well-being cultivated through mindfulness practices has the potential to foster contentment, subsequently enhancing non-material values.

IS MINDFULNESS REALLY FOR ME?

For those new to mindfulness, it is essential to have some understanding of what is involved. The practice is not for the faint-hearted. Those who decide to give it a try must be clear that it is not a quick fix. Lasting change requires sustained motivation and commitment over the long term. Any mindfulness-based initiative should offer informative orientation meetings and materials to enable informed choices. Orientation sessions create an opportunity for participants to fully understand the course structure, goals, and expectations. This clarity fosters commitment and motivation, increasing the likelihood of active participation and engagement (Hölzel et al., 2011b). Ensuring the safety and ethical treatment of participants is paramount. Orientation sessions prior to mindfulness training can be opportunities to discuss issues of safety and confidentiality, as well as addressing concerns related to physical and psychological well-being.

It is important to note that while mindfulness meditation can offer various benefits, it may not be appropriate for everyone, especially in certain circumstances. Assessment and screening are necessary to identify contra-indications of mindfulness – situations or conditions in which the practice of mindfulness may not be suitable or could potentially have adverse effects. Individuals with severe mental health disorders such as schizophrenia, severe bipolar disorder, or dissociative disorders may not benefit from mindfulness practices and could experience exacerbation of their symptoms.

Mindfulness should be integrated into clinical treatment plans carefully under the guidance of mental health professionals (Khoury et al., 2013). Individuals with a history of severe trauma or PTSD may find mindfulness practices triggering. Mindfulness practices often involve an explicit focus on bodily sensations and emotions, which can be distressing for those with unresolved trauma. Trauma-sensitive approaches are recommended (Treleaven, 2018).

In some cases, mindfulness practices that involve focusing on the present moment can increase anxiety or trigger panic attacks in individuals with acute anxiety disorders. Mindfulness should be adapted to the individual's needs, and relaxation techniques may be more appropriate initially (Roemer et al., 2015). While mindfulness-based interventions have been used in addiction treatment, individuals in the early stages of recovery or actively using substances may struggle with mindfulness practices. These individuals may require specialised interventions focusing on addiction treatment (Witkiewitz & Bowen, 2010).

Some physical health conditions, such as epilepsy or certain cardiovascular issues, may be aggravated by deep relaxation techniques used in mindfulness. It's essential for individuals with such conditions to consult with healthcare professionals before engaging in mindfulness practices (Black & Slavich, 2016). Mindfulness is a valuable practice with numerous benefits, but it is not universally suitable for all individuals or situations. It is crucial to consider individual needs, consult with healthcare or mental health professionals, and adapt mindfulness practices accordingly to ensure their safety and efficacy.

CHAPTER SUMMARY

This chapter considered intention and motivation to engage in mindfulness practice. Some commonly reported research outcomes were also presented. It was noted that the intentions that underly one's motivation to practice are an important facet of mindful awareness. Traditionally, establishing intention within a certain ethical framework was outlined.

Research studies suggest wide-ranging potential outcomes associated with mindfulness practice, including individually focussed benefits such as:

- Improved mental heath
- Better physical health
- Enhanced well-being
- More effective cognitive functioning and emotional regulation

in addition to global and social health outcomes such as:

- More effective relationship functioning
- Enhanced pro-social behaviour

- Increased empathy
- Heightened self and other focused compassion
- Reduced stereotyping and bias
- Environmental sustainability.

Nevertheless, it is crucial to recognise that mindfulness is not a universal remedy, and there are instances where, for many individuals, it may not be the most suitable practice to pursue.

SECTION II
Practice

5

CLARIFYING INTENTION

PRACTISING WITH INTENTION

Sometimes the obvious questions are not so obvious. Why practise mindfulness? More specifically, why should *you* practise mindfulness? How might it serve you? What might you miss by not practising? Socrates is thought to have said, "The unexamined life is not worth living." In a similar vein, Jon Kabat-Zinn reminds us, "*the little things and the little moments, they aren't little. They're life!*" (Moyers, 1993; 38:50). This call to live life, to experience all it has to offer – from the devastating losses to the ecstatic highs and everything in between – are all vital moments to be lived. From a mindfulness perspective, we only have "moments" to live. As we will explore further in Chapter 12, there are no guarantees regarding how long we will live. It is special to be here. As *Homo sapiens*, the ones that "know," conscious awareness appears to be unique to our species. To live a life that reflects such "knowing," infused with awareness of its transience and specialness, is one of the gifts of mindfulness.

Clarifying intention

Please refer to the audio-guided Intentions Practice.

What appeals to you about practising mindfulness?
What motivates you to practise?
What is important in your life that greater mindfulness could help to support?
What could it offer you?
What are the consequences of not being mindful?

DOI: 10.4324/9781003453598-8

There is a world of difference between practising mindfulness and "thinking about" practising mindfulness. We could consider "thinking about" as part of the "doing" mode of mind. This "doing mode" tends to become the "default mode" for most of us, such is the value placed on thinking. Mindfulness practice is different to thinking. We are not attempting to stop thinking or prevent thinking; instead the practice of mindfulness encourages us to simply "observe" thinking and switch to a mode of mind more aligned to directly "sensing" or "being" (e.g. McGilchrist, 2018; Teasdale, 2022; Williams, 2010). This allows us to experience life as it unfolds, moment by moment, and to train awareness to come back to the present moment each time attention wanders away. "Thinking about" sensing draws us away from the immediacy of the present. "Thinking about" what we are experiencing has the illusion of bringing us more in touch with the present moment but in effect creates an added layer between what is happening (e.g. hearing birdsong or feeling the movement of the breath) and directly sensing it.

FORMAL AND INFORMAL MINDFULNESS PRACTICE

When it comes to the practice of mindfulness, we can distinguish between "formal" and "informal" practices. The distinction typically refers to the form of practice we are engaged in. The body scan (Chapter 6), mindful movement (Chapter 7), and sitting meditation (Chapter 8) are commonly referred to as "formal" practices. Informal practice, which can be *any* activity engaged in with kindly awareness, can serve both as an extension of the formal practice, as well as a bridge back to formal practice. However difficult or challenging we may find it to clear some time in our day for formal meditation, we can stay in touch with our intention for practising mindfulness through periods of informal practice.

Remembering to re-member

"Remembering" is a key feature of the earliest definitions of mindfulness. Although mind wandering is universal, there is a greater likelihood of "remembering" the more we connect to the body (sensations) and other direct experience through both formal and informal practice.

ANY ACTIVITY CAN BECOME A MINDFULNESS PRACTICE

It can be unrealistic to seek to maintain a seamless continuity of awareness for long periods. Although the intention to do so may be helpful and motivating, it is likely to quickly become demotivating and frustrating. We often need to remind ourselves that it is natural for the mind (for attention) to wander. There is tremendous evolutionary value in this, as it allows us to identify what is important and disregard what is unimportant. The problem is that we are often not aware of what is on our mind much of the time. The fact that attention wanders isn't necessarily a problem if we can learn to recognise it and gently redirect it when it may be more helpful to. It may be possible under retreat or retreat-like conditions to maintain mindfulness more of the time; however, "more time being mindful" isn't necessarily the goal. How we meet moments of "mindlessness" is just as important as maintaining awareness of the present moment through the body (sensations), thoughts, emotions, and impulses to act. So even when not being mindful, there is an opportunity, when we notice this, to reconnect to the present moment. And then we are being mindful again!

Although formal meditation can provide clear boundaries for practising mindfulness, any activity can become a mindfulness practice. A key aspect of what makes any activity "mindful" is how intentional we are about paying attention in a kindly, open, and curious way. So, whether we are showering, brushing our teeth, having a cup of coffee, or waiting at a bus stop, we can become aware of what we are experiencing and how we are relating to what's happening.

Experimenting with giving attention to one or more "sense doors" (e.g. seeing, touching, hearing, tasting, smell) can be a natural way to make any activity more mindful. When walking, for example, we might choose to prioritise sensations of touch (of our feet on the ground), or the movement of the entire body, or sounds, or smell. Focusing awareness on any sensory aspect of experience can become a way into greater presence and connection with whatever activity we are engaged in. (In the Buddhist tradition, the mind is a sixth sense, one we can become aware of by paying attention to thoughts and emotions.)

The extent to which one may be able to "open" to experience depends on many factors – both external and internal. External factors include environmental conditions, such as the temperature of the room; adequate sitting equipment; reducing noise disturbance or interruptions from mobile phones; time available for practice; whether one is alone or in a group, and so on. Internal factors include one's expectations, current state, and understanding of the practice, for example, to feel relaxed or at ease; subtle or overt pressure to gain insight or achieve something; fatigue or drowsiness; physical comfort/discomfort or pain; one's mood, for example, feelings of agitation, irritation, frustration, or boredom. None of these factors need be obstacles *per se*, as long as, with the help and stability offered by a clear intention to pay attention, one can recognise what is happening and skilfully respond. Indeed, this is precisely one of the main reasons why we practise – to experience a range of mind–body states to which we can "practise" responding wisely and compassionately. (A couple of minutes if you are a beginner is enough to start with.) This will often entail cultivating qualities of heart, such as kindness, gentleness, patience, and trust, as well as other attitudinal qualities of mindfulness (Kabat-Zinn, 2013) that can support us in opening to experience.

Mindfulness as a warm bath!

There are many metaphors of mindfulness that can help to communicate something of the quality of the practice. One may be to consider mindfulness practice like taking a warm bath! From this we might get a visceral sense of just how nourishing and containing the practice can be. Approaching practice in this way can help overcome seeing it as a chore – precisely the mode of mind that can undermine even the intention to practise.

CREATING HELPFUL CONDITIONS AND NEW HABITS

A key aspect of maintaining a regular mindfulness practice is creating and maintaining the conditions that support and encourage mindfulness. For example, the environment in which you live and work can have various "push/pull" influences over your decision-making to engage in mindfulness practice. This is a point taken up by James Clear (2018) in his book *Atomic Habits*. It can be both skilful and helpful to create the conditions for new habits by making them 1) obvious, 2) attractive, 3) easy, and 4) rewarding.

This might mean creating a dedicated practice space in your home or workplace (1) and making it warm, comfortable and inviting (2), by sourcing blankets or cushions, including perhaps some plants and natural furnishings. A regular, protected time for practice each day can help in making it easier (3) and more likely that you practise, as sometimes thinking about practice can make it less likely to happen. Be playful with time, as "clock time" isn't necessarily a fair representation of quality practice. It can be helpful to hold the amount of time you spend practising lightly, for example, by not setting any time limits but instead committing to spending some time in meditation posture. At other times, it might be helpful to set a timer and practice for a specific length of time. Finally (4), the extent to which we cultivate the attitudinal qualities of mindfulness will ultimately determine how rewarding we find the practice. We may also notice the positive impact on our relationships even after brief practices. We have a lot of influence over how nourishing and restorative the practice is for us. However, this is something we usually need to work at quite consciously at the beginning.

Everyday tasks, chores, or activities can become opportunities to practice mindfulness. The difference is intention, attention, and attitude. We can deliberately make any activity – whether it is hanging clothes on a washing line or brushing your teeth – a mindful one simply by bringing kindly awareness to it. Although there may be resistance to the chore or task itself (compounded by thoughts and feelings about the activity), it is always possible to intentionally focus on more neutral aspects of the activity, for example, sensations of the breath or sensations of the body in movement, with kindness and curiosity.

The "attention economy" is a term attributed to political scientist and cognitive psychologist Herbert Simon (1971), who recognised that attention is a finite resource. He also astutely recognised (long before the advent of the iPhone) that "a wealth of information creates a poverty of attention" (Simon, 1971, p. 40). With so many competing demands on our attention, making conscious choices about where to direct it can save us from becoming passive recipients of what we take in and the risk of becoming depleted. We have a lot of say over where we place our attention and for how long. This might be a helpful reminder, particularly when we might feel overwhelmed, over-exposed, or exhausted by various forms of social media and news reports.

Frequently, what is not interesting or entertaining gets dismissed as "boring." What is not useful or relevant can be classed as redundant and attention freed up to be more usefully directed elsewhere. The potential danger here, particularly in this information age, is that we may seldom take opportunities to pause, to recharge, or to take stock. In essence, we may have forgotten how to be. The ability to stop, to appreciate what Henry David Thoreau (1854) called the "bloom" of the present moment, is something special and to be savoured. This appreciation of "non-doing" has enormous health benefits, especially given the addictive quality of "driven-doing" (Williams, 2010). Many of us may need to re-learn the art and skill of non-doing and the benefits of rest.

What is "boredom," anyway?

It seems that one of the common reactions we can have towards ourselves, other people, situations, or things is that of boredom. Sometimes we are just not that interested! This isn't a mistake or a failing on our part but rather how we seem to be hardwired. When we become aware of boredom, we can deliberately bring awareness to the thoughts, feelings, physical sensations, and any impulses we may have. For example, we can ask ourselves, "Where, exactly, does boredom show up in the body in this moment? Does this feeling have a shape or particular colour associated with it? Does it stay the same or does it change from moment to moment? What role are my thoughts playing in my experiencing of this as 'boring?'" Strange though it may sound, cultivating curiosity towards boredom can become quite fascinating!

TRAUMA SENSITIVITY

Even if you are new to mindfulness, you are always the expert when it comes to knowing yourself and making wise choices. There is no "right" way to practise mindfulness. What any two people might need when it comes to their practice might be entirely different. For example, one person may long for stillness; another might find movement practice more helpful. It is vitally important (for the long-term development and sustainability of your practice) that you respond to what you are noticing within yourself when practising. This will help you to make informed choices about what to focus on, for how long, and in what way, for example, giving oneself permission to open the eyes, to let go of the practice entirely, or to get up and move instead of sitting still. Any or all of these may be skilful choices. There is no "one size fits all" when it comes to practising mindfulness. As you begin to trust how you feel and adjust the practice guidance according to what feels right for you, the practice itself should feel more nourishing.

Each of us has a unique personal history and set of experiences that will inform the development of our mindfulness practice. Research published by the WHO (Kessler et al., 2017) suggests that at any one time, 10% of us will be living with the effects of a serious trauma or life event. We are also likely to experience several traumas in our lifetime. Knowing this is likely to be helpful to us as we engage in mindfulness practice, especially if we encounter difficulties or challenges such as falling asleep, irritation or agitation, or unexplained feelings of sadness or pain. This is part of the mystery and challenge of mindfulness practice: that when we sit down or lie down to practice, we never quite know what will happen. The question then becomes, how do we work with whatever arises within the context of mindfulness practice? Is it possible to bring a curious, kindly attention to the body/mind, or would it be more skilful to let go of the practice for a time? Bringing kindly awareness to what we are experiencing within the practice is integral to mindfulness. This is an important point, especially at times when our expectations of what we would like to get out of the practice (i.e. our thoughts) take over and "lead" our actual experience.

WORKING WITH PHYSICAL PAIN AND DISCOMFORT

Even though we may have started the practice in a relatively stable, still, and comfortable posture, it may not take long before we notice some physical discomfort. This is normal. We can work with physical discomfort in several ways. The first and most obvious thing we can do is to move and ease out the body, before settling back into stillness once again. In fact, any movement we make during the practice can simply be folded in as part of the sitting practice – bringing awareness to the intention to move and the movement itself, as well as any after-effects of moving. If discomfort persists, you can always experiment with adopting a different posture, for example, standing, walking, or lying down.

An alternative to moving is to bring a sense of curiosity and interest to the details of whatever sensations you are experiencing. This means deliberately shining the spotlight of attention directly on whatever part(s) are calling your attention. For example, noticing temperature – whether the sensation is hot or cold or neither. Perhaps it has a particular shape or boundary that can be traced in your mind's eye? Are the sensations predominantly ones of tingling? Burning? Pins and needles, or numbness? If what you are noticing is an absence of sensation, how is this? Sometimes, a sensation might be associated with a particular colour. How is it to notice this? It is important to choose the extent to which you are willing to explore difficult or more challenging sensations. A gentle, playful attitude when directing your attention will be helpful, especially not forcing any aspect of the practice. You are the expert; you get to choose how much and for how long to explore.

Another option is to experiment with the breath. Again, there are a couple of options we can choose here. We can choose to simply focus entirely on the breath, using the breath as an anchor for attention, as we cannot both "think about" pain, for example, and feel the breath's sensations at the same time. Whenever we discover we have been pulled into thinking about the pain (which frequently serves only to intensify our experience of it), we gently reconnect to the breath once again. Alternatively, much as in the body scan (see Chapter 6), we can imagine directing the breath "into" and "down to" regions of more intense sensation. It is important when working in this way to remember that we are not trying to get rid of the unwanted sensation(s). Rather, we are simply allowing the breath to support ourselves in staying present to whatever we may be experiencing, from moment to moment. In this way, we are changing often habitual tendencies to want to deny, suppress, or push away things we don't like or don't want. As we have seen, this can often just create additional layers of stress, tension, and difficulty – what is sometimes called "secondary suffering."

As well as these options within the practice itself, it can be helpful to build up to sitting for longer periods over time. This is especially important when periods of stillness might exacerbate pain. Listening to the body and making wise, compassionate choices within periods of formal practice will be most supportive. For these practices to remain nourishing and beneficial to you over the long term, you will likely need to be especially gentle and patient with yourself.

WORKING WITH PSYCHOLOGICAL AND EMOTIONAL PAIN

As well as experiencing physical pain and discomfort, we may also experience forms of psychological pain (e.g. sadness, grief, anger, fear, painful memories, self-criticism, shame, blame, or guilt). It is important to remember that "no emotion is final" and that there are several ways we can work with painful emotions. MBCT (Mindfulness-Based Cognitive Therapy; Segal et al., 2013) was developed as a skilful response to patterns of thinking and feeling that can trigger depressive relapse. This relies not just on gaining understanding about universal patterns of depression but also gaining experiential insight in shifting attention into the body. Focusing attention to explore the resonance of thoughts and feelings in the body can be a novel way of working for many of us who are "in our heads" most of the time. This is subtle work and relies on establishing a connection to the body that can often take time. In many ways, the eight weeks of MBCT are just an introduction to working with emotion through the body. Along with developing greater awareness of the body, cultivating attitudinal qualities of openness and kindness are just as important.

RESPONDING TO TIREDNESS AND FATIGUE

Just as there are several ways of working with physical and psychological pain, so too with tiredness or fatigue. Of course, at a fundamental level, this is often an indication that we are in some ways sleep deprived, a common complaint due to the various demands and pressures we may be facing, from screen time to the early morning commute to childcare to health needs – anything that might otherwise interrupt a good night's sleep. It is essential to prioritise and protect sleep (as much as possible) as a cornerstone of good mental and physical health. If sleep is difficult or impossible for us (e.g. due to an underlying condition), engaging in periods of conscious rest is just as important.

ATTITUDINAL QUALITIES OF MINDFULNESS

The ability to recognise and cultivate certain attitudinal qualities within the practice of mindfulness is arguably one of its key benefits. Over the initial months and years of practising mindfulness, we can begin to recognise what our default state of mind/heart is when we discover that our attention has wandered and "see" how this plays out in how we "speak" to ourselves. Part of the "work" of mindfulness is in making these patterns more explicit and better known to us. We do so not necessarily with the intention of changing things but more with the intention of getting to know and understand ourselves more fully. The paradox of mindfulness (as we saw in Chapter 3) is that such an orientation to the practice can allow change to happen, precisely by not forcing it.

Practice: cultivating kindness

Extending kindness to others often comes more easily than being kind to ourselves. This can become especially clear to us when practising mindfulness and becoming aware of our "inner dialogue." We might discover that we would never dream of speaking to other people the way we do to ourselves. The good news is that there is a way to change this; we can learn to be kinder and gentler with ourselves. When we begin to truly see the destructive tendencies of negative self-talk and self-focused rumination, we are on the cusp of change.

We can begin to extend a kindlier attitude to ourselves in several ways. One way is through giving thoughtful attention to the space in which you practise. Ensuring that the space is clean, bright, and comfortable, with good ventilation, is one way to start looking after yourself. Another way is through giving ourselves plenty of time to find our way "into" the practice. Taking care of the body by ensuring you are warm and comfortable in whatever posture you choose. Remember, we don't need to rush any of this. Even the transitions into and out of formal practice are vital moments of our lives.

MINDFULNESS AND HUMOUR

We know instinctively (and now scientifically) that, like smiling, laughing is good for us (Dunbar et al., 2012). It boosts our heart rate, reduces stress, and even improves work productivity. Laughing releases endorphins and the "happy" hormones such as dopamine and serotonin. It also suppresses stress hormones like cortisol. These effects are linked to a better mood, reduced pain, lower blood pressure, a stronger immune system, and lower stress levels and rates of depression. Similarly, laughter yoga, developed by Indian physician Dr Madan Kataria (Hoare, 2022) is an approach that actively seeks to cultivate joy and release stress through movement and breathing exercises which deliberately encourage laughing.

The capacity to laugh at life (including oneself) involves a willingness to change perspective. Of course, this is not always possible or appropriate. Laughter may be helpful, and at other times, the naming of personal challenge will require a more sober and measured response. The image of a clown who can laugh, cry, and get up after falling symbolises our capacity to meet experience, pleasant or painful, with a degree of equanimity. As the genius of silent comedy, Charlie Chaplin, so succinctly put it, "In order to truly laugh, you must be able to take your pain and play with it" (Osincup, 2024).

Mindfulness approaches have been successful in helping those struggling with depression, anxiety, and pain of various kinds. More recently, in courses like "Mindfulness for Life" (Kuyken, 2024), there has been greater emphasis on positive psychology to help us move towards a state of flourishing. To this end, it is vital to cultivate our connection to mindfulness practice as ways to foster qualities of joy, gratitude, and loving kindness. To this end, Kastner (2024) has demonstrated that a humour-enriched mindfulness-based programme was effective in increasing mindfulness, benevolent humour, and psychological well-being and in reducing sarcasm, cynicism, stress, and gelotophobia (fear of being laughed at), compared to controls.

HOW LONG SHOULD ONE PRACTICE? WHAT THE RESEARCH SAYS …

There does appear to be a small but significant positive correlation between the amount of mindfulness practice one engages in and the reported benefits of engaging in MBSR or MBCT (Parsons et al., 2017). This would suggest there is no need to limit the time we spend associated with learning other kinds of new skills or interests. Understandably, with such specifications of time, the mind may easily get caught up in attempting to "bank" or accumulate time. On the other hand, we could easily miss an entire practice session due to sleepiness. The whole notion of time collapses within the practice of mindfulness itself, as 5 minutes can seem like an hour and an hour like the "click" of your fingers – especially if we find it helpful and enjoyable. Psychology professor and neuroscience researcher Amishi Jha writes about many potential benefits that can accrue with just "12 minutes" of mindfulness practice (Jha, 2021). A more useful notion than focusing on time might be the sincerity of one's intention, regardless of time. Alertness plays into this – so, intention, attention, attitude *over time.*

A somewhat counter-intuitive piece of advice from meditation teacher Sharon Salzberg is to simply adopt a meditation posture, letting go of setting any time constraints whatsoever. Such freedom within the practice can make all the difference, especially when we may feel we don't have time. Even if all we have time for is to adopt a meditation posture, it can act as a reminder to be present and a way of reconnecting to intention. Another way we can view the practice of mindfulness is that of "inclining the mind" towards certain attitudinal qualities – a way of being with ourselves and others. We almost always have to be intentional about this; otherwise we are likely to continue to get caught up in habitual busyness, as well as default attitudes and modes of mind that are more associated with "doing" or "driven doing" than simply "being."

In a novel approach at the time (2010), Matthew Killingsworth and Daniel Gilbert from Harvard University sent research participants text messages at random times during the day and asked where their mind was in that moment. The results were astounding. People reported their minds to be wandering almost half of the time (46.9%). Furthermore, participants were also asked to say how their mood was. This provided an extra insight into the nature of mind wandering. Most people who reported their mind had been wandering had low mood. This led the authors to conclude, "a human mind is a wandering mind, and a wandering mind is an unhappy mind." As we saw in Chapter 3, Farb et al.'s (2007) research revealed brain configurations underlying a default, narrative mode of mind on the one hand and one that reflected being more present, through activation of brain regions associated with sensory processing and the body, on the other. It is important to recognise that both modes of mind have their place, for example, the creative potential and ease offered by mind wandering, and that it can also lead to unhappiness if left unchecked.

LETTING GO OF THE PRACTICE

The Austrian writer Rainer Maria Rilke beautifully observed that our deepest fears are like dragons, guarding our deepest treasures. The idea that there may be great treasure to be found by getting to know the deepest parts of ourselves requires a certain willingness to do our own inner work. However, we need to do this inner "work" with much patience, kindness, and skill. For example, there may be times when it feels simply too difficult or challenging to engage in formal practice. We may choose to opt out or let go of the practice for many different reasons, such as feeling extremely agitated or sleepy. It is important in such moments to allow yourself to let go of the practice entirely, without criticising yourself or giving yourself a hard time. At other times, it may be possible to engage in periods of informal practice instead, such as walking. When we do feel motivated and steady enough in ourselves to "work with" difficult mind/body states, we can deliberately choose to make them a focus in our practice.

PERIODS OF NOT PRACTISING

Regardless of your intention, there will be times when your practice might stall, or you have not been able to practise for some time. The attitudinal qualities of mindfulness are especially important at these times. Although there may be a familiar pattern to criticise and judge yourself harshly, this is a moment to practice kindness and understanding. Especially in the early months of developing a regular practice, it can be helpful to anticipate and expect that your practice may wane – even as you continue to value it highly. Our experience has shown that how we re-engage with the practice after periods of not practising are opportunities to become *even clearer* about the "why" of practising mindfulness. Given that our lives are constantly changing, with different challenges and experiences, we return to the practice never quite the same. This can be an opportunity to reconnect and clarify one's intention for practice.

During busy or difficult periods, it may be enough to simply acknowledge your intention to engage in the practice, especially if demands are preventing or blocking you from practising. We can always work on the foundational attitudinal qualities of the practice (e.g. patience, acceptance, non-striving; Kabat-Zinn, 2013), even if we cannot focus attention long enough to engage in the practice itself. It is possible to bring kindly awareness to "not practising" or to our resistance to practising – paradoxically, this is also being mindful.

Equally, practising during times of upheaval may be very difficult or impossible. One helpful approach might be to focus attention on moment-to-moment aspects of experience and even narrating these: *"now I am walking downstairs, now I can feel my hand on the banister and my feet contacting the stairs. Just this next step … I can feel my hand sliding on the banister."* This involves coming back to the immediacy of physical sensations when the mind wanders away. *"Still feeling the contact with the banister, shifting weight, lifting my leg, taking the next step."* Finally, talking about your mindfulness practice with fellow practitioners or mindfulness teachers on a regular basis can be very helpful in sustaining motivation and clarity about "why" you are practising. Inspiring talks or attending teacher-led retreats can also help to nourish and sustain you in your practice. Frequently, teachers of standard 'eight-week' mindfulness programmes will offer "retreat days" as part of their teaching calendar, and it is often possible to join these once you have a well-established practice. Retreat days can offer a timely re-setting of intention and offer inspiration whenever the practice is feeling stuck or stalled.

THE ATTITUDINAL FOUNDATIONS OF MINDFULNESS

The seven attitudinal foundations of mindfulness, developed by Jon Kabat-Zinn (2006), form a framework that fosters a receptive, creative, and less judgemental approach to our mindfulness practice. These foundational attitudes, along with two later additions, are underlying principles of mindfulness.

Non-judging: This foundation encourages observing thoughts and experiences without assigning value judgements. It involves letting go of the tendency to label thoughts as good or bad, right or wrong, and instead, cultivating a neutral awareness.

Patience: Mindfulness practice involves recognising the natural unfolding of experiences and allowing them to manifest in their own time. Patience in mindfulness means acknowledging and accepting the pace of personal growth and understanding.

Beginner's Mind: Cultivating a "beginner's mind" involves approaching each moment with openness and curiosity, as if encountering it for the first time. This attitude promotes receptivity and prevents preconceived notions from clouding perception.

Trust: Trust refers to developing a basic confidence in experience. Although things may be unclear for us, or we may not understand why we may be feeling a certain way, if we can allow things to be as they are *for now*, clarity will come – or the situation will change. Trust also involves trusting in a fundamental lawfulness of nature and the transformative potential of mindfulness itself.

Non-striving: Instead of striving for a particular outcome, mindfulness encourages being present and fully engaged in the current moment. Non-striving involves letting go of the pursuit of specific results and embracing an open and accepting attitude.

Acceptance: Acceptance involves acknowledging thoughts and feelings without resistance or judgement. It is about allowing experiences to be as they are, even if they are challenging, and fostering a compassionate response to oneself.

Letting go (non-attachment): Letting go in mindfulness means releasing attachments to thoughts and emotions. It involves allowing experiences to come and go without clinging to them or pushing them away, promoting a sense of emotional freedom.

Gratitude: Gratitude involves recognising and appreciating the positive aspects of one's life. In the context of mindfulness, it serves as a powerful attitudinal foundation that enhances the overall experience of the present moment. When individuals cultivate gratitude, they shift their focus from what may be lacking to what is already present and meaningful. This shift in perspective aligns with the core principles of mindfulness, encouraging individuals to be fully present and engaged with the richness of their current experiences.

From an academic standpoint, research on gratitude and mindfulness has demonstrated positive outcomes, including improved well-being, mental health, and interpersonal relationships (Wood et al., 2010). The integration of gratitude into mindfulness practices amplifies the potential for holistic personal development.

Generosity: Generosity involves the selfless giving of time, resources, or kindness to others. In the context of mindfulness, cultivating a generous attitude fosters a sense of interconnectedness and compassion. When individuals engage in acts of generosity, they not only contribute to the well-being of others but also experience a deep sense of fulfilment.

Academic literature on the intersection of generosity and mindfulness suggests that engaging in altruistic behaviours positively impacts mental health and overall life satisfaction (Dunn et al., 2008). The integration of generosity into mindfulness practices expands the focus beyond personal well-being to the interconnectedness of all beings, reinforcing the notion that mindfulness extends beyond individual introspection to a broader sense of community.

CHAPTER SUMMARY

- There is no one way or "right way" to practice mindfulness.
- You are the expert when it comes to knowing yourself (even if this is currently an underdeveloped skill).
- Mindfulness is about making wise choices.
- Wise choices mean responding in a kindly way to whatever is happening in any given moment. It is the opposite of reacting.
- Developing kindness is key to developing and sustaining our practice over the long term.
- The attitudinal foundations of mindfulness are an essential feature of mindfulness training.

6

FINDING YOUR GROUND
The body scan practice

In a fluctuating, hectic, unstable world, most people would benefit from finding greater steadiness and calm to have the resources to meet experience as it is, moment by moment. The body scan invites us to tune into our physical sensations, to come to our senses, which is an important aspect of creating a flourishing life. As Segal and Farb (2024) have clearly demonstrated, sensing balances overthinking, and overthinking can often cause unhelpful stress.

In relation to mindfulness of the body and its importance, here is what the founder of Buddhism said 2,500 years ago:

> *If one thing, O monks, is developed and cultivated, the body is calmed, the mind is calmed,* discursive thoughts are quieted, [my emphasis] *and all wholesome states that partake of supreme knowledge reach fullness of development. What is that one thing? It is mindfulness directed to the body.*
>
> (Anguttara Nikaya; cited in Thera, 2010, p. 9)

This is an ancient insight confirmed by modern neuroscience describing the relationship between the default mode network (DMN) and the sensing network. For example, in their book *Better in Every Sense*, Segal and Farb (2024) explain that the brain has two networks – the rapid problem-solving default mode network (habit) and the sensory mode network, which is devoted to fresh learning and insight. Given the universal tendency to live in our heads and experience life through concepts, we recommend "sense foraging" or, in Jon Kabat-Zinn's words, "coming to our senses." One method of bringing greater balance to these two

DOI: 10.4324/9781003453598-9

brain networks, among many others, is to bring attention to the body as a whole world of sensations.

MINDFULNESS IS, IN ITS ESSENCE, ABOUT PRACTICE, BUT PRACTISING WHAT EXACTLY?

According to Jon Kabat-Zinn, mindfulness practice fosters the learning that arises from paying attention in the present moment, on purpose, and non-judgementally (Kabat-Zinn, 1994). The body scan meditation applies this concept to the body. Many mindfulness courses (e.g. Mindfulness-Based Stress Reduction (MBSR) and Mindfulness-Based Cognitive Therapy (MBCT)) start with the body scan as the main "formal" practice, which is then done daily at home after the first week of the course.

According to Buddhist scholar Bhikkhu Anālayo (2020), Kabat-Zinn learned meditation from Robert Hover, who taught vipassana meditation retreats in the tradition of U Ba Khin, a Burmese meditation teacher. Kabat-Zinn's decision to teach these meditation practices outside of a religious context stemmed from his desire to introduce them as therapies for pain reduction (Helderman, 2019). The meditator is directed to sweep their attention through the body, resting in various regions of the body systematically. Importantly, there is no instruction to change the state of the body; this is not a relaxation exercise. The body scan is a mindfulness exercise, designed to bring the attention to experience in the present moment.

HOW TO PRACTICE THE BODY SCAN MEDITATION

The body scan meditation as taught in MBSR lasts for 45 minutes. In this practice, the meditator is invited to lie down. Kabat-Zinn purposely decided to have the practitioner lie down because many of his first patients were in too much pain to complete a 45-minute seated meditation (Anālayo, 2020). However, it is perfectly fine to do the practice in a sitting position or even while standing. It may be that for many people, lying down encourages a sense of ease and a letting go of activity – in other words, an invitation to simply let go, to enter and dwell in what is called "being" mode.

This is "a different way of knowing that … helps you to step outside of your mind's natural tendency to over-think, over-analyse and over-judge" (Williams & Penman, 2011, pp. 34–35).

In this first formal practice, students are asked to carve out some time each day to lie down and to gently and clearly attend to the body just as it is. This can be very challenging for busy people who may ask, "how can I spend this time 'doing nothing'?" when there are so many pressing demands on their time. This implicit encouragement and permission to rest is an important aspect of this practice. Many people find it difficult to sleep enough hours and are often sleep deprived and in desperate need of rest. In yoga practice, there is a comparable exercise called "yoga nidra" which also encourages deep rest (Stanley, 2021).

It is important to be warm and comfortable. You may want to place a pillow or folded blanket under your knees to help take any stress or strain off your back. You can also use a shallow pillow or folded towel under your head, blanket over your torso or anything else that makes you feel more comfortable. Some teachers suggest a yoga position called "savasana" with the legs straight and the arms out to the side, palms facing upward, but there are other options, for example, the semi supine position with the knees bent and the feet flat on the ground. The main thing is that you feel comfortable and the body feels well supported, so feel free to experiment with different postures.

Although relaxation is the opposite of stress (Benson & Klipper, 2000) and an important state to encourage, this is not the aim of the body scan. Rather the intention is to bring an open, friendly, and curious attention to whatever is present in experience from moment to moment. This includes the experience of the mind wandering from the intended focus (and coming back, time after time). For the duration of the body scan, the meditator is instructed to maintain awareness of physical sensations in different regions of the body. If at any point awareness shifts away and the participant becomes distracted, they are instructed simply to return to the body and continue with the practice.

The meditation begins with finding a helpful anchor, such as the breath movements in the belly, and this can be the place to be returned to whenever one feels lost or troubled. Other possible anchor points might be the contact of the body with the ground or sensations in the hands. Then, from this anchor, the attention is generally invited to move into the feet, noticing any sensations present in the toes. Then the meditator slowly moves awareness to the heels, ankles, and upward. The instruction is simply to notice and be aware of any sensations that are present (including the absence of sensation). Sensations are anything that is noticed in the body, like tingling, cramping, tightness, heat, coolness, buzzing, pulsing, itching, throbbing, or numbness.

Why is noticing sensations in the body beneficial? It helps bring our attention into the present moment, since we can only feel or sense what is taking place in the "here and now." Implicit within the body scan is an understanding that physical sensations are also often tied to emotional states. You may not even realise that stress and other emotions, such as anger or sadness, cause physical symptoms like tightness in your chest, headaches, and heartburn. Recognising where we hold stress in the body is important because we often only become aware of this when we are exhausted or experience pain. This can be the body's reminder to us to take care. The practice invites us to stay present to the body even when we don't like what we're experiencing, such as pain and discomfort. After moving in this way systematically through the entire body, the meditator is then instructed to link the parts together and feel the body in its entirety. In addition to the value of noticing sensations in the body, this practice is a perfect nursery ground for cultivating the attitudinal foundations (Kabat-Zinn, 2013).

Often, people ask "how long should a body scan meditation take?"

It depends on how much time you have and your preferences. There is no strict time limit; however, giving yourself about 20–40 minutes to connect to the body and get into the practice is recommended. Because the body scan practice can be lengthy, it is important not to become disheartened if you lose focus or fall asleep. This often happens, even to experienced practitioners.

If you're short on time, even a 5- or 10-minute body scan meditation can be beneficial. Most people find listening to a recorded guidance very helpful for this practice, at least to start with in the early weeks and months of doing it, and so you can choose the length of the recording accordingly. *Please refer to the audio-guided Body Scan Practice.*

INTENTIONS OF THE PRACTICE

Perhaps surprisingly, the aim of the body scan is not to achieve a state of relaxation, nor any other special state. Of course, experiencing relaxation is highly desirable as it is the opposite of stress (see Benson & Klipper, 2000). So, it's lovely to feel relaxed, but it is not our intention. We can practise the body scan however we are feeling. The body scan helps us to develop three fundamental skills for paying attention: directing our attention, sustaining our attention, and learning how to shift our attention (Teasdale, 2014).

It doesn't matter what sensations you become aware of – the important thing is, as best you can, to tune into the *direct* sense of the body, rather than getting *entangled* in thinking about it. We also learn how to work with the various challenges that can arise in any mindfulness practice, whether that is physical, for example, pain, tension, falling asleep, or discomfort; emotional, for example, sadness, boredom, frustration; or mental, for example, the mind creating fantasies or worries.

If you're struggling to feel like you benefit much from a body scan practice, consider your intentions and attitude toward the practice. Are you rushing or approaching the practice with specific goals in mind?

It's best to stay open-minded and curious, rather than going into meditation with specific goals. If your practice is worsening your stress, try making your sessions shorter and taking the pressure off yourself.

As the first longer practice, we see the importance given to the body in mindfulness-based programmes. MBSR emphasises the possibility for all people of touching states of greater wholeness, and this requires coming home to the body. This approach can be seen as a valuable counter to many modern attitudes to the body, such as preoccupation with appearance, feelings of inadequacy, self-infatuation, or alienation.

The body scan is also an opportunity for the skilled teacher to infuse the practice with the attitudinal foundations of mindfulness such as trust, non-striving, patience, non-judging, and letting go (Kabat-Zinn, 2013).

POTENTIAL LEARNING FROM
THE BODY SCAN

Consistent practice is crucial for reaping the benefits of meditation. This is not easy, and having support is very helpful. So, do consider practising with others, finding a qualified teacher, committing to a regular practice time, and letting go of unrealistic expectations (Birk, 2020). *Please refer to the audio-guided Body Scan Practice.*

RECLAIMING YOUR LIFE

Engaging in a body scan meditation allows individuals to tune into bodily sensations, fostering a deeper connection with the present moment and enhancing the sense of being alive. Kabat-Zinn (2013) describes this process: "When you tune into them (sensations), you are reclaiming your life in that very moment, and your body as well, making yourself more real and more alive. You are living your life in real time, as it unfolds, moment by moment in awareness. You are present for it and with it and in it. Your experience is *embodied* (original italics)" (p. 77).

CULTIVATING WHOLENESS
AND "BEING" MODE

In addition, the body scan reveals the "doing" mode, *"characterised by judging everything, comparing the way things are with the way you want them to be, and striving to make them different from how they actually are. This mode often involves being on automatic pilot, getting lost in thoughts taken too literally and personally, living in the past or future, and avoiding what you don't like"* (Williams & Penman, 2011, p. 105).

In *Falling Awake*, (Kabat-Zinn, 2018a) Jon Kabat-Zinn suggests that practising radical acceptance during the body scan encourages individuals to embrace the present moment and let go of resistance, facilitating a deeper connection with themselves and their surroundings. The body scan practice facilitates the development of concentration and attentional flexibility by encouraging a sustained focus that is intentionally moved throughout the body. The body scan can also enable individuals to perceive their bodies as integrated wholes nested within larger spheres of relationality, fostering a sense of interconnectedness (Kabat-Zinn, 2018b).

Rebecca Crane has highlighted four key skills honed through the body scan: connecting with present-moment physical sensations, intentional attention placement, skilful management of mind wandering, and acceptance of experiences as they arise (Crane, 2017, pp. 112–113). In addition, crucially and fundamentally, this simple practice is the training ground of helpful and grounded attitudes towards ourselves such as trust, patience, and non-striving (Kabat-Zinn, 2013). Unlike active practices like progressive muscle relaxation (PMR), the body scan emphasises acceptance of bodily sensations without attempting to alter them in any way (Dreeben et al., 2013a). This practice may help us avoid the risk of perceived failure by encouraging individuals to be with whatever experience is arising, moment by moment.

In terms of the original MBSR objectives, the body scan's acceptance-oriented approach can help individuals cope with chronic pain by recognising its transient nature and fostering a more positive relationship with bodily sensations. Kabat-Zinn's insights into the body scan practice underscore its transformative impact on individuals' relationships with their bodies, mind states, and overall well-being. By tuning into what he calls the "body scape," individuals develop a refined sensitivity and vivid awareness of their physical sensations, which becomes emotionally nuanced and stabilising over time. This heightened awareness is reflected in anecdotal reports from mindfulness practitioners who note significant shifts in their experience of chronic pain, fear, and illnesses like cancer or heart disease as they commit to daily body scans over weeks (Kabat-Zinn, 2018b). Through this practice, individuals learn to approach their body and mind states non-reactively and non-judgementally, which Kabat-Zinn (2013) describes as an "intrinsically fulfilling" experience. He emphasises that this approach to presence enables people to confront even challenging emotions like fear, loneliness, and confusion, fostering a sense of acceptance and healing: to see that such mind and body states are indeed workable and, ultimately, profoundly healable.

Kabat-Zinn also speaks to the body scan's practical benefits, such as countering mental "drivenness" by pausing to reconnect with the body: "Just getting down on the floor for a while … can slow down or stop the forward momentum of the head and all its drivenness" (2018b, p. 77). He encourages us to imagine the body as a "musical instrument" that the body scan helps "tune," or as a "house" that the body scan opens up, allowing "the fresh air of awareness" to clear it (2018b, pp. 80–81). These metaphors highlight the body scan as a mindful tool for both understanding and revitalising not just the body but our whole integrated mind–body system, promoting an intrinsic sense of calm, openness, and balance.

BENEFITS OF THE BODY SCAN

Although MBSR and MBCT have been studied extensively as programmes and shown to have multiple benefits for both physical and mental health, the body scan meditation has been studied less on its own as it is only one tool used within the MBSR and MBCT programmes. Generally, research studies of mindfulness include the entire programme (e.g. Grossman et al., 2004). However, the following studies indicate a number of benefits from body scan practice.

1. *Stress and nervous system regulation*: helps mitigate the fight-or-flight response, reducing cortisol levels and promoting relaxation by activating the parasympathetic nervous system (Ditto et al., 2006; Schultchen, 2019b).
2. *Managing anxiety*: enables individuals to identify and release anxiety-induced tension, reducing overall anxiety and improving emotional well-being (Carmody & Baer, 2008, Goyal, 2014).
3. *Chronic pain management*: encourages an accepting attitude toward pain, reducing its psychological impact and improving coping mechanisms, even with brief sessions (Ussher, 2014).
4. *Improving sleep*: reduces tension and fosters calmness, alleviating anxiety that impedes sleep (Gu et al., 2015), and is effective when integrated into cognitive-behavioural therapy for insomnia (CBTI) (de Bruin et al., 2020).
5. *Enhancing self-awareness*: promotes recognition of internal experiences, fostering a non-reactive approach to thoughts and emotions, and enhancing psychological well-being (Miriams et al., 2013; Fischer, 2017).

6. *Boosting cognitive performance*: improves attention, concentration, and decision-making by enhancing interoception (awareness of internal bodily sensations) (Zanesco, 2018).

7. *Cultivating a renewed relationship* with ourselves that is kind and creative (Keng at al., 2011).

HOW TO INCORPORATE BODY SCAN MEDITATION IN YOUR LIFE

Establish a routine and choose a suitable time for practice. Some people like to check in first thing in the morning before getting out of bed. Other people prefer doing a body scan meditation before sleep so they can sleep better. See what works best for you. Embrace imperfection in meditation and aim for consistency rather than perfection.

Do the best you can. There is no aim, no right or wrong way to do it, and no reason to worry that you might not be "good" at it.

For some people, the thought of taking 30 minutes to do any sort of meditation is very stressful. Depending on your time availability, you can extend or shorten the time it takes to do a body scan. You may want to do mini-body scans where you quickly scan your body to see where you are holding tension. For example, some people hold their jaws very tight.

By integrating body scan meditation into your daily life, you can experience the numerous benefits it offers for physical and mental well-being.

RISKS AND SIDE EFFECTS

A leading expert in trauma recovery, Bessel Van der Kolk, comments that "trauma victims cannot recover until they become familiar with and befriend the sensations in their bodies" (Van der Kolk, 2014, p. 100). David Treleavan, who has highlighted the need for "trauma sensitive mindfulness" agrees: "The body scan … can produce great benefits for participants. For instance, in her research with trauma survivors, Trish Magyari found that body scans were the most helpful aspect to some survivors in their trauma recovery" (Treleaven, 2018, pp. 143–144).

At the same time, Treleaven (2018) highlights how bringing attention to physical sensation can be challenging or dysregulating for anyone who has experienced trauma and may induce shame from a sense of failure from feeling numb or few sensations or an inability to concentrate. For this reason, Treleavan advises that "survivors need to feel in choice. Modifications can include positioning oneself in different postures (e.g. sitting up), keeping one's eyes open or lying on one's side" (2018, p. 143).

Letting people know what to expect and managing expectations can also be helpful, as well as checking in with participants after the practice.

It is also important to "normalise numbness during a body scan or affirm someone's choice not to linger on a particular area of the body" (Treleaven, 2018, p. 144).

For individuals with post-traumatic stress disorder (PTSD) or severe anxiety, it may be advisable to commence any kind of meditation under the guidance of a therapist.

CHAPTER SUMMARY

In conclusion, the body scan is a foundational practice which can begin to teach the practitioner many important skills and invaluable shifts of attitude. It is a direct way of coming to our senses, moving from analysing to sensing, which is a key mindfulness skill.

7

MOVEMENT AND STILLNESS
Taking the practice into everyday life

Evidence-based mindfulness programmes such as Mindfulness-Based Cognitive Therapy (MBCT) and Mindfulness-Based Stress Reduction (MBSR) include a focus on integrating mindfulness with physical activity. These programmes encourage individuals to bring a sense of curiosity and interest to physical sensations, movements, and especially any reactions to these, during gentle exercise or everyday activities. This form of mindfulness practice aims to deepen the mind–body connection, enhance physical and mental well-being, and cultivate a sense of presence.

Mindful movement is a practice that reveals and extends the possibility of bringing mindful awareness to all the moments of our day. Mindful walking and gentle stretches can create a more continuous experience of dropping into the present moment even in the midst of busy lives. "It provides an extended laboratory (or playground) to explore your mind in all its intricacies" (Williams & Penman, 2011, p. 118).

In examining the practice of mindful movement, it is evident that various cultures have long integrated physical activity with mental training. For instance, the ancient Indian practice of yoga emphasises the union of body and mind (Feuerstein, 2012). Similarly, Chinese traditions such as *Tai Chi* and *Qi Gong* (sometimes known as ch'i kung), as well as Japanese martial arts like *aikido* and *karate*, highlight the synergy between physical movement and mental focus (Jahnke et al., 2010; Nakamura, 2013). In contemporary Western contexts, additional methodologies aimed at a holistic mind-body development have emerged, such as the *Alexander Technique* (Jones, 1998) and the *Feldenkrais Method*

DOI: 10.4324/9781003453598-10

(Buchanan, 2002). Track, field, and team sports, including football, baseball, and basketball, increasingly make use of psychology to enhance physical performance (Mumford 2016, Gallwey 2024). In addition, in dance forms like *tango*, originating in Argentina, there is an implicit embodiment of this principle of intertwining physical movement with mental training (Pellegrini, 2016).

Engaging in mindful movement practices, such as gentle stretches, encourages individuals to cultivate presence, purposefulness, and non-judgemental awareness, akin to mindfulness practices like body scans or sitting meditation (Kabat-Zinn, 2003). "Movement can have as profound and soothing an impact on the mind as the body scan" (Williams & Penman, 2011, p. 118).

Recognising the embodiment of our experiences, it becomes apparent that achieving greater wholeness, a central aim of mindfulness-based programmes (MBPs), necessitates the inclusion of our physical selves (Kabat-Zinn, 2011). Furthermore, proper care for our bodies is paramount for both disease prevention and the recovery process from injuries and illnesses (Lengacher et al., 2019). Mindful movement, as a concept, underscores not only an awareness of the body but also the significance of nurturing it, attending to its cues, and respecting its limitations (Kabat-Zinn, 2013). It is essential to recognise that mindful movement is about cultivating awareness, with all the fruits that this brings, and not about competition, whether with oneself or others.

WHAT KIND OF MOVEMENT IS USED IN MINDFULNESS-BASED PROGRAMMES?

In MBSR and MBCT there is a primary focus on mindful movement based on hatha yoga movements. When Kabat-Zinn devised his MBSR programme, he was himself a practitioner and teacher of yoga. In *Full Catastrophe Living* (which describes the MBSR programme), Kabat-Zinn (2013) states that "Yoga *is* meditation." An intriguing suggestion! In "MBCT distinctive features," Rebecca Crane comments that "the practices taught are commonly drawn from hatha yoga postures but may also be drawn from other disciplines such as qigong or tai chi, depending upon the practice experience of the teacher" (Crane, 2017, p. 115). Some teachers particularly value the calming and soothing qualities that can often be experienced in qigong (chi kung) when moving with the breath (see e.g. Karunavira, 2021). *Please refer to the audio-guided practices on Mindful Yoga Introduction, Mindful Yoga (1) and (2), Mindful Movement based on Chi Kung, Stretch and Breath Practice.*

KEY ASPECTS OF MINDFUL MOVEMENT

1. Attention to bodily sensations

During mindful movement, individuals focus on the physical sensations associated with each movement. This includes changes in temperature, noticing the feeling of muscles stretching, the contact of feet with the ground, or the rhythm of the breath. This can offer a very clear and welcome focus for the mind.

Example: In yoga, paying close attention to how various parts of the body feel in a pose and how the breath moves through the body.

2. Slow and deliberate movements

Movements are often performed slowly and deliberately to facilitate deeper awareness and connection with the body. This may be very different to how we usually move – with a driven task orientation or simply on autopilot.

Example: In tai chi, the slow, graceful movements help to cultivate a focused and calm mind.

3. Non-judgemental awareness

Practitioners are encouraged to observe their bodily sensations and movements without judgement or striving to change them. This fosters acceptance and reduces the tendency to criticise oneself.

Example: While walking mindfully, noticing how the body feels with each step without trying to alter the gait or speed; or while stretching, acknowledging the body's natural limits in that moment.

4. Integration with breath

Mindful movement often incorporates awareness of the breath, using it as an anchor to maintain presence and focus.

Example: In mindful walking, synchronising steps with the breath can enhance the sense of rhythm and grounding.

5. Enhancing the mind–body connection

By bringing mindfulness to physical activities, individuals can develop a greater sense of embodiment and a deeper connection between mind and body. We can sense when we are physically pushing beyond what is helpful in a posture in a way that reflects how we can often be doing this on the mental and emotional level at other times. We can also notice times when we are not using enough effort, and this might help us see other ways in which we limit ourselves in life. Movement practice has this aspect of helping participants learn about life tendencies through the way they are played out and reflected in a grounded and clear way in the movements themselves.

Example: In mindful stretching, feeling the stretch deeply in the muscles and noticing how it affects the overall sense of wellbeing. Are you pushing or straining in any way? Does this feel familiar? Or are you holding back for some reason? Again, does this feel like a known pattern?

6. Promoting relaxation and stress reduction

Mindful movement practices are designed to reduce stress by encouraging a state of calm and presence.

Example: Practising qigong can help release physical tension and foster a sense of inner peace.

INTENTIONS OF MINDFUL MOVEMENT

A key intention is to bring awareness to an often-neglected aspect of our experience: the body and its sensations. Through establishing a greater connection, we can learn to listen more attentively to the messages of the body and start to take greater care of ourselves. As in any mindful practice, we can weave in the attitudinal foundations described earlier (see Chapter 5), learning how to stretch without striving or forcing, or noticing this when we do. With the guidance of a teacher (in person or virtual), we can practise qualities such as Beginners Mind, Patience, Acceptance, Non-judging, Trust, and Allowing (Kabat-Zinn, 2013).

During mindful movement, we are invited to focus on the physical sensations generated by simple movements and, crucially, how we are *relating to* these sensations. Is there resistance, striving, pushing, holding back, liking, not liking? This is where much potential for insight lies. For example, we can investigate how much effort we are making in each movement, and in this way, notice patterns such as pushing or holding back. These patterns may then become more visible at other moments when going about our everyday tasks. In between movements, we can take a pause to sense the impact of the movement on the body, thoughts, and mood.

Near the end of an individual stretch, we can find our "edges," a soft edge with the arising of some intensity in the body. Here we might feel able to explore and stay with the sensations being felt. In contrast, we may encounter a "hard edge," which is the body saying, "Enough!" At this point, any further stretching or effort may cause harm. This signal is to be respected. (see Burch & Penman, 2013). Learning over time how to work with moments of discomfort is a key mindfulness skill. Extending insights that arise from physical challenges then paves the way for exploring emotional difficulties and generally waking up to some of our only too familiar life tendencies as we see them played out in the movements before our eyes, so to speak! This connection between emotional states and physical sensations is explicitly explored in MBCT, originally developed to prevent depressive relapse.

WALKING PRACTICE

This is an ancient movement practice which involves becoming aware of the body and its sensations as we walk along a short track or circle. When we walk mindfully, we are bringing attention to the physical sensations of walking, especially to the soles of the feet. We practise becoming fully present with each step, letting go of any sense of destination, of needing to get somewhere, and repeatedly coming back to where we are. Once we become familiar with this, we can then drop into informal moments of mindful walking in everyday life (e.g. going upstairs at home or the walk from the carpark to the office).

Key elements of mindful walking

1. Attention to bodily sensation

Mindful walking involves paying close attention to the sensations in the body as it moves. This includes feeling the ground under your feet, the movement of your legs, the swing of your arms, and the rhythm of the breath.

Example: Noticing how each foot lifts, moves forward, and contacts the ground.

2. A deliberate pace

The speed of walking may vary according to intention: thus, if the mind is sleepy and dull, a quicker pace may be helpful, or if wanting to calm our system, we could explore a slower pace. Walking slowly and deliberately helps deepen awareness.

Walking slowly and deliberately can help to deepen awareness and allow for a more thorough observation of bodily sensations.

Example: Taking smaller steps and moving at a pace that allows you to notice and appreciate each part of the walking process.

3. Breath awareness

Integrating breath awareness into the practice, mindful walkers often synchronise their steps with their breathing. This helps maintain focus and grounding in the present moment. If this integration feels restricting or controlling, coordinating with the breath may be paused for a short while and then picked up again later.

Example: Taking a step with each inhale and another step with each exhale. Or breathing in as you lift your back foot and breathing out as you place the foot on the ground in front of you.

4. Non-judgemental observation

Observing sensations, thoughts, and feelings without judgement is a core component of mindful walking. This means inviting an intention to accept whatever arises during the practice without trying to change it.

Example: Noticing a thought about an unfinished task and gently bringing your attention back to the sensation of walking.

5. Engagement with the environment

While the primary focus is on the body's sensations, mindful walking also involves being aware of the surroundings. This can include noticing the sights, sounds, and smells around you.

Example: If walking outside, observing the colour of the leaves, the sound of birds, or the feel of air against the skin. Simple beauty can arise as we slow down and come to our senses.

Steps to practice mindful walking

Please refer to the audio-guided Walking Practice. Firstly, find a suitable location. Choose a safe and comfortable place to walk, whether it's indoors or outdoors. This could be a quiet path, a park, or even a long hallway. Begin by standing still for a few moments. Take a few deep breaths and bring your awareness to your body. Feel the connection between your feet and the ground. Then begin walking at a pace that feels appropriate for your bodily and emotional state, paying attention to each part of the movement, from lifting your foot to placing it back on the ground.

You can also synchronise your movement with your breath. For instance, you could take one step with each inhalation and one with each exhalation.

As best you can, keeping your mind focused on the sensations of walking. If your attention wanders, you may find stopping for a few moments helpful, then gently bringing it back to the feeling of your feet touching the ground or the rhythm of your breath.

Finally, gradually expand your awareness to include your surroundings. Notice the environment without losing touch with the sensations in your body.

Mindful walking is a powerful practice that integrates mindfulness with the simple act of walking. It offers numerous physical and mental health benefits by fostering present-moment awareness, enhancing the mind–body connection, and promoting a sense of peace and well-being. Whether practised alone or as part of a broader mindfulness programme like MBSR or MBCT, mindful walking is an accessible and effective way to incorporate mindfulness into daily life.

MINDFUL MOVEMENT IN A LYING DOWN POSITION

In this practice, we are going to explore movement in a lying down position.

Movement practice can also be done standing or sitting in a chair, so decide what would suit your body when you come to practice. If you have any injuries or medical concerns, speak with your medical advisers before starting the practice. The first movement is to move from sitting or standing to the floor. It may be helpful to use a chair as a support to make the movement on to the ground.

Whatever position you choose, what is most important is that you listen to the messages of your own body. You are the expert here! Please treat this guidance as just one possible suggestion. As your own best expert, you decide how long to stay in a posture, when to stop, or indeed when not to do a posture at all. A resting position is always a valid option available to you during the practice.

In mindful movement, we can explore our experience in just the same way as in other practices like the body scan and sitting meditation. We may notice patterns of striving, pushing, holding back, and judgements about what we can and can't do that may reflect familiar traits in our everyday life. We may notice our minds commenting, comparing, criticising. We may find ourselves thinking, "it's too slow" or "too fast," or "I'm getting bored, why am I doing this?" or "this is so calming and enjoyable!" Whatever form your thoughts may take, the invitation is simply to notice them and come back to the body and its world of physical sensations.

As we move into the gentle stretches, we can sense when we have reached a limit and how we relate to it. Can we explore that sense of limit, move towards it and then away from it, or do we feel we have to get beyond it? Perhaps we believe that we must reach a certain goal and put great effort into reaching it? Who is setting this goal?

Please bear in mind that this is not an exercise class. We are not in the gym, however useful that may be. We are not even in a yoga class, unless it's very mindful yoga! In relation to the breathing, it's important that as you stretch you maintain your capacity to breathe. In fact, if you find that your breathing is held or strained, it may be a sign that you are trying too hard. In such moments, it may be more helpful to relax the effort you are making.

Movement practice allows us to explore these themes and much else besides. Especially we can learn about how to take better care of ourselves by listening deeply to the messages of the body and respecting the wisdom of the body.

THE BENEFITS OF MINDFUL MOVEMENT

Many people report that mindful movement helps them focus more easily than while practising a stillness practice such as the body scan. People often report less mind wandering and more attention to what is arising in the present moment. Especially at the beginning of someone's contact with mindfulness, this can help to build confidence, a sense that "I can do this!" Since it seems more accessible, the question may arise: why is the body scan commonly introduced before mindful movement? Perhaps this points to the importance of developing non-judgemental and non-striving attitudes in the body scan so that these traits, which are so commonly associated with physical movements, are more noticed and let go when movement practice is introduced.

When we move our body and adjust the postures in which we hold our body, we also *shift the activity of our autonomic nervous system*, which influences reactions like our heart rate, blood pressure, and fight-or-flight response. This means that mindful movement can offer us a way to shift our emotions and moods, from the outside in.

PHYSICAL BENEFITS

- *Flexibility*: Enhances mobility and reduces injury risks through stretching exercises (Gard et al., 2014).
- *Strength*: Builds muscular strength and endurance via resistance and body-weight exercises (Malarkey et al., 2013).
- *Balance*: Improves coordination, reducing fall risks (Malarkey et al., 2013).

- *Cardiovascular health*: Boosts heart and lung function through activities like aerobic yoga (Cramer et al., 2014).

MENTAL BENEFITS

- *Stress reduction*: Promotes relaxation and reduces stress via mindful awareness and endorphin release (Huang et al., 2020).
- *Anxiety relief*: Calms the nervous system, alleviating anxiety symptoms (Pilkington et al., 2005).
- *Improved mood*: Combines exercise, mindfulness, and social support to reduce depressive symptoms (Huang et al., 2020). Mindful movement promotes positive mental health (Spaccapanico et al., 2024).
- *Emotional regulation*: Strengthens mind–body awareness, cultivating peace and emotional stability (Zou et al., 2018).

COGNITIVE AND PSYCHOLOGICAL BENEFITS

- *Cognitive function*: Enhances memory, attention, and executive function through mental engagement (Lu et al., 2016).
- *Resilience*: Develops adaptive coping strategies and emotional regulation (Halladay et al., 2015).
- *Self-esteem*: Improves confidence and body image via physical accomplishments (Gard et al., 2014).

OVERALL IMPACT

Mindful movement integrates physical activity and mindfulness to strengthen the mind–body connection, fostering overall health and well-being. Further research is encouraged to expand our understanding and application of these practices for holistic wellness.

HOW TO CULTIVATE MINDFULNESS IN ANY MOVEMENT

Engaging in mindful movement offers a dynamic alternative to seated meditation, appealing to individuals may prefer a more active approach to mindfulness. Whether you're walking, running, swimming, or weightlifting, you can infuse your exercise routine with mindfulness by tuning into the sensations of your body and the rhythm of your breath. Here are some strategies to incorporate mindfulness into your physical activity. These are derived from the systematic review by Birdee et al., 2016.

1. Clarify your intentions:

Before beginning your exercise session, reflect on your reasons for engaging in mindfulness practice. Are you seeking to enhance focus, manage emotions, or improve overall well-being? Aligning your intentions with your exercise goals can provide motivation and direction.

2. Bring awareness to any distractions:

To fully immerse yourself in mindful movement, disconnect from external distractions such as music, phone calls, or digital devices (not always so easy in gyms!). Embrace the present moment by focusing solely on your activity, the surroundings, and the direct sensations, thoughts, and emotions arising in each moment.

3. Tune into body sensations:

Direct your attention inward and become attuned to the sensations in your body as you move. Notice areas of tension or ease, warmth or cool sensations, changes in muscle engagement, and any subtle shifts in posture or alignment.

4. Harness the power of the breath:

Use your breath as an anchor to guide your awareness during exercise. Pay attention to the rhythm and depth of your breath, allowing it to serve as a constant point of focus amidst the ebb and flow of movement.

5. Experiment with different focal points:

Explore various focal points of attention beyond your breath, such as the cadence of your footsteps or the sensation of movement in specific muscle groups. Experiment with different anchors to sustain and bring creativity into your mindfulness practice.

6. Cultivate open awareness:

Practice open awareness by expanding your attention to include your surrounding environment. Notice sensory experiences like the temperature of the air, sounds in the environment, and visual stimuli around you. Remembering to pause for a few moments regularly during the practice allows this more open awareness to manifest itself.

7. Embrace acceptance:

Adopt an attitude of acceptance and non-judgement towards your exercise experience. Embrace the present moment, acknowledging any discomfort or resistance with compassion and understanding. The goal is the cultivation of awareness itself.

8. Foster self-compassion:

Invite a sense of kindness and appreciation towards yourself during workouts. Rather than comparing yourself to others or criticising your performance, acknowledge your efforts and celebrate your commitment to self-care.

By integrating mindfulness into your movement practice, you can enhance both physical fitness and mental well-being, cultivating a deeper sense of presence and connection with yourself and the world around you.

CAUTIONS WHEN PRACTISING MINDFUL MOVEMENT

If there any pre-existing physical problems. for example, back or joint pain, it is important to consult a physician or therapist before engaging with the practice.

Some students may find that movement practice may uncover body issues, for example, shame, incapacity, unacknowledged injury, or limitations. This points to the benefits of learning mindfulness with an experienced guide who can explore these issues that may arise.

1. *Physical injuries and health conditions*: Mindful movement practices, such as yoga and tai chi, involve physical activity that may not be suitable for individuals with certain health conditions or injuries. For example, those with severe joint problems, uncontrolled high blood pressure, or recent surgeries may need to modify or avoid certain movements to prevent exacerbating their condition (Saper et al., 2017; Cramer et al., 2014).

There is always a risk of over-exertion or injury: Participants may push themselves too hard in an attempt to achieve specific postures or movements, increasing the risk of over-exertion, muscle strain, or injury. Instructors should emphasise the importance of self-awareness, gentle pacing, and respecting one's physical limits during mindful movement sessions (Cramer et al., 2014).

2. *Psychological vulnerabilities*: Engaging in mindful movement practices can sometimes evoke strong emotional or psychological responses, particularly in individuals with trauma histories or acute mental health issues. Practitioners with conditions such as severe depression, psychosis, or post-traumatic stress disorder (PTSD) may find certain aspects of the practice distressing or triggering (van der Kolk, 2014). This important topic was explored in relation to body scan practice (see Chapter 6). Movement practice may be safer and less triggering than the body scan or sitting for some psychological disorders, for example, anxiety. Certain participants may feel uncomfortable or resistant to the emphasis on the mind–body connection inherent in mindful movement practices. This discomfort may stem from past experiences, cultural factors, or a general disconnection from the body. Instructors should create a supportive environment that encourages participants to explore their experiences without judgement (Stanley et al., 2015).

3. *Spiritual or religious concerns*: Some individuals may have cultural, spiritual, or religious beliefs that conflict with the philosophical or cultural origins of certain mindful movement practices. Instructors should ensure that the practice is presented in a secular and inclusive manner, respecting diverse beliefs and backgrounds (Bautista et al., 2022).
4. *Potential for overstimulation*: Mindful movement practices involve heightened sensory awareness and regulation of bodily sensations, which may overwhelm individuals who are highly sensitive or prone to sensory overload. Instructors can provide guidance on grounding techniques and self-regulation strategies to help participants manage arousal levels during practice (Kabat-Zinn, 2013).

TRAINING ISSUES WHEN TEACHING MINDFUL MOVEMENT

Feeling confident to guide movement practices may be difficult for many of us who have not got a regular movement practice of our own. Due to their training, many mindfulness teachers (especially psychologists and therapists) are more comfortable working with the mind than the body. They may say "I am not a yoga teacher! How can I teach movement practice in an effective and safe way?" This lack of confidence can lead to mindful movement being the Cinderella of mindful practice, especially in MBCT. This is a great shame as the practice has so many important lessons to teach.

Greater access to training and a commitment to personal practice is the way to help mindfulness teachers to feel more confident to offer movement practice.

CHAPTER SUMMARY

- Mindful movement in MBCT and MBSR is a holistic practice that integrates mindfulness with physical activity, promoting a balanced and embodied approach to well-being.
- By fostering present-moment awareness, non-judgemental observation, and a deeper connection with the body, mindful

movement can significantly enhance both physical and mental health.

- Any movement has the potential to become a mindful movement practice if done with intentionality, awareness, and kindness.

8

OPENING TO EXPERIENCE
The sitting practice

Mindfulness meditation practice is often depicted by someone sitting cross-legged in meditation posture. It is important to understand that this is just one possible way of sitting. The physical configuration of the body while sitting is just one aspect of the practice. More importantly, what is happening in the body/mind during the practice and especially, how we relate to this, is where the real potential for calm, stability and insight lies. This section will give an overview of some of the basics of sitting meditation, including posture and different types of sitting equipment. Ways to structure your sitting practice and the underlying principles upon which this is based will also be outlined.

SITTING POSTURE

There is no hierarchy when it comes to the posture one adopts when practising mindfulness. Although the sitting posture is most readily identifiable with meditation, when it comes to mindfulness practice, the "external" posture is less important than the posture one adopts "internally." One can be mindful in any position – whether sitting, standing, lying down, or walking/in movement. Perhaps the real benefit of the sitting posture is that it can be sustained for relatively long periods of time (not that this is necessarily the goal), with somewhat less temptation to fall asleep (as when lying down). It also has the advantage of being more energy efficient than moving or standing.

Sitting is one of four postures in which to cultivate mindfulness of the body (standing, lying, and walking/moving being the

DOI: 10.4324/9781003453598-11

others traditionally referred to). Sitting also supports the investigation and cultivation of other ways of establishing mindfulness – feeling tone; thoughts and emotions; and the recognition and contemplation of universal phenomena, such as impermanence and causality (as described in the Satipatthana sutta, Anālayo (2003)). The posture should support our intention to bring awareness to the present moment through the cultivation of calm and stability, leading to insight.

When sitting in a chair, adopting a comfortable and upright posture, with feet flat on the floor, arms and shoulders relaxed, with hands resting comfortably on your thighs or together in your lap is recommended. Ideally, your knees should form a 90-degree angle when both feet are flat on the floor. (If your feet don't touch the floor, it can be helpful to place your feet on a small block or wedge for extra height and stability. This will enable you to sit for longer periods of time and ensure the body is well supported.)

A relaxed posture is best – one in which the spine is tall, without straining. Sometimes it can be helpful to place a cushion at the lower back, as well as to use the support of the back of the chair. At other times, especially when feeling sleepy, sitting away from the back of the chair (so that the spine is self-supporting) can aid a sense of alertness. This can be especially supportive if we notice a tendency to "collapse" inward/downward in the posture, due to tiredness. A collapsed posture (e.g. slouching) can also act as a reminder to re-establish mindfulness of the body as part of the practice.

You may also wish to experiment with sitting on the floor, either with meditation cushions (known as "zafus" in the Japanese Buddhist tradition) or using a meditation stool or bench.

There are typically two ways of using meditation cushions or meditation benches. The first, which is much easier for most people, is with knees bent and lower legs resting to the sides of the cushion(s), or legs extending underneath the bench. Alternatively, it is possible to sit with legs bent in front of the body, ideally with knees in contact with the floor or supported by firm cushions. This three-point posture (bum on seat, both knees making contacting with the ground/cushions) should feel comfortable and stable and require little effort to maintain for long periods. It may be necessary to sit forward on the cushions and to use two or more stacked cushions to achieve this posture. Feel free to experiment and have your posture checked by a mindfulness teacher if unsure. A trained eye can make helpful suggestions to aid comfort and avoid problems later.

When exploring the cross-legged posture, it is extremely important to avoid any degree of forcing the body and take great care of your knees. Many of us are not used to sitting on the ground, which requires more flexibility in the hips. Of course, it is possible to develop more flexibility, especially in the hips, through yoga or Pilates practice. The kneeling posture, described above, is an easier place to start for many people.

It is very important to take care of the body while sitting. Some meditation traditions emphasise not moving during meditation practice but instead to use the desire to move as an opportunity to investigate what is happening in the body–mind. Feel free to experiment with movement and stillness within the practice, especially if you are new to it. There is no one-size-fits-all. As best you can, be open and experiment with how rigidly you seek to maintain any meditation posture. It may represent a more goal-oriented frame of mind and could result in pain or injury. Even though it can be revealing to see the "play" of the mind in relation to more challenging sensations, taking care and being gentle with yourself within the practice is most important. After all, you will be much more likely to continue with the practice itself if you feel physically comfortable and well supported and give yourself permission to move when needed.

When sitting, we are cultivating the capacity to "hold our seat" no matter what the mind and our thoughts might be saying about the practice (e.g., "I'm really bored with this, I want to stop!" or "I'm no good at this, I'm not making any progress."). Deliberately meeting such thoughts with kindness, gentleness, and curiosity is core to maintaining our seat. Although from the outside we may look like we are "just sitting," the bigger story is that we are becoming more aware – of patterns of physical sensation, thinking, feeling, and impulses to act that we might ordinarily shy away from, ignore, or get lost in. It is our reactivity to what we notice when sitting that offers the biggest potential for insight. Again, it is important to emphasise that our reactions in themselves are not "wrong." They are usually very understandable patterns we have developed over time. Mindfulness simply offers us countless opportunities to notice these. From this place of greater awareness, we gain more insight into ourselves and greater choice about how we might want to respond.

WAYS TO STRUCTURE THE SITTING PRACTICE

There is usually an implicit structure to audio-guided mindfulness practices — whether of the body scan, mindful movement, or sitting. This consistency of sequencing and language both demarcates the transitions within the practice, and creates a sense of psychological safety and predictability. These can be helpful boundaries when engaged in inner work of this kind.

SETTLING AND CONNECTING TO INTENTION

Regardless of the type of practice, reconnecting with "why" one is choosing to practise ("intention") is usually a good place to start as you settle into a comfortable and stable posture (*please refer to Introduction to Section II for more details about "intention"*). *Please refer to the audio-guided Intentions Practice.* Once settled, it can be helpful to spend some time exploring the physical sensations of posture. For example, where, exactly, is the body in contact with the floor? What regions of the body are being directly supported by the seat/cushion/stool? Where are the arms resting? Is there tension in the body? If so, where exactly? Is there a sense of relaxation in the body? Where? The purpose of these questions isn't so much to come up with a verbal response but rather to support you in guiding and maintaining awareness of the body. Depending on the amount of time you have set aside for practice, you might spend just a few moments connecting to the body in this way, or it could become the focus of the entire practice period. Paying attention to the body and arranging the posture with care is always time well spent.

CHOOSING A SPECIFIC FOCUS OR "ANCHOR" TO ATTEND TO, OR OPENING AWARENESS?

Typically, after spending some time settling into the posture, audio-guided mindfulness practices will invite you to choose a clear focus of attention for the next part of the practice. This may be sensations in a particular region of the body (e.g. sensations in the hands or feet), sensations of the breath (e.g. movement of the chest or abdomen with each in-breath and each out-breath), attending to sounds or a visual object (e.g. a picture or flower or entire visual scene). Again, the invitation is simply to allow your attention to rest, moment by moment, with sensations in relation to one specific "object'." Although you will likely notice being repeatedly pulled into thinking (e.g. thoughts or judgements about these sensations, or other kinds of discursive thought, imagery, or daydreaming), the practice involves simply noticing these tendencies and gently returning attention to the chosen object once again. *How* we do this is vital. This is where cultivating compassionate qualities is essential to the practice becoming a nourishing and sustaining one. These are the attitudinal qualities of mindfulness, as mentioned earlier (Kabat-Zinn, 2013). An entire practice period might consist of patiently, from time to time, escorting attention back to the breath or some other "anchor" of attention. This initially requires a lot of effort and is known as "focused attention" (FA) practice. It is also possible to choose one "primary" anchor or focus of attention (e.g. the breath) and to allow a "secondary" anchor (e.g. sounds) to play a supportive role in being present.

ATTENTION AS A "SPOTLIGHT" OF AWARENESS

When thinking about directing attention to different aspects of experience, the metaphor of a theatre "spotlight" can be helpful. A spotlight helps us in directing attention to what is most salient or important in any given moment – in terms of the stage or theatre, it points to where the action is. Likewise, we can direct the spotlight of our attention to one or more aspects of experience in any given moment.

Within focused attention practice, you might also choose to experiment with changing the focus of attention, spending some time "foregrounding" one aspect of your experience, for example, the breath, before moving on to something else, for example, sounds. *Please refer to the audio-guided Sitting Practices (1), (2) and (3).*

The sitting practice and focusing attention

Taking some time now to settle into a comfortable posture, whether sitting, lying or standing. (Although this is called the "sitting prac-tice," we can choose to practise in any posture.)

Deliberately spending some moments resting attention on the sensations of contact between the body and whatever is support-ing the body. Perhaps feeling sensations of weight – heaviness or lightness in relation to the body as a whole, or perhaps in relation to different regions – the legs, the back of the body, the head. Are there any feelings or thoughts in relation to what you are experienc-ing? Are there sensations of weight in the arms and hands? Perhaps also registering sensations of warmth or coolness in the body in this moment and noticing what the mind does with such information – maybe judging, comparing, complaining? Just noticing this. Maybe also exploring sensations of warmth or coolness in a particular region of the body. Are there different temperature zones in the body as you experience it now? As best you can, allowing your experience to be exactly as it is. (Of course, if you need to move or get an extra blanket for warmth, feeling free to do so, bringing awareness to any of these decisions and movements.)

When you are ready, inviting you to bring awareness more con-sciously to the breath, if this is your chosen anchor, or to some other chosen anchor such as your feet on the floor, your hands, or sensations of contact of your seat. Perhaps noticing how the breath moves the body – at the chest, the abdomen, the back of the body. If using the breath, resting for some moments with breath move-ment throughout the body. After some time, deliberately choosing one place in the body to come up close to the breath, perhaps at the abdomen, allowing movement here to take centre stage. If, for any reason, the breath is not a comfortable place for you, then feeling free to choose an alternative "anchor" point such as the soles of your feet or your hands or listening to sounds appearing and disappearing.

THE SITTING PRACTICE AND OPENING AWARENESS

A development of the sitting practice is to "open" awareness to the entire attentional field in what is known as "open awareness" (OA) or "choiceless awareness" practice. Within OA practice, it is not necessary (or possible!) to attempt to keep everything you are experiencing in mind all at once, but rather you allow your attention to rest with whatever is most obvious or salient in any given moment. For example, in one moment, it may be awareness of the breath, in the next, birdsong or a car engine, the next, a fragment of thought or memory. In this way, rather than setting out ahead of time to prioritise one single aspect of experience, we simply register and acknowledge the unfolding of experience as it presents itself, moment by moment. If we notice the tendency to get drawn into thinking about or judging some aspect of our experience, we can just notice this as one aspect of what is unfolding and open awareness once again to the entire attentional field. If we notice that our attention is starting to "drift" or that the mind becomes very active or agitated, it may be sensible to return to FA practice to allow the mind to settle once again. OA practice is also sometimes known as "just sitting" or "zazen" within the Zen tradition. What could be simpler? Though as we'll see, "simple" doesn't mean "easy"!

Open awareness/choiceless awareness practice

Begin by settling attention on the body and/or breath for some moments. Perhaps sensing into the contact points of the body in this moment – the ground, seat, or surfaces supporting the body.

At a certain point of your choosing, deliberately opening awareness to the entire attentional field. What is most salient in this moment? Sounds? Physical sensations in a particular region of the body? Thoughts?

No need to hold everything in awareness all at once. Allowing whatever is most obvious or salient to be held in a non-reactive attending, from moment to moment. After some time practising in this way, returning attention to a more deliberate focus or "object" of attention, such as sensations of the breath or sensations of the body with whatever is supporting the body, for example, feet on the floor or the contact of the chair. Perhaps taking one or two more intentional breaths to finish.

Although FA practice may have more benefits in terms of attention training, minimising the tendency to become distracted and having a beneficial calming effect on the body/mind, OA practice can enhance our capacity for "clear seeing." OA practice can allow us to recognise persistent patterns of thinking/feeling/doing which we have more opportunities to see when not distracted by a busy mind. It is for this reason that traditionally, FA precedes the development of insight or wisdom, which is associated more with OA.

Periods spent either focusing attention or opening awareness are profoundly beneficial. Although focusing attention sets the stage for opening awareness, you may naturally find yourself moving between these practices within one practice session. You might decide to "bookend" your practice with a period of FA practice, regardless of whether you are intending to practice with open awareness. Additionally, giving yourself some time to settle into the practice initially, before practising with focused attention, can be helpful. There is no need to rush any aspect of the practice, as doing so likely reflects more of a "doing mode" (Williams, 2010) perspective.

TRAUMA SENSITIVITY WHEN SITTING

Being still can be a major challenge, especially where there has been a history of trauma (Treleaven, 2018). For some, it may be that mindful movement is a more accessible place to start. Exploring gentle yoga stretches or chi kung may be a very helpful alternative to being still. As we gradually cultivate deeper and more extended states of calm, we also develop our capacity to look at the detail of our lives. This greater "seeing" opens the potential to react less in an automatic, unhelpful way and respond in a kinder, more creative manner, which benefits us and those around us.

It may not be realistic to expect yourself to sit still right away. Instead, you might choose to adjust your posture by changing position slightly, weaving any movement into the practice "as part of" the practice. We can do this by noticing the impulse to move, the movement itself, as well as the after-effects of moving.

THE ROLE OF MOVEMENT WITHIN SITTING PRACTICE

Sitting for any length of time can be physically challenging, especially if living with chronic pain or other health conditions. The use of movement as a precursor to periods of more formal sitting practice can help to create more supportive conditions by waking up the body/mind, loosening the body out, and softening around any physical tension or agitated pent-up energy. Equally, giving oneself permission to move or to change one's position or posture during the practice can also be extremely supportive and necessary. What appears to be important at such times is to "weave" the movement into the sitting practice, so that it becomes part of the practice, rather than seeing this as "opting out" from the practice. We can do this by noticing the intention to move (before actually moving), then moving with awareness, noticing the changing sensations in the body as we do so. (*Practice question: What signals is the body sending you to move? Where, precisely, in the body do you notice this? What thoughts and feelings are you aware of?*) We can also bring awareness to the after-effects of moving (*Practice question: How does it feel in the body/mind now that you have moved?*). We can, of course, always let go of the practice altogether, at any time.

BECOMING MINDFUL OF FEELING TONE

A more recent development within the world of secular mindfulness has been that of feeling tone (Williams & Penman, 2023). Feeling tone refers to the very immediate, involuntary sense of experience as either "pleasant," "unpleasant," or "neither pleasant nor unpleasant," This continuous flow of moments of feeling tone can, however, be made more conscious. It is a pivotal moment in the perceptual process, as once something is judged to be either pleasant or unpleasant, we usually default to further elaborating on the experience. This is where our reactions of attachment (wanting to hold onto the experience/wanting more) or aversion (wanting to avoid or be rid of the experience) can take over and create more difficulties for us. The more conscious we can be of our tendency to want to hold onto an experience or push away aspects of experience, the more we can avoid being automatically pulled into the experience. It is not that these tendencies are wrong per se, rather that they often become the trigger for rumination and/or avoidance. Once established with the earlier practices of the body scan, mindful movement, and sitting practices, we recommend weaving "feeling tone" into your regular practice. *Please refer to the audio-guided Feeling Tone Practice.*

KINDNESS PRACTICE(S)

Mindfulness practice is unlikely to be sustained without cultivating kindness. As Jon Kabat-Zinn (2005, 2013) and others have noted, if we are not "hearing" the word "heartfulness" at the same time as we hear the word "mindfulness," we are unlikely to have a full understanding. The cultivation of kindness is key to sustaining a mindfulness practice and allows it to be a nourishing one, over and above a purely cognitive attention training.

By "kindness" we mean a body–mind–heart state that is associated with feelings of warmth, care, and security. Understood or more accurately "felt" in this sense, kindness practice becomes a nourishing and sustaining act of self-care. For many of us, a practice that directly addresses tendencies towards harsh self-judgement and self-criticism can be liberating. However, chances are that many of us need to deliberately engage in this as a practice and remain patient as we build this inner resource over time.

Traditionally, "loving-kindness" (also known as "Metta") practices involve experiencing the effects of cultivating kindness towards oneself and/or others. If directing kindness toward oneself is too difficult or challenging, we can practise by cultivating and sending kindness towards others first. If the idea of sending kindness towards others is too difficult, we can allow ourselves to be the sole recipient. If cultivating kindness toward oneself and others is too challenging, we can start with a deceased loved one, favourite historical figure, a pet, or a plant. The recipient of our kindness practice is less important than developing our capacity to get in touch with and cultivate this quality within ourselves. Kristin Neff and Christopher Germer (2018) have written about the dangers of what they call "backdraft" or "blow-back" in people for whom cultivating kindness is particularly challenging. Even the idea of generating feelings of kindness and gentleness towards ourselves may create a lot of resistance. We don't need to force any of this and can begin with bringing a sense of kindly curiosity towards our *resistance* to kindness. This might take the form of, "Oh, isn't it interesting that as I even think about being kind to myself, I notice a lot of resistance to it. I wonder where in my body I am feeling this resistance?" This "move" into the body and away from thinking about why one might be feeling resistance to cultivating kindness is skilful and an act of kindness.

How we understand kindness is key. Many of us may have an automatic resistance to generating kindness or being kind to ourselves due to a sense of self-indulgence (or that somehow, it feels "selfish"). We may think, "How can I spend time generating kindness to myself when there is so much suffering in the world? When others need my attention. I need to act!" The truth of the matter is that unless we are well resourced ourselves, which means knowing how to extend kindness to ourselves first, our compassion (compassion = kindness in action) is likely to either fluctuate, be short lived, or be prone to compassion fatigue and burnout. Kindness as a way of being and compassion as a response to suffering is a resource that we can share with others. The more we ourselves are resourced and nourished by kindness, the more we have available to share with others. *Please refer to the audio-guided Kindness Practice.*

Kindness practice

Inviting you to take some moments to settle into a comfortable posture.

Allowing attention to rest with the sensations of weight, gentle touch, or pressure between the body and the surfaces supporting the body in this moment.

If you feel comfortable with moving attention to the breath, perhaps feeling the movement of breath at a particular location in the body for a few minutes.

At a certain point of your choosing, inviting you to deliberately bring a sense of kindness and gentleness towards yourself. Allowing these feelings to become alive in you. Sometimes, the repetition of certain phrases can be helpful in generating feelings of kindness. Again, the specific phrases themselves are not so important. What is important is that you find some formula of phrasing that allows you to access and dwell in a state of kindness and well-being. Some examples of phrases are given below:

"*May I be happy.* May I be well. May I be safe.
May I find peace and be at ease.
May I be filled *with (loving) kindness.*"

It's important to say that we don't need to feel the effects of these phrases immediately. Rather trusting that this kind of inner work is more about "inclining the mind" towards such feelings. This process is like planting seeds. We need to trust that although we may not see anything happen immediately (or for many months), over time, something may begin to germinate and ultimately grow.

Some people take to loving-kindness practice like ducks to water. Others may have very different reactions and encounter resistance or find this kind of practice difficult in some way. Luckily, "explicit" kindness practices are not the only way to develop more kindly awareness, especially if strong feelings of frustration or a sense of failure arise. For example, we might consider how we offer kindness to ourselves and others on a daily basis, often without realising. Cleaning our teeth, choosing our clothes, feeding ourselves, and taking care when crossing the road are a few examples. It is also worth noting that in "formal" practice, we are encouraged to bear in mind the Attitudinal Foundations (Kabat-Zinn, 2013; see Chapter 5) such as patience, allowing, and non-judging. This means that whatever kind of mindfulness practice we engage in, the suggestion is always to bring a friendly attitude of allowing and letting be to all aspects of our mind–heart/body that arise in awareness.

THE "MOUNTAIN" PRACTICE

The stability, beauty, and grandeur of a mountain can be a helpful image when sitting or standing. We can draw on these qualities of "mountain" to inspire the tone and feel of our practice. If standing, perhaps bringing the image of a familiar mountain to mind, allowing it to inform the quality of your stillness. Perhaps feeling the height of the body extending upward, as you sense into the groundedness and rootedness of your feet in contact with the floor and earth below. Similarly, when sitting, we can feel the stability that the lower legs and pelvis offer – our stable base – much as the base of a mountain supports its rising slopes and lofty peak above.

We can allow the image of whatever mountain we are familiar with to inspire us as we continue to sit or stand mountain-like, the height of the body extending upward as it rises out of the pelvis and extends through the back of the neck and head. In this practice, we are drawing on the qualities of mountain as a metaphor for how we can be in relation to whatever arises, either internally (our thoughts, feelings, physical sensations, impulses) or externally (our physical environment). Just as a mountain "just sits" no matter what weather conditions, seasons, or visitors might prevail, so too might we practise "just sitting," meeting whatever arises with calm equanimity as best we can – for however long we choose. *Please refer to the audio-guided Mountain Meditation Practice.*

THE "LAKE" PRACTICE

Just as the image of a mountain can offer a sense of presence, stability, and rootedness to the earth, a lake can offer us qualities of calm, stillness, and depth that we can draw on in our practice. Harsh weather can wreak havoc on the surface of a lake, churning it up to look more like rough seas. Similarly, your body–mind might feel like a small boat on the surface of a great lake, being buffeted by strong winds and waves, rudderless and directionless. You may even feel somewhat nauseated by the effects of whatever you are facing or thinking about. This is where most of us live, pushed around by our thoughts and feelings on the surface of things.

However, as we descend to the depths of the lake and look back, it seems possible to come into a different relationship with whatever chaos be happening on the surface. We can use the lake metaphor to inspire us in relation to whatever may be going on for us. It's important to recognise that we are learning to come into wise relationship with whatever challenges may be present by deliberately choosing to view things from a more expansive awareness. The lake metaphor invites us to adopt a different position in relation to difficulty, descending beneath the surface of things to a depth and capacity of awareness that can offer us a changed perspective.

CHAPTER SUMMARY

- Care should be taken to find a sitting posture that supports both comfort and alertness.
- Although stillness can be tremendously supportive while sitting, it is important to allow for movement at times within the practice as an expression of self-care.
- Focused attention practice is usually helpful when the mind is quite busy, agitated, or distracted.
- Open awareness/choiceless awareness practice does not set any predetermined focus for the attention but rather allows whatever arises in the moment to become the focus.
- Formal periods of kindness practice offer a practical way to nourish oneself and develop self-compassion. This can become a wellspring from which to extend kindness to others.

9

WEAVING IT IN

Shorter mindfulness practices

One of the real challenges of establishing a mindfulness practice is weaving it into everyday life. The transitions between periods of formal mindfulness practice and making breakfast, driving to the office, or doing the shopping can seem a long way away from our meditation cushion or mat. The invitation in this chapter is to begin to explore how we might weave formal mindfulness practice into everyday life. We can do this through shorter (even momentary) formal practices, as well as remembering that any activity or period of inactivity can be an opportunity to practise bringing kindly awareness to the moment we are in.

We have recorded a selection of both brief and short practices. *Please refer to the audio-guided Brief and the Short Practices.* We distinguish between "brief" practices and "short" practices. Both have their place. Both can be extremely helpful at different times. As our colleague at the Centre for Mindfulness Research and Practice (CMRP) at Bangor University, Trish Bartley, describes them, brief practices are literally meant to be a "touch-and-go," less than a minute in duration. It only takes a moment to reconnect to the body, to step out of "autopilot" mode. We notice whatever may be going on in the body–mind in that moment and simply become aware. These practices need to become so embedded in our lives that they become equally "automatic," that is, reliable ways to connect to ourselves and the wider context in any given moment.

DOI: 10.4324/9781003453598-12

RECLAIMING YOUR LIFE – ONE MOMENT AT A TIME

At first you may notice a lot of resistance to stopping and pausing – this is normal. This resistance may be felt in the body, like the halting of forward momentum, or in the mind in the form of thoughts ("Why do I need to stop? I don't want to stop!"). Resistance can also take the form of unpleasant feelings, such as frustration or irritation. It is important at such times to remember that our awareness can hold it all. Awareness itself does not differentiate or judge, it simply reflects and acknowledges what is already here. You are invited to practise pausing and stopping amid the busyness of your life as often as you can, stepping out of autopilot to reclaim your life – one precious moment at a time.

FINDING YOUR "ANCHOR"

An anchor affords safety and stability while allowing for some movement. Within the context of mindfulness practice, an anchor offers us a place to rest our attention, a place to come back to when the mind wanders. This can be particularly useful when things are difficult or when feeling stressed. There may be times during the day when deliberately connecting to some aspect of present moment experience might serve us well as an anchor. Investing time in developing a sense of connection to one or more "anchors" (such as sensations of the breath at a particular location in the body, sounds, hands, or feet-on-floor) can offer a fresh perspective on whatever else may be happening in that moment. Without an anchor, the tendency can be to get swept away by the currents of ruminative thinking or becoming overwhelmed by a torrent of thoughts and emotions or body sensations.

One possible "anchor" is to bring your attention to sensations of the breath at a particular location in the body (only choose this anchor if the breath feels accessible to you and you are not currently experiencing any breathing difficulties). The breath can act as a kind of "moving target" for the mind (Segal et al., 2013). The mind itself is rarely still, especially when caught up in rumination or obsessing or dominated by unhelpful patterns of thinking/feeling. Directing attention to the moving target of sensations of the breath at such times can serve to widen the lens of attention – perhaps just enough to offer some perspective. Experiencing the effects of gently taking attention to a reliable "anchor" is a profound act of kindness and self-care, especially at those times when the mind may be racing and full of thoughts. Although knowing this might be helpful, it is through experiencing this repeatedly that we discover its true value.

FINDING YOUR ANCHOR

We invite you to explore what anchor works for you.

Remember: we are not trying to achieve anything special here. The invitation is to simply spend some time connecting to different aspects of your present moment experience – to identify which aspect might act as a reliable, accessible place you can return your attention to.

Settling into a comfortable posture – sitting, lying down, or even standing:

- Exploring sensations in your feet with/without moving them – can you return your attention here when it wanders?
- Exploring sensation in your hands, whether while still or moving them – can you return your attention here?
- Exploring the breath as an anchor – can you feel the sensations associated with breath movement at a particular location in the body, for example, the tip of the nostrils, the chest, abdomen, or in the body as a whole? You do not have to breathe in any special way – it is best to allow the breath to happen naturally, without trying to change it or alter it in any way. The breath knows how to breathe itself.
- Physical sensations of posture can also act as an anchor. Noticing the sensations of contact between your body and the chair/cushion/mat or mattress – allowing this be a place where you can return attention to.

It is important not to get too discouraged when the mind wanders. The objective here isn't to keep attention "fixed." Rather, gently returning attention back to whatever anchor you've chosen, as many times as you notice attention has drifted away. As many things are likely to distract us during the day, can we remember to support ourselves by coming back?

Another way to think about having a reliable, accessible "anchor" for the body/mind is to have some way to "ground" attention in, and connect to, the present moment. Understood this way, we can "ground" our attention by connecting to some aspect of present moment experience (e.g. the sensations of contact of the feet on the floor or sounds). This is likely to offer an alternative focus to whatever may be happening in the body/mind and can be a way to take care of ourselves. Having an alternative focus for the mind (especially when our thoughts may be "racing") can lead to developing a sense of confidence and stability over time.

WAYS OF CONNECTING TO THE BREATH AND BODY

One of the simplest ways to become mindful is to become mindful of the body and physical sensations, including the breath. The body is always present – even when the mind may be frequently miles away. We often live in our heads so much we can forget that we even have a body, until perhaps hunger or pain acts as a reminder. This appears to have been the case for one of the main characters in James Joyce's (1914) short novel *Dubliners*. As Joyce writes, "Mr. Duffy lived a short distance from his body." Joyce knew there are times we can forget we even have a body. However, we can connect with the body at any moment – all that is required is to remember, to literally "re-member" the body. If attention is in the body and on physical sensations, we are *de facto* present. Understandably, different thoughts or other aspects of present-moment experience will likely take our attention away again, so we really need to allow for this. Patience and kindness are key. As soon as we have re-connected to the body, we are present again.

THE "PAUSE"

Our colleague at CMRP, Trish Bartley, first described the "Pause" as part of a set of brief practices designed for cancer patients

(Bartley, 2011). This involves intentionally bringing awareness to the present moment by asking a simple question, *"How am I feeling right now?"* This need only be very brief, as little as a few seconds. The intention is simply to become aware and to step out of "automatic pilot." This is similar to "Step 1" of The Breathing Space (outlined further below). The benefit of such a brief practice is that it can interrupt habitual ways of operating, leading to new possibilities. If you find that you are getting pulled into thinking about how you are feeling, see if you can come back to simply acknowledging the feeling itself and how this feels in the body (e.g. tingling, lightness, heat, pressure). This can be done at set times, perhaps linked to certain tasks or using a timer, or randomly throughout the day, as an act of self-care. You get to choose, and no one needs to know! *Please refer to the audio-guided The Pause Practice.*

FOF-BOC

A very brief way of connecting to the body while sitting is through embodying the acronym "FOF BOC." "FOF-BOC" refers to "Feet-on-floor, bum-on-chair" and originates from the Mindfulness in Schools Project (2022) in the U.K. What could be more basic than feeling one's feet on the floor? Although incredibly simple, this brief practice can also be very powerful. *Please refer to the audio-guided F-O-F B-O-C Practice.* Whether sitting or standing, we can choose in any moment to take awareness to the contact between our feet on the floor and bum on the chair. This gives us a very definite focus for attention, to connect with whatever physical sensations may be available to us there in any given moment.

As the neuroscience of mindfulness suggests, we are shifting our mode of mind as we do this. Instead of operating from a mode of mind predominantly associated with thinking about experience, the mind shifts to "experiencing" or sensing. The distinction between "thinking" and "sensing" is critical to the effectiveness of these short practices. "Thinking" often involves "thinking about" something or someone and is associated with the conceptual mind. "Sensing" involves a willingness to direct attention to what is coming in through our sense doors – touch, taste, smell, sight, and sound. Although sensing is coordinated by the brain, no further thinking or mental elaboration is necessary when we give ourselves over to sensing. As with any of these practices, we develop our understanding of them over time.

Transitions between formal and informal mindfulness practice:

Bringing "kindly awareness" to the transitions between formal and informal mindfulness practice can be especially helpful. The automatic tendency to operate on "autopilot" can be strong. The good news is that we can make this a regular part of our practice, that is, intentionally moving from formal meditation posture into standing or walking, or "taking our seat" on the meditation stool or cushion in a way that will support the cultivation of awareness as we begin to settle into the practice. Everything can become a mindfulness practice, even the transitions into and out of practice.

THE "3-STEP BREATHING SPACE" (SEGAL ET AL., 2013)

Developers of Mindfulness-Based Cognitive Therapy (MBCT) for depression, Zindel Segal, John Teasdale, and Mark Williams (2013) have developed a short practice that encapsulates many key aspects of the eight-week MBCT programme itself. A helpful visual model of the 3-Step Breathing Space takes the form of an hourglass.

In Step 1 of the Breathing Space: we are invited to step out of autopilot, to become aware. We deliberately bring awareness to our thoughts, feelings, and bodily sensations. Without this first step, we might simply continue to operate automatically, perhaps without considering the consequences for ourselves or others.

In Step 2 of the Breathing Space: we gather attention to a point of single focus, such as the breath. We narrow the focus of attention around the breath, experiencing the sensations associated with the in-breath and the out-breath for a few breath cycles. If the breath is not comfortable for any reason, we can explore other possibilities as we suggested earlier (feet, seat, hands, or sounds). This stage of gathering is represented by the narrowing of the hourglass.

In Step 3 of the Breathing Space: we widen the focus of attention beyond the breath (or other focus) to include an awareness of sensations throughout the body, to our thoughts, feelings, and the wider context or environment we find ourselves in. From this place of greater awareness and perspective, we re-engage with the activities of our day. *Please refer to the audio-guided 3-Step Breathing Space Practice.*

THE "S-T-O-P" PRACTICE (CFM, 2017)

Developed by colleagues at the Center For Mindfulness (CFM) at UMass, the S-T-O-P practice incorporates many of the key elements of mindfulness. The "S" stands for stopping. This can be a radical act, especially when the fervour, speed, and momentum of everyday tasks take over. The "T" stands for taking a few mindful breaths. You might bring awareness to the movement of the breath at a particular location in the body – the nostrils, chest, or abdomen for example – and follow the sensations there. The "O" stands for observing whatever may be happening in mind and body. What thoughts are present? What feeling or mix of feelings are present for you in this moment? Do you notice any impulse(s) to move or act? The "P" stands for proceed – making a deliberate decision to continue, with awareness. This may lead to choosing a new direction based on greater clarity revealed through stopping. This can also be an opportunity to bring greater kindness to yourself or whatever situation you may find yourself in. *Please refer to the audio-guided S.T.O.P Practice.*

EATING

Although one of the great pleasures in life, the act of eating can easily become automatic and unconscious. With so many things competing for our attention, there are plenty of ways to distract ourselves while eating. We need scarcely any attentional resources to ingest and digest our food, meaning we can miss the whole experience. If you've ever had the experience of clearing your plate while watching T.V., only to realise you never really "tasted" your food (and maybe felt a bit cheated!), you might be persuaded to engage in this mindful eating practice. *Please refer to the audio-guided Eating Practice.*

The raisin exercise

You will need two raisins and clean hands!

The first mindfulness practice in MBSR and MBCT, the "raisin" exercise is an opportunity to practise mindful eating and acts as a prelude to truly "tasting" and experiencing life. It's helpful to bring a sense of playfulness and curiosity to this practice, being open to what it might reveal to you.

Choosing one of the raisins, simply allow it to rest in the palm of your hand. Imagine that you had never seen anything quite like this before, as if you had just dropped in from Mars and were seeing such an object for the first time. (Of course, it *is* the first time you've seen *this* raisin!) Take some moments to register its size and shape, its colour and weight. Next, perhaps taking the raisin between thumb and forefinger of the opposite hand, spending some time paying closer attention to its skin – its ridges and folds; perhaps holding it up to the light – registering its colour and how light is reflected on its surface. *If you notice that you have a lot of thoughts about the raisin, coming back gently to the immediacy of seeing, perhaps giving the label "thinking" to any thoughts or judgements you might have about the raisin or about this exercise.*

Next, perhaps closing the eyes and bringing it close to your ear – does it make a sound when you press it? Coming back to seeing briefly once again. If you choose to, preparing to eat the raisin by pressing it against your lips. Do you notice any changes taking place in the mouth in preparation for tasting? Feeling its skin against yours here at the lips, bringing attention to sensations of touch. Now, if you feel OK with doing so, placing the "object" in your mouth. Noticing how it is received by the tongue. Perhaps with eyes still closed, giving your full attention to exploring its surfaces with your tongue. Noticing contact with the gums and teeth as you do so. Perhaps noticing the impulse to bite into the object and any thoughts that you might have in relation to the object or this exercise. Now finally, when you're ready to, taking one mindful bite into the surface of the raisin. What flavours do you notice, if any?

Continuing to chew slowly and mindfully until ready to swallow the remainder of the raisin. Perhaps positioning it at the back of the mouth in preparation for swallowing. When ready to, consciously swallowing the raisin and tracking its journey as best you can, down the back of the mouth and throat, as it makes its way to the stomach. Savouring the resonance of this experience and perhaps noticing the after-effects in the mouth and the work of the tongue in "sweeping up"! Perhaps registering the fact that you are now precisely one raisin heavier!

With the second raisin, perhaps eating this the way you might ordinarily eat. Noticing the contrast between these two experiences of eating.

WALKING/SOLES OF THE FEET PRACTICE

Much like eating, walking is another habitual activity that requires very little attention – unless, of course, you're learning or re-learning to walk, in which case it takes enormous focus and will-power. Walking meditation can be practiced either "formally" or "informally," indoors or outdoors. As part of "formal" practice, one might choose a short distance as defined by the width of your bedroom, for example. Then, following a period of standing still, settling attention on the contact between the soles of the feet and the floor, begin lifting, moving, and placing the feet very deliberately and mindfully (see Chapter 7 for more guidance on mindful walking). *Please refer to the audio-guided Mindful Walking Practice.*

INTERPERSONAL MINDFULNESS

Any encounter with another human being is special. We are inherently a social species, and our survival on the planet depends on one another. If you've ever spent time apart from other people in silence, for example while camping or on retreat, you'll recognise how precious a thing it is to reconnect and to be able to communicate with others. Mindfulness practice can make us particularly sensitive in our interactions with others, and this can become its own kind of practice. We can bring awareness not only to our own thoughts, feelings, and physical sensations when in the presence of others but right into our communications themselves. When we allow our interactions to be informed by mindfulness practice, it has the power to change and deepen our understanding of ourselves, others, and our relationships.

Mindful listening and speaking practice

You may be interested in experimenting with bringing mindfulness into your way of relating to others – either formally or informally. If you decide to practise mindful communication in a formal way, find a time and a space where you and a partner will not be interrupted. Decide who will speak first and who will listen first. Choose a topic that is meaningful for you. It may be a current concern or difficulty, perhaps a relationship issue or anything that is currently occupying your time and attention. If you are new to mindfulness, perhaps choosing something on a scale of difficulty that is around a 3–4 on a scale of 1–10.

Speaker role: *Whoever is in the speaking role speaks for approximately 5 minutes.* As best you can, bring awareness to the language you use and how this feels as you give voice to whatever it is that you are speaking about. It is fine to pause from time to time to reconnect to what feels most important to communicate. There is no right or wrong. See if you can bring a non-judgemental awareness to whatever you hear yourself saying.

Listener role: Whoever is in the listening role *just listens!* This means giving yourself full permission to be present for whatever is being said without the need to respond or reply in any way. You are free from having to demonstrate you are listening or give advice. Trust that your willingness to be present and to really hear what is being said will be enough.

After 5 minutes, take some moments to pause in silence together, acknowledging whatever has been spoken and heard. When ready, swap roles – the speaker becomes the listener for the next round.

After another brief pause, take some time to discuss together what you may have learned from this listening and speaking exercise, from the perspective of speaker and/or listener.

INTERPERSONAL STYLES OF RELATING

Bringing greater levels of awareness into our relationships can be illuminating. How we are with others and how others are with us can be a major source of stress. The value of registering the effect spending time with others has on us can be a vital step towards greater levels of health and wholeness. There are several predictable patterns of relating that we tend to develop with others over time. The main styles we highlight here are avoidant, aggressive, passive, passive-aggressive, and mindful. These terms in themselves point towards what may be healthy/unhealthy about each style. (Further information on each of these relationship styles can be found in Kabat-Zinn, 2013.)

The possibility of bringing mindfulness into relationships offers the possibility of changing the dynamics of how we relate to others and, in turn, how others relate to us. Mindfulness can allow us to better identify the kind of relationship dynamic we are currently in and use this information to change how we are. Unfortunately, we cannot change the other person(!) but frequently changing how we relate can often lead to unexpected changes in others as well. There is no guarantee of change, but it starts with us. We could feel despondent about this – "why is it (always) me who needs to change first?" Or we could grasp the possibility and freedom that awaits when we step into our own power in the relationship and change how we are in the relationship.

A frequent obstacle to developing a daily mindfulness practice is experiencing a sense of guilt and feeling selfish that we are taking time for ourselves, when we could use our time to do more for others. The truth of the matter is that there is no end to the amount we could do for others, but we also need to ensure we don't lose sight of ourselves either. Seen in this light, the decision to take care of ourselves while caring for others becomes an act of profound common sense.

CHAPTER SUMMARY

- In this chapter we distinguish between "brief" and "short" practices and describe several options. They offer a way of weaving mindfulness into everyday life.

- Brief practices offer a way to connect to the present moment and may last from seconds to a few minutes.
- Short practices usually last for several minutes and can be mode specific, such as eating, sitting, or walking, or they can incorporate a specific image.
- Much can be learnt from bringing mindfulness into our relationships with others and the world and it represents the application of mindfulness from the inside to the outside.

SECTION III

Application

10

MINDFULNESS IN THE MAINSTREAM

Our hope is that the previous segments of this book offer readers a comprehensive understanding of mindfulness, and a straightforward guide to establishing a personal practice. The forthcoming section will delineate the current scope of applied settings, summarising the advancements achieved through recent decades of research and practical implementation, proposing the relevance of mindfulness amidst the multifaceted crises confronting humanity in our age. This chapter begins by providing an overview (as we write in 2025) of the current landscape, acknowledging both the possibilities and limitations of mindfulness in the mainstream as things currently stand, while also offering recommendations for the future trajectory of the field.

Three decades ago, the term "mindfulness" remained relatively unknown within mainstream discourse. In 2015, the Mindfulness Initiative in the U.K. released an influential All-Party Parliamentary report gathering a significant and growing evidence base and advocating for the integration of mindfulness across various public domains, including education, the workplace, healthcare, and the criminal justice system. Since then, substantial empirical evidence has continued to garner acknowledgement and validation for the significance of mindfulness within mainstream institutions across diverse public and private-sector domains. The scope for mindfulness now extends beyond these sectors, including recognised benefits of the practice for elite athletes and military veterans and growing recognition of its potential in fostering sustainable behavioural shifts, advancing climate action, and promoting societal peace and equity.

DOI: 10.4324/9781003453598-14

However, mainstream integration of mindfulness has also brought forth its share of challenges that form an agenda for the next phase of the work. There are critiques that mindfulness could potentially be used as a checkbox exercise within educational institutions and workplaces, aimed at equipping individuals to cope with overwhelming workloads and mitigate burnout rather than addressing the root causes of unhealthy and unsustainable working conditions. The contemporary mindfulness movement has primarily developed within academic circles, which has been a necessary trajectory towards acceptance within the mainstream. Stepping back at this juncture enables us to address consequential issues relating to an exclusivity in its language, costs, and pedagogy. This chapter explores diverse contemporary uses before delving into the less illuminated pitfalls, shedding light on what is called for now in broadening the work beyond mainstream settings.

EDUCATION

Numerous educational institutions have implemented mindfulness initiatives for students, integrating practices such as mindful breathing into their overall curriculum and delivering specifically tailored mindfulness-based programmes designed to appeal to a younger audience. These programmes aim to bolster students' concentration, emotional regulation, and general well-being. The transition from childhood to adolescence presents distinctive cognitive, emotional, and social hurdles. Mindfulness interventions offer a promising avenue for nurturing resilience and supporting mental well-being in the education of young people and a potential toolbox for improving the mental health of children and adolescents.

One prominent area of investigation in the literature is the impact of mindfulness on emotional regulation in young individuals. Studies such as the work by Huppert and Johnson (2010) have demonstrated that mindfulness training in schools can lead to improvements in well-being. By providing tools for recognising and accepting emotions without judgement, mindfulness equips young people with adaptive strategies to navigate the complex emotional landscape of adolescence.

Such practices have also been linked to enhancements in cognitive functions for young people, particularly the attention regulatory sub-systems of alerting and conflict monitoring. Research findings suggest that engagement in concentrative meditative training positively influences such systems, with implications for academic performance (Baijal, 2011).

Meta-analyses have provided evidence supporting the effectiveness of mindfulness interventions in alleviating symptoms of anxiety and depression in young individuals (Zoogman et al., 2015). The cultivation of mindfulness appears to offer a preventive and therapeutic approach to addressing common mental health challenges during the crucial developmental period of adolescence.

While the existing research provides valuable insights, it is essential to acknowledge methodological considerations and challenges in studying mindfulness interventions. Variability in intervention protocols, outcome measures, and the duration of follow-up assessments poses challenges in comparing and generalising findings across studies. Moreover, the need for long-term investigations to understand the sustained impact of mindfulness interventions on youth well-being is evident.

Funded by the Wellcome Trust, the MYRIAD (My Resilience in Adolescence) Trial (Kuyken et al., 2022) initiative embarked on an inquiry into methods of bolstering the mental well-being of adolescents aged 11–16 over a period of 8 years. Building upon prior research demonstrating the efficacy of mindfulness for adults, researchers sought to investigate its potential effectiveness in younger populations. Specifically, the project aimed to ascertain whether mindfulness training implemented within school settings could serve as a viable, cost-effective, accessible, and scalable means of fostering mental health and well-being in adolescents. A large cohort was investigated, engaging over 28,000 children, 650 teachers, and 100 schools, and collecting 20 million data points.

Mindfulness training demonstrated a positive impact on school climate, fostering an atmosphere of mutual respect. However, despite improvements in school climate, universal schools-based mindfulness training did not significantly enhance overall mental health or well-being compared to standard social-emotional teaching. Many young people did not fully engage with the mindfulness training curriculum, with low compliance rates observed for required mindfulness practice homework. Implementing mindfulness training within the schools proved challenging, requiring dedicated staff, adequate resources, and efforts to dispel misconceptions about mindfulness. Additionally, training teachers to deliver mindfulness effectively was demanding and time-consuming, with only a minority achieving high levels of proficiency.

Findings suggested that mindfulness training may be more beneficial for certain groups of children, such as older teenagers, while potentially less effective for those with more pronounced mental health issues. Those who actively participated in mindfulness practices reported better mental health outcomes and improved mindfulness skills over time (Kuyken et al., 2022). In addition to student benefits, mindfulness training also offered advantages for teachers, with those undergoing training experiencing lower levels of burnout compared to their non-trained counterparts.

Ultimately, the approach to "scaling up" the delivery of mindfulness in schools across large cohorts in a relatively short time did not lead to significant impact. However, prior research has shown that well-trained, motivated teachers working with similarly motivated students can have positive effect. Moving forward, more research is needed to explore the nuances of which interventions work best for different groups of children, ensuring a more tailored and effective approach to promoting adolescent mental health. It may be that the most effective way to employ mindfulness to support resilience in young people is through a systemic impact on school culture and ethos.

Educators play a crucial role in shaping the learning experiences of students, but the demanding nature of the profession often leads to elevated levels of stress and burnout. Mindfulness interventions may support the well-being of teachers. Mindfulness is integrated into teacher training programmes to help educators manage stress, improve classroom dynamics, and foster a positive learning environment. This approach recognises the impact of teacher well-being on student outcomes.

By incorporating mindfulness practices into their routines, teachers may develop coping mechanisms and emotional regulation skills, contributing to improved mental well-being. Teachers participating in the Cultivating Awareness and Resilience in Education (CARE) programme experienced enhancements in various aspects of well-being, including efficacy, reduced burnout and time-related stress, and increased mindfulness compared to the control group. Evaluation data indicated that teachers regarded the programme as both feasible and effective for alleviating stress and enhancing performance, affirming its acceptability and efficacy (Jennings & Frank, 2013).

Effective classroom management is essential for creating a conducive learning environment. Mindfulness practices have been investigated for their impact on teachers' emotional regulation and ability to manage challenging situations in the classroom. Studies such as those conducted by Roeser et al. (2013) indicate that mindfulness training may enhance teachers' emotional well-being, resilience, and responsiveness to student needs. This suggests that mindfulness may positively influence classroom dynamics and teacher–student interactions. Studies suggest that teachers who engage in mindfulness practices may create a more positive and supportive classroom environment, which, in turn, can impact students' social-emotional development and academic performance.

The research evidence on mindfulness for schoolteachers has practical implications for teacher well-being, classroom management, and professional development. Integrating mindfulness into teacher training programmes and ongoing professional development may offer a holistic approach to supporting educators and in turn the young people they serve. Research has shown that mindfulness can create a culture or ethos within an education setting that benefits both teachers and students. Future interventions could therefore be less focussed on individual well-being and more systemically directed to the cultivation of a wholesome relational environment.

THE WORKPLACE

Many companies (e.g. Google, General Mills, Goldman Sachs, Unilever) have implemented mindfulness programmes for employees to address workplace stress, enhance focus, and promote a positive work culture. These programmes often include mindfulness workshops, meditation sessions, and stress reduction initiatives, as well as full mindfulness-based programmes specifically tailored to the workplace environment. See, for example, the experience of Google as described by Tan (2013).

One primary focus of mindfulness in the workplace literature is its impact on stress reduction and employee well-being. Studies demonstrate that mindfulness interventions can lead to significant reductions in stress levels among employees in high-stress working environments (Jha et al., 2014). Mindfulness-Based Stress Reduction (MBSR) programmes, when implemented in workplace settings, have been associated with improvements in psychological well-being and a decrease in reported stress-related symptoms.

Employee satisfaction and commitment to the organisation are critical factors for organisational success. Research suggests that mindfulness practices can positively influence job satisfaction and organisational commitment. A study by Wongtongkam et al. (2017) found that employees participating in mindfulness programmes reported higher levels of job satisfaction and a greater sense of commitment to their organisations. This underscores the potential role of mindfulness in fostering a positive workplace culture.

Mindfulness has also been linked to cognitive performance and creativity in the workplace. Mindfulness practices can enhance cognitive flexibility and problem-solving skills (Colzato, 2012) and bolster working memory and selective attention (Jha et al., 2014). This has implications for workplace productivity and innovation, as employees with improved cognitive function are better equipped to navigate complex tasks and generate creative solutions.

Mindfulness has also been integrated into workplace leadership training programmes to enhance the emotional intelligence and resilience of leaders. This can contribute to better decision-making, improved team dynamics, and overall organisational well-being. A study by Langer et al. (2014) suggests that leaders who incorporate mindfulness into their leadership style exhibit improved decision-making, communication, and conflict resolution skills. Moreover, organisations that prioritise mindfulness have been associated with enhanced employee engagement, reduced absenteeism, and increased overall organisational performance.

As organisations increasingly recognise the potential benefits of mindfulness, the practical implications of implementing mindfulness programmes in the workplace are gaining significance. Future research should focus on identifying optimal strategies for integrating mindfulness into organisational culture, addressing potential barriers to implementation, the most effective mode of delivery, and the scalability of mindfulness interventions across diverse workplace settings.

HEALTHCARE

Those working as healthcare professionals are vulnerable to experiencing high levels of stress, burnout, and compassion fatigue. Mindfulness interventions have attracted significant interest in the healthcare sector due to their potential to improve the well-being and resilience of those in caring professions.

Mindfulness training can enhance resilience among healthcare professionals, enabling them to better cope with the demands and challenges of their work. A study by Kemper et al. (2015) found that mindfulness and compassion were positively associated with resilience and lower levels of sleep disturbance for young healthcare professionals. Nurses who participated in a mindfulness programme reported reductions in stress, anxiety, and depressive symptoms, as well as enhanced feelings of well-being (Irving, 2009).

Similar benefits have been demonstrated across various settings, including hospitals, clinics, and academic institutions. A meta-analysis by Burton et al. (2017) found that mindfulness-based interventions were associated with significant reductions in burnout and psychological distress among healthcare providers.

In the clinical context, it is imperative for healthcare providers to exhibit a heightened sensitivity towards patients' distress, a willingness to acknowledge personal fallibility, a commitment to enhancing technical proficiency, an adherence to evidence-based practices, and a clarity regarding their own values. These attributes collectively empower practitioners to engage with their patients in a compassionate manner, demonstrate technical competence, maintain a strong presence, and exhibit insightful decision-making abilities. Epstein (1999) reported that primary care physicians who underwent mindfulness training demonstrated improvements in patient-centred communication and clinical empathy.

There are inspiring examples of how mindfulness can support healthcare professionals in their work. For example, since 2018 in England, high-intensity psychological therapists working within the NHS Talking Therapies service (formerly IAPT) have been offered a 12-month training in MBCT funded by the UK government (Health Education England). At the time of writing, the 7th cohort is being organised. In the United States, Drs Mick Krasner and Ron Epstein have developed mindfulness programmes for physicians with real-world impact on levels of stress, compassion fatigue, and burnout (Krasner, 2024), and in the UK, the Mindful Self Care Programme has been developed by Maura Kenny for those working in high-stress environments.

Further research is needed to better understand the specific mechanisms through which mindfulness exerts its effects in healthcare settings and to identify optimal intervention strategies for different healthcare professions and contexts.

THE CRIMINAL JUSTICE SYSTEM

As criminal justice agencies seek innovative approaches to address rehabilitation, reduce recidivism, and enhance the overall well-being of individuals involved in the system, mindfulness has emerged as a potential tool. Some correctional institutions have introduced mindfulness programmes for inmates and staff, aiming to reduce aggression, manage stress, and promote rehabilitation. These programmes often include meditation and mindfulness-based interventions to support emotional regulation.

Research has investigated the impact of mindfulness interventions on inmate well-being and behaviour. Studies have shown that mindfulness programmes implemented in correctional facilities can lead to improvements in psychological well-being, emotional regulation, and reductions in aggressive behaviour among inmates (Himelstein et al., 2019). This suggests that mindfulness may serve as a valuable tool for enhancing the rehabilitative potential of correctional environments.

Incarceration often brings about high levels of stress and emotional distress among inmates. Mindfulness-based interventions have been shown to be effective in reducing stress and enhancing coping skills. Research by Samuelson et al. (2017) indicates that mindfulness training can lead to significant reductions in perceived stress levels and improvements in coping mechanisms, providing inmates with valuable tools to navigate the challenges of incarceration.

Individuals within the criminal justice system often grapple with mental health issues and substance abuse disorders. Mindfulness-based interventions have been explored as a complementary approach to addressing these challenges. Studies such as those by Bowen et al. (2014) suggest that mindfulness can play a role in reducing symptoms of depression, anxiety, and substance abuse, thereby contributing to a more comprehensive approach to rehabilitation within the criminal justice context.

One of the key outcomes of interest in prison settings is the impact of mindfulness on reducing rates of recidivism. While research in this area is still evolving, promising findings suggest that mindfulness interventions may have a positive influence on post-release outcomes. Participation in mindfulness programmes may be associated with a reduction in the likelihood of reoffending (Parrish & Maull, 2017). This points to the potential of mindfulness as a preventive strategy in breaking the cycle of criminal behaviour, leading to further incarceration.

Integrating mindfulness into rehabilitation programmes may offer a holistic approach to addressing the multifaceted needs of individuals involved in the criminal justice system. Additionally, providing correctional staff with mindfulness training can contribute to a more compassionate and empathetic approach, fostering a rehabilitative rather than punitive environment.

As the field continues to evolve, future research should focus on refining mindfulness interventions tailored to the unique needs of criminal justice populations. Longitudinal studies are needed to assess the sustained impact of mindfulness on post-release outcomes, and further exploration of the potential role of mindfulness in diversion programmes and alternative sentencing approaches is warranted.

SPORTS AND ATHLETICS

Mindfulness is increasingly incorporated into sports psychology to help athletes manage performance anxiety, improve focus, and enhance overall mental resilience. Athletes may practice mindfulness techniques to stay present during competitions and cope with pressure. Notable sport stars who utilise mindfulness and meditation include Novak Djokovic, the LA Lakers, the Seattle Seahawks, Kobe Bryant, Misty May-Treanor, and Kerri Walsh.

The intersection of mindfulness and athletic performance has been a focal point of research. Studies such as those conducted by Gardner and Moore (2007) have suggested that mindfulness training can positively influence attentional focus and concentration, which are both crucial components for success in sports. Athletes engaging in mindfulness practices have reported improvements in their ability to maintain concentration under pressure, ultimately contributing to enhanced performance outcomes.

Athletes often face high levels of stress and pressure, both during competition and in training. Mindfulness interventions have been explored as tools for stress management and developing effective coping strategies. Research by Birrer and Morgan (2010) indicates that mindfulness training can lead to reductions in anxiety and improvements in emotional regulation among athletes. This suggests that mindfulness may play a crucial role in helping athletes navigate the psychological challenges inherent in competitive sports.

In addition to performance-related benefits, mindfulness has been investigated for its role in injury rehabilitation and pain management among athletes. Studies such as those by Solberg et al. (2019) suggest that mindfulness practices can contribute to improved pain tolerance and psychological well-being during the rehabilitation process. Mindfulness-based interventions may provide athletes with valuable tools to cope with the physical and emotional aspects of injuries, facilitating a smoother recovery and return to play.

Mindfulness interventions have also been explored in the context of team sports, addressing aspects of communication, cohesion, and overall team dynamics. Research by Tassi et al. (2023) suggests that team-based mindfulness training can enhance collective efficacy, trust, and communication within sports teams. This indicates that mindfulness may not only benefit individual athletes but also contribute to a positive and cohesive team environment.

The research evidence on mindfulness in sports holds practical implications for athletes, coaches, and sports organisations. Integrating mindfulness into training regimens may offer a holistic approach to athlete development, focusing not only on physical prowess but also on mental resilience. Future research should explore optimal strategies for incorporating mindfulness into sports programmes, consider individual differences among athletes, and assess the scalability of mindfulness interventions in various sports settings.

MILITARY AND VETERANS' SERVICES

Mindfulness-based interventions are used to support the mental health and well-being of military personnel and veterans. These programmes may assist in managing symptoms of post-traumatic stress disorder (PTSD) and promoting overall resilience.

The military and veteran populations encounter distinct challenges related to their service experiences, including exposure to trauma and the demands of a highly structured and often stressful environment. Mindfulness has gained attention as a potential intervention to address the mental health needs of military personnel and veterans. This review aims to synthesise the growing body of research evidence on the effectiveness of mindfulness in promoting resilience, mitigating mental health challenges, and enhancing overall well-being in military and veteran populations.

PTSD is a prevalent mental health concern among military personnel and veterans. Research such as the work by Kearney et al. (2013) has investigated the impact of mindfulness interventions on PTSD symptoms. Findings suggest that mindfulness-based programmes can lead to significant reductions in PTSD symptoms, including intrusive thoughts, hyperarousal, and avoidance behaviours. The cultivation of present-moment awareness and non-judgemental acceptance may contribute to improved coping mechanisms for individuals grappling with the aftermath of trauma.

Anxiety and depression are common mental health challenges in military and veteran populations. Mindfulness-based interventions have been explored as potential strategies for alleviating symptoms of anxiety and depression. Studies such as those conducted by Johnson et al. (2016) indicate that mindfulness interventions can be effective in reducing symptoms of anxiety and depression among military personnel and veterans. Mindfulness practices may offer individuals tools to manage negative thought patterns, regulate emotions, and enhance overall emotional well-being.

Resilience is a critical factor in the mental health and well-being of military personnel and veterans, influencing their ability to navigate stressors and challenges. Research by Smith et al. (2011) suggests that mindfulness training can contribute to the development of resilience and adaptive coping mechanisms. By fostering a non-reactive awareness of thoughts and emotions, mindfulness may enhance individuals' capacity to bounce back from adversity and maintain psychological well-being in the face of stressors.

Sleep disturbances are prevalent among military personnel and veterans, often linked to stress and trauma exposure. Mindfulness-based interventions have been explored as a potential approach to improve sleep quality. Studies such as those by Herrmann et al. (2020) suggest that mindfulness practices can lead to improvements in sleep patterns and overall sleep quality. Mindfulness may address the hyperarousal and intrusive thoughts that contribute to sleep disturbances, offering a holistic approach to promoting better sleep hygiene in these populations.

Traumatic brain injury (TBI) is a common occurrence in military settings and can have lasting effects on cognitive and psychological functioning. Research by Barnes et al. (2019) has explored the role of mindfulness in supporting individuals with TBI. Preliminary findings suggest that mindfulness interventions may contribute to improvements in cognitive function, emotional regulation, and overall well-being in individuals with TBI, offering a potentially valuable adjunctive therapy.

The research evidence on mindfulness in military and veteran populations has practical implications for mental health interventions and support services. Integrating mindfulness into existing mental health care frameworks may offer a holistic approach to addressing the unique challenges faced by military personnel and veterans. Critics in this area raise the opposing underlying epistemologies between mindfulness and military combat, pointing to the focus mindfulness traditions have on non–violence. This conflict is addressed more fully at the end of this chapter. Future research should explore optimal strategies for tailoring mindfulness interventions to the specific needs of these populations, considering factors such as deployment history, combat exposure, and the presence of co–occurring mental health conditions.

BROADENING MAINSTREAM MINDFULNESS

The past 20 years of evidence-based practice have been successful in introducing mindfulness within mainstream institutions, including the UK National Health Service, the criminal justice system, education, and the workplace. The usefulness of a mindfulness-based approach in areas such as the management of health and well-being, resilience, emotional and behavioural regulation, leadership, and effective communication is now well established. We are now able to step back from this body of work and see how an over-focus on the individual may have contributed to the perpetuation of unhealthy systemic structures and the unhelpful upholding of the status quo.

It has been suggested that in some cases, mindfulness has been employed as a metaphorical "band aid" that has not addressed unhealthy organisational frameworks and social norms that have placed the responsibility for resilience in the face of distress with the individual, rather than recognising and holding accountable systems of power and control. The emphasis on individual well-being and self-improvement may in some instances have neglected broader social and structural factors that contribute to mental health issues, such as systemic inequalities and societal injustices.

There is a critique that mindfulness in some settings may have become commodified, with its practices and teachings marketed as quick-fix solutions for stress reduction or personal enhancement (Purser, 2019). Presented in this way, mindfulness can appear to overly prioritise personal well-being and happiness. By promoting a narrow definition of success and happiness, mindfulness may inadvertently perpetuate harmful ideologies of productivity and achievement, while neglecting the complexities and interconnectedness of human experience.

Mindfulness has rapidly entered the mainstream over the last 20–30 years. Based on solid research and linkage to policy, much work has been dedicated to best practice and upholding integrity and standards of quality in the mindfulness field. The development of Good Practice Guidelines and professional bodies such as the British Association of Mindfulness-Based Approaches (BAMBA) and its international counterparts regulate the field and inform public understanding of quality in standards. The development of the Mindfulness-based Interventions: Teaching Assessment Criteria (Crane et al., 2013) at Bangor University along with a significant body of research exploring effective pedagogy in mindfulness teaching have mapped out a framework for what good quality mindfulness delivery looks like. An ongoing consideration in the development of new directions of travel is how to find ways of upholding quality and integrity while balancing space for innovation and increased accessibility.

In *Disrupting White Mindfulness*, Karelse (2023) argues that mindfulness, as it is commonly practised in the West, has been appropriated from its cultural origins, particularly from Buddhist traditions, without proper acknowledgement or understanding of its historical and cultural contexts. This appropriation perpetuates colonial legacies by erasing the contributions of non-Western cultures to mindfulness practices. As we look back over the past two decades, we can see that the work done was of its time. Research and teaching of mindfulness has in some settings reflected and reinforced white cultural norms and values, resulting in the exclusion or marginalisation of people from diverse racial and ethnic backgrounds. A key focus for the next phase of the work is to open to new themes around social justice and planetary health including a more nuanced, co-created, and socially engaged approach that acknowledges cultural origins, addresses systemic inequalities, and promotes collective well-being alongside individual flourishing.

LIMITATIONS OF CURRICULUM-BASED APPROACHES

Our understanding of effective pedagogy in the teaching of mindfulness is in transition. Teachers are moving away from standardised curricula toward more flexible, innovative, and adaptive approaches. This shift reflects the growing recognition that mindfulness is not a one-size-fits-all practice; instead, its effective integration into diverse contexts requires customisation to meet the unique needs, cultures, and experiences of participants.

Traditional mindfulness teaching methods often rely on structured curricula, such as the well-established eight-week formats of Mindfulness-Based Stress Reduction (MBSR) and Mindfulness-Based Cognitive Therapy (MBCT). While these programmes are evidence-based and provide clear guidance for teachers and learners, they can be overly prescriptive, limiting adaptability. Critics argue that strict adherence to predefined lesson plans (which does not match the spirit of these approaches in any case) may fail to address the dynamic and culturally diverse needs of participants, particularly in non-clinical or community-based settings (Crane et al., 2017).

EMERGING TRENDS IN MINDFULNESS PEDAGOGY

The evolving pedagogy of mindfulness has always emphasised flexibility, creativity, and responsiveness, prioritising the lived experiences and needs of learners. Teachers are increasingly tailoring mindfulness practices to the specific goals, contexts, and challenges of participants. For example, workplace mindfulness programmes may focus on short, accessible exercises to manage stress during the workday, while youth programmes might integrate playful, movement-based activities to engage children. This personalisation helps participants find resonance with mindfulness, enhancing its relevance and effectiveness.

Mindfulness teaching is becoming more culturally responsive, recognising the diverse ways contemplative practices are understood and practiced globally. Pedagogies aim to honour and incorporate participants' cultural values and neuro-diverse processing styles, avoiding the imposition of standardised practices that may feel alien or disconnected.

Digital tools and apps are playing an increasing role in mindfulness pedagogy, enabling adaptive learning. Platforms like Headspace or Insight Timer offer modular content, allowing users to choose practices aligned with their specific needs, such as stress relief, focus, or sleep. Interactive features, such as feedback systems and guided customisation, further enhance the adaptability of these resources.

Moreover, the focus on innovation calls for collaboration across disciplines and cultures, incorporating insights from psychology, education, and social work as well as knowledge from diverse lived experience to co-produce more holistic and impactful mindfulness interventions. Educators must balance the need for evidence-based practices with creative exploration, ensuring that mindfulness remains grounded while evolving to meet contemporary challenges.

The pedagogical shift in mindfulness teaching – from curriculum-driven models to more flexible, adaptive approaches – represents a necessary evolution in response to the complexities of modern life. By understanding the barriers to accessibility to mindfulness to date, embracing personalisation, cultural sensitivity, experiential learning, and collective engagement, mindfulness education can become more accessible, inclusive, and impactful. This transition not only enhances the relevance of mindfulness in diverse contexts but also reflects its foundational principles of awareness, compassion, and responsiveness to the present moment.

CONCLUSION

Mindfulness is now firmly established within mainstream settings, including

- The workplace
- Healthcare
- Criminal justice
- Sports and athletics
- Military and veterans' services

The chapter also shines a light on the way the work has developed over the past two decades as it rapidly entered the mainstream and offers an overview of areas that are evolving in the next phase of this work. The following chapters present a broader, more socially engaged potential for the application of mindfulness to the global challenges that are facing our world at this time.

11

MEETING THE META-CRISIS WITH MINDFULNESS

In earlier sections, we explored the reasons behind the widespread popularity of mindfulness, reviewed some of the evidence supporting its effectiveness, and examined possible mechanisms of action. We then discussed how to cultivate a personal mindfulness practice and offered suggestions for supporting this process. In the final chapters, we shift focus to how mindfulness can help us navigate some of the most pressing challenges of our time – environmental, social, political, and cultural.

We are currently living in what has been described as the "age of the meta-crisis" (Schmachtenberger, 2023), a period marked by a convergence of interconnected global crises. These crises include climate change, environmental degradation, and species extinction, as well as rising political polarisation, geopolitical tensions, and ongoing conflicts. Additionally, the rapid development and potentially destructive impact of artificial intelligence (AI) technologies highlight the need for us to hold on to those human qualities that enable us to protect the planet rather than contribute to its destruction.

Although mindfulness is clearly neither a panacea nor a magic wand, as we have seen, there is emerging evidence that paying attention in ways that enhance awareness of these issues (noticing what is happening both internally and externally) helps our ability to respond. Israeli writer/historian Yuval Noah Harari sees meditative practice as central to navigating contemporary life: *"we need to get to know ourselves better and we need to develop this mental flexibility. Not as a kind of (side) hobby … This is really the most important quality or skill to just survive the upheavals in the coming decades"* (Skipper, 2018).

DOI: 10.4324/9781003453598-15

Throughout this book so far, we have described several aspects of a mindfulness-based approach to life. As well as opening to pleasant moments and allowing ourselves to be nourished by them, difficult and challenging aspects are also part of life, and we have innate tendencies to crave pleasant and push away unpleasant experience. Our choice therefore is not whether to experience difficulties, but rather how we might respond when difficulties arise, as they surely will. This premise holds as we turn now to exploring how the mindfulness revolution might be relevant to the meta-crisis.

GUIDANCE ON HOW TO READ THIS CHAPTER

Before embarking on this adventure, discovering what may seem like a radical approach to the challenges faced by the world, it is worth laying out an explicit framework to equip us with the resilience required to face such issues without leading to feelings of overwhelm. The challenges outlined may at points feel insurmountable. It may even feel like mindfulness simply leads to a greater awareness of all that is wrong in the world. Follow your own inner guidance and wisdom as you read, taking regular pauses and perhaps engaging in the practices outlined. You may even notice a subtle change in the way you are relating to what you read. In essence, this is an opportunity for you to apply the learning from Section II.

WHAT IS A "META-CRISIS" ANYWAY?

Human beings have always faced challenges of threat and uncertainty. Indeed, the management of threat seems to be intrinsic to all life. However, there are now several, real existential threats that we will need to navigate to ensure human survival. The most obvious and pressing is that of climate change and global warming. Added to this, with increasing geopolitical tension, war, and nuclear capabilities; political polarisation and social inequities; and the negative potential of AI, it seems clear that for all our advances, humanity is faced with challenges on multiple fronts. At an individual level, this appears to be reflected in growing levels of stress, a lack of meaning, and increased rates of depression, heart disease, and cancer.

A recent international study by the National Bureau of Economic Research (Giuntella et al., 2023) which surveyed approximately half a million people in midlife (in some of the most economically prosperous nations on the planet) reported that 80% of respondents felt their lives lacked meaning. This was a resounding result in terms of the aim of the study – to determine whether adults do, in fact, experience a "midlife crisis." This suggests that there is something fundamental about the way we are living now that is not serving us. Scientist-philosophers such as Iain McGilchrist (2019) have concluded that as a species, we have lost our way through the gradual dominance of the left hemisphere (of the brain), with its precise categories of thinking being applied in all aspects of life. This has led to the left hemisphere usurping the guiding role of the right hemisphere with its capacity to see things in wholes rather than component parts, with greater breadth and flexibility. According to McGilchrist, mindfulness, as well as other activities such as reading poetry, spending time in nature, and dancing, can help to activate the right, more holistic hemisphere. This would allow the right hemisphere of the brain to do what it does best – hold complexity and ambiguity and foresee the implications of actions that get missed by the left in its total focus on completing tasks. In terms of our response to these multiple crises, the inner capacities cultivated through mindfulness could scarcely be more relevant (Kabat-Zinn, 2019).

MINDFULNESS AND SOCIAL JUSTICE: RACISM, BIAS, AND PREJUDICE

Bringing awareness to issues of bias, prejudice, and racism in all their forms can help to illuminate the landscape of how our behaviours are learned, assimilated, and handed down historically, as well as being innate features of what it is to be human. We know about the evolutionary/survival value of in-group and out-group biases (e.g., Baumeister & Vohs, 2007), as well as the confirmation bias (e.g., Klayman, 1995; Wason, 1960), which means we seek out like-minded people to confirm our own views and opinions. This likely then becomes self and group-serving and gratifying, confirming one group's existence on the planet in quite fundamental ways (values, ideals, worldview) without being "checked" or needing to accommodate others' views. The rise of anti-immigration sentiment in the U.K. (which was a major influence on its decision to leave the European Union), is just one example. Recent developments in the United States too have echoes of developments that led to the rise of fascism and xenophobic nationalism in Germany prior to World War Two (Browning, 2018).

What would a mindful approach to racism look like? Founded on the same attitudinal qualities of openness, curiosity, and kindly awareness, it might start with an acceptance that simply by virtue of being socialised in one culture or society rather than another, we have inherited certain biases of perception that likely favour "people like us" over others. Mindfulness might also allow us to recognise some common, core features of being human, such as a desire for safety, freedom, love, and connection, as well as to live in peace without fear of threat or intimidation. Mindfulness can also help us to recognise those places of contraction in the body/mind when faced by other views or ways of seeing – of difference. The body can be a tremendous ally in bringing curiosity and kindness to what is being noticed and offer an alternative to endless cycles of thinking and rumination.

> **Practice**
>
> Taking a moment to feel your responses to what you are reading. Let your eyes rest by closing them or looking out of a window. Noticing how your body feels, relaxed or tense. And how are you feeling? Can you identify any thoughts or images passing through your mind?

CLIMATE AND BIODIVERSITY

How do we engage mindfully with climate change? Whether we choose to see the effects of increasing temperatures as human-induced or not, the environment is reliably predicted to become increasingly hostile and challenging to all living things. We have already learned that "a wandering mind is an unhappy mind" (Killingsworth and Gilbert, 2010). However, there is also evidence to suggest that "a wandering mind is a less caring mind" both towards ourselves and others (Jazaieri et al., 2016). Mindfulness can support us in remaining open to and aware of our reactions to learning about the effects of climate change.

> In 2022, a record 32.6 million people were forcibly displaced by the effects of climate change. The overall figure is expected to double by 2050 (Internal Displacement Monitoring Centre, 2023) and reach 1.2 billion in a "worst case" scenario (Institute for Economics and Peace, 2023).
>
> What reactions do you notice (in the body, feelings, thoughts) when reading such figures? One set of reactions in the domain of "feelings" may be of shock, followed quickly by a sense of despair. Perhaps this is accompanied by sensations of heaviness in the chest or stomach? Thoughts may be something like, "I don't like reading this (headlines)," or "We need to change this." Mindfulness is the cultivation of kindly awareness to whatever we notice. As we allow our experience to be as it is, feelings may evolve to a sense of sorrow. This may change further to a sense of joining and solidarity in recognising this as a sorrow we share with others.

We might then allow our grief to inform our actions in support of the planet. If we get stuck in despair, mindfulness can help us to acknowledge this and take care. This may result in bringing greater levels of awareness to actions such as what we choose to eat, purchasing more locally sourced food and produce, and engaging in more conscious consumption, including noticing when these patterns become habitual, unconscious, or simply a form of distraction. This is not about judging any patterns of behaviour we do become aware of, rather to "see" these very clearly first of all before deciding what, if anything, we might change. We may extend this to decisions that directly affect the environment. Finally, we find the view expressed by Irish writer/

philosopher John O'Donohue (Tippett, 2008) to be deeply compelling. *"I think it makes a huge difference when you leave your house: whether you think you are walking into 'location', which is simply 'dead space' which you are crossing so that you can get to where you need to go; or whether you believe you are walking into a living universe. If you believe the second, then your walk becomes a different thing."*

Political polarisation and economic crisis

I believe finding ways to be quiet together will be fundamental to the healing process. I'm hoping that we can get people on both sides of the aisle to move away from the turbulence that is dominating the surface of our politics, and the media covering our politics.

Congressman Tim Ryan (in Boyce, 2019)

We are in desperate need of a new politics and a new way of engaging in political debate that moves us outside of self-perpetuating echo chambers where we hear and see what we expect to hear and see. Political discourse is often framed in overly combative ways, as "either/or" choices based on an underlying simplistic formulation of right and wrong. This continues to simplify and "dumb down" the electorate into binary choices, when in practice what is called for are frequently "both/and" positions incorporating multiple perspectives. We regularly encounter tough decisions and grey areas in our own lives that can help to guide us when discerning how to relate to simplified media narratives in political discourse.

How can mindfulness help? There is a well known exercise from MBSR based on the Japanese martial art of Aikido, which was developed to represent different styles of communication – particularly when it comes to very direct, confrontational styles such as insisting we are right or submitting to another (which we often encounter in political debates). It involves a conscious "stepping in" to meet the communication offered by someone in an open, curious, grounded, "mindful" state – very alive to what is coming your way. Of course, mindfulness practice is dependent on at least one member of the communication remaining open

– otherwise no compromise or evolution of understanding is possible. Rather than seeking to defeat opposing views, it may be helpful to be open to considering different perspectives on the same thing – neither right nor wrong, thereby allowing new perspectives to emerge.

Mindfulness is increasingly supporting members of parliament, as well as political and administrative staff around the world, to resource themselves in their work. It is also beginning to inform the development of government policy itself – from primary and secondary education to all forms of healthcare, well-being, and the criminal justice system. This is perhaps best exemplified by the Mindfulness Initiative (U.K.) following the establishment of the Mindfulness All-Party Parliamentary Group (MAPPG) within the Westminster Parliament in England. Inspired by this initiative, governments and public institutions are increasingly exploring the integration of mindfulness into public policies, especially in the areas of education, healthcare, and workplace well-being. This includes initiatives to promote mental health and resilience on a broader societal level. Wales is another example of a country where mindfulness principles are being integrated into public policy and politics.

Government and public institutions play a pivotal role in society, often navigating complex challenges and demanding work environments. Individuals working in government settings face unique challenges related to stress, decision-making, and organisational dynamics. Mindfulness has emerged as a potential tool to enhance well-being, resilience, and overall performance. Mindfulness interventions may lead to significant reductions in perceived stress levels among employees in government and public sectors. By cultivating mindfulness, individuals may develop coping mechanisms and resilience to navigate the challenges inherent in political communication.

WAR AND THE INTER-GENERATIONAL EFFECTS OF WAR

At the time of writing (2025), two wars are dominating Western media coverage – the war in Ukraine and the war in Gaza.

There are fears that more of the surrounding regions of Palestine and Israel will be drawn into the conflict there, including Iran. Meanwhile, tension between North and South Korea remains precipitously high. Given the nuclear capabilities of these nations, the threat to the continued existence of humanity is at a critical stage. The legacy effects of these wars, even if a peaceful solution is found, will be profound and transgenerational.

Set against such devastation, displacement, and ongoing destruction, how could mindfulness possibly help? The ability to acknowledge the effects of war on all levels – physical, psychological, socio-cultural, and economic – can be a pivotal first step in taking care of ourselves. For example, mindfulness can allow us to begin to process and work with the felt sense of trauma in the body, if conditions of security allow. A significant recent development in the field is "trauma-informed" mindfulness teaching. This recognises the fact that those who have experienced trauma may be re-traumatised if the trauma has not been acknowledged. However, beginning to slowly and carefully process the effects of trauma in the body (at the person's own pace) through gentle movement practices or the cultivation of various "anchors" that can help to support awareness of the present moment can allow the subtle work of integration of such traumatic experiences to begin. A recent development in this area is that of Mindfulness-Based Trauma Recovery for Refugees (MBTR-R) (Kincade, 2023).

IMMIGRATION

A challenge resulting primarily from climate change and war is the mass displacement of people, causing significant immigrant populations. The rhetoric around immigration is frequently over-simplified and one-sided, rarely offering a more nuanced weighing up of information in relation to those who feel threatened, be they immigrants or locals. When there are real challenges faced by both sides, including social welfare entitlement; provision of food, housing, and medicine; and the ability to work and access education, transport, and heating, there can be an understandable demand that the state prioritise and look after its own citizens first. There are real pressures on resources, and choosing whom to prioritise will therefore always be a focus of concern and debate.

Political parties that advocate for a nation's most vulnerable citizens have traditionally been set in opposition to those that prioritise the freedom of the individual to determine where its funds are spent. There is an onus on political parties to communicate and direct funds where needs are greatest, balanced against a communication strategy that clearly explains the moral and ethical reasoning behind financial decision-making and resource provision. How can mindfulness help? The compassionate aspect of mindful awareness might allow us to see and respond to both our own and others' suffering. A powerful effect of learning mindfulness in groups is a shared sense of universal experience and "common humanity." Each one of us suffers. This is a fundamental truth about human existence. Mindfulness helps us to see clearly, which means seeing the effects of unexamined narratives or learned prejudices. Mindfulness entails a compassionate, openhearted questioning and curiosity in relation to all things. In relation to immigration, we might ask, how would a mindful society respond to the question of immigration?

"Just like me"

Taken from the Buddhist tradition, this compassion practice invites us to spend some time seeing the similarities between ourselves and others. This allows us to broaden the scope of our awareness from personal concerns and unconscious biases to including others, especially those who may superficially appear to be very different.

THE "ATTENTION ECONOMY," THE IMPACT OF AI AND SOCIAL MEDIA

The world of advertising has realised for many decades that the ability to capture a buyer's attention is key to sales. Whether a pithy slogan or slick commercial campaign, we are constantly exposed to media that attempts to draw our attention in. In a super-charged, media-dense world, the ability to stand out from the crowd is prized in the information age. Given that a sale can take place in the matter of seconds on the basis of a single "click," attention is indeed the "new gold" (de Kwant, 2019).

Social media and commercial platforms thrive on our ability to scroll, follow, and "like" the people, products, and services that reflect our idealised self. Although this can be engaged in with awareness, the intelligence and design of these platforms and algorithms ensures that many of us remain engrossed in these digital worlds far longer than initially intended.

Equally, the effects of social media can be devastating. Mindfulness in schools should include bringing greater awareness and intentionality to the use of social media platforms. Esther Ghey, mother of murdered transgender teenager in England, has called for mindfulness to be made available for all children for just this reason (ITV, 2023).

Johann Hari (2023) writes about his hard-won efforts to wean himself away from his dependence on social media, which he claims to have contributed to the loss of his capacity to pay attention. He also identifies speed, exhaustion, and pollution. Hari comments that "I found strong evidence that our collapsing ability to pay attention is not primarily a personal failing on my part, or your part, or your kid's part. This is being done to us all. It is being done by very powerful forces. Those forces include Big Tech, but they also go way beyond them. This is a systemic problem" (Hari 2023, p. 9).

Social media provides a superficial image of social engagement which is deeply compulsive and likened to other addictive substances that tend to dictate to us (the root meaning of the word *ad-diction*). Mindfulness practice can help us to foster greater levels of awareness in our use and engagement with social media and give ourselves permission to take regular breaks from forms of media that may be unhelpful or harmful. For example, forming an intention to take a breathing space or other mini meditation at regular intervals and upon opening social media pages can offer a helpful perspective when choosing to engage.

How does one build a more flexible mind?

I practice meditation, I practice vipassana. I do two hours every day of meditation. I go to a lot of retreats, up to 60 days every year, and it works for me. I won't say that it will work the same for everybody. Different techniques work for different for people ... But we should be more clear about the goal: we need to get to know ourselves better and we need to develop this mental flexibility ... This is really the most important quality or skill to just survive the upheavals in the coming decades.
Yuval Noah Harari (Skipper, 2018).

FROM REACTING TO RESPONDING

The theory of evolution highlights our inherent human tendencies when confronted with threat or danger. Millennia of survival-driven reactivity have predisposed our species to instinctively respond with "fight," "flight," "freeze," or "fawn" behaviours to protect ourselves from harm. However, in the context of the meta-crisis, these automatic reactions are not likely to be as suitable or effective as they would have been when facing a sabre-toothed tiger. In modern day terms, "flight" reactivity may present as a collective burying of heads in the proverbial sand, business as usual. "Freeze" has been likened to the denial that there is a problem at all, and certain kinds of activism that may be polarising, combative, and exhausting may be a form of "fight" reactivity.

Activism is generally defined as intentional actions taken by individuals or groups to bring about social or political change. These actions are typically organised, sustained, and oriented towards specific goals or outcomes. Activism is characterised by its proactive nature; it involves planned, deliberate strategies aimed at addressing root causes of injustice or inequality. Activism requires collective action, which is strategically designed to influence public opinion, policy, or social norms. Activism can take various forms, including protests, advocacy, lobbying, educational campaigns, and civil disobedience.

Reactivity, on the other hand, refers to immediate, often impulsive responses to stimuli or events. Reactive behaviour is typically characterised by emotional responses – such as anger, fear, or frustration – that emerge in response to perceived threats or challenges. In the context of social or political issues, reactivity may manifest as spontaneous protests, riots, or social media outbursts. While reactivity can provide an immediate expression of dissent or resistance, it is usually less organised and more volatile than activism.

Activism can emerge from reactive moments. For example, a spontaneous protest following a triggering event, such as the killing of George Floyd in America, can evolve into more organised, sustained activism addressing broader issues like systemic racism and police violence. Activists may also capitalise on reactive moments to galvanise public support and draw attention to their causes.

Reactive behaviour is often driven by emotional dysregulation and a lack of conscious cognitive processing, which can limit the potential for sustained or strategic social change. Health crises such as obesity, medication use, and the opioid disaster may be forms of "flight." Turning away from underpinning anxiety fed by the meta-crisis may lead to forms of addiction and avoidance necessary to keep the reality of the social and environmental state of the world at bay.

MINDFULNESS: THE NEXT WAVE

Mindfulness is widely regarded as a hallmark of "third wave" psychological therapies, reflecting its evolution within behavioural and cognitive approaches. This classification emerged in response to limitations identified in earlier therapeutic models, related to the need for more holistic and process-oriented frameworks. In the historical progression of psychotherapy, the "first wave" of behavioural therapy in the mid-twentieth century focused primarily on observable behaviours, relying on principles of classical and operant conditioning. The subsequent "second wave," represented by cognitive-behavioural therapy (CBT), incorporated cognitive processes, emphasising the identification and restructuring of maladaptive thought patterns contributing to emotional distress.

The "third wave," emerging in the 1990s, introduced a significant paradigm shift. This approach extends beyond symptom reduction, aiming to cultivate psychological flexibility and broader well-being through acceptance and experiential strategies. Unlike earlier waves, third wave therapies focus on one's relationship to thoughts and emotions rather than their specific content, helping individuals engage with their internal experiences non-judgementally. Central to this shift is the incorporation of mindfulness emphasising present-moment awareness and acceptance. Third wave therapies also emphasise aligning actions with personal values, fostering a sense of purpose and fulfilment.

Mindfulness plays a foundational role in several third-wave interventions. In acceptance and commitment therapy (ACT), mindfulness is integral to promoting acceptance of distressing thoughts while encouraging value-driven actions. Dialectical behaviour therapy (DBT), originally developed for borderline personality disorder, incorporates mindfulness to enhance emotional regulation and interpersonal effectiveness. Mindfulness-Based Cognitive Therapy (MBCT) blends traditional cognitive strategies with mindfulness practices, offering a preventive approach for recurrent depression.

The 2024 International Conference on Mindfulness: Mindfulness in a Changing World, hosted by Bangor University and the Mindfulness Network, presented an emerging focus on social and environmental factors as a potential "fourth wave" in psychological and mindfulness-based interventions. This conceptual wave extends the scope of mindfulness beyond individual well-being to encompass collective, ecological, and systemic dimensions. Rooted in the recognition of interconnectedness, the fourth wave emphasises the role played by the broader social and environmental systems in which individuals exist, thereby acknowledging the urgent psychological and practical challenges of the modern world and recognising the inherent interconnection between personal and collective well-being.

The concept of mindfulness as part of the fourth wave arises against the backdrop of global crises and interacting elements of the "meta-crisis." While the third wave primarily focuses on personal transformation through acceptance and self-awareness, critics argue that it insufficiently addresses the socio-political and ecological contexts that shape individual suffering. By integrating mindfulness with social justice, sustainability, and collective action, the fourth wave seeks to bridge this gap. This wave is influenced by developments in ecological psychology, critical mindfulness studies, and indigenous wisdom traditions that emphasise interconnectedness and collective responsibility.

The fourth wave of mindfulness is grounded in the principle of interdependence and what Vietnamese Nobel Prize winner Thich Nhat Hanh beautifully termed "interbeing" (Hanh, 1993). This perspective highlights the profound connections between personal, societal, and environmental well-being and encourages individuals to move beyond individualistic mindsets and cultivate awareness of their role within larger ecosystems. By fostering a sense of interconnectedness, mindfulness in this context becomes a tool for understanding the mutual influence between human actions and the broader environment.

Another central principle is compassionate action, which extends traditional mindfulness practices of acceptance and compassion into tangible efforts to address social and environmental injustices. This involves engaging in ethical practices and mindful activism that challenge systemic inequities and promote sustainable living. Compassionate action (e.g., Gilbert et al., 2017) emphasises the importance of translating inner mindfulness into outward, socially responsible behaviours.

Mindfulness is also reframed as a means of fostering sustainability and stewardship in the fourth wave. Practices are designed to cultivate ecological awareness and promote harmony with nature. These include behaviours that minimise environmental harm, such as mindful consumption and sustainable lifestyle choices. This positions mindfulness as an integral part of creating an environmentally conscious and sustainable society. Furthermore, the fourth wave prioritises community-centred practices, moving beyond the self-focused nature of traditional mindfulness programmes. These approaches emphasise collective engagement, such as shared rituals, collaborative dialogue, and cooperative problem-solving. By fostering relational mindfulness, the fourth wave seeks to build stronger communities that are united in addressing common challenges.

The principles of social and environmental mindfulness are increasingly reflected in a variety of emerging practices and frameworks. For instance, nature meditation and mindful consumption aim to strengthen individuals' connections with the natural world, cultivating a sense of stewardship and responsibility towards the environment (Barrett et al., 2016). Similarly, mindful activism integrates mindfulness into activist efforts, helping to sustain resilience and compassion in the face of systemic challenges. Practices such as mindful protest and reflective spaces for activists allow individuals to maintain emotional balance, reduce reactivity, and engage constructively in high-stress situations. Community-based interventions further align with this approach, highlighting the importance of collective engagement in addressing social and environmental issues.

Despite its promise, the concept of the fourth wave is not without its critics. One concern is the potential for "greenwashing," where ecological mindfulness is superficially adopted without addressing the underlying systemic inequities or root causes of environmental degradation. This raises questions about the authenticity and depth of such practices. Another challenge lies in the risk of overburdening mindfulness with excessive objectives. Sceptics caution against stretching mindfulness to address too many domains without sufficient empirical grounding. Mindfulness is not a panacea and in isolation is not sufficient, but it does enable us to engage in the world in more skilful ways. Practices aimed at cultivating wholesome mind qualities need to be combined with work at organisational and institutional levels to create systemic change.

As the fourth wave of mindfulness gains momentum, further research is needed to evaluate its scalability and impact. Integrating mindfulness into policymaking could institutionalise its principles and expand its reach. Additionally, interdisciplinary collaboration among psychologists, ecologists, and social scientists will be critical in refining the framework and exploring its applications.

The fourth wave represents a significant evolution in contemplative practices, addressing the interconnected challenges of a globalised world. By linking personal transformation with collective responsibility, it offers a holistic vision of health and flourishing that extends to societies and ecosystems. This approach under-scores the importance of fostering resilience, compassion, and sus-tainability in addressing the social and environmental crises of the twenty-first century.

CHAPTER SUMMARY

In this chapter we outlined some serious challenges facing all life on earth. We also suggested that, however emotionally demand-ing it may be, there are advantages to resourcing ourselves through mindful practices so that we can start to recognise and respond to these challenges. Acknowledging the personal resonance of these issues for us can inform decisions in relation to making more skil-ful, pro-social choices such as seeking connection or taking action.

12

BEYOND SUFFERING AND FLOURISHING

How mindfulness meets the human condition

In earlier chapters in this section, we looked at some of the applications (and limitations) of mindfulness in the mainstream (Chapter 10) and broadened this to how mindfulness might support us in meeting the multiple challenges facing us at this inflection point in human history (Chapter 11). In this final chapter, we expand the application of mindfulness beyond suffering and flourishing. Instead, we take a broader view to consider how mindfulness might be relevant to some basic existential questions such as death, identity, and meaning. These themes are universal to being human, though often exist only on the periphery of awareness until some life event brings them to the fore. These themes also underlie many of the crises we face, both individually and collectively. For example, the existential threat of death underpins not only our individual lives but also the life of the planet in the form of climate change. In this chapter we advocate, much as the poet Rilke (1903/2012) did, to "live the questions now," In doing so mindfully, it is hoped that our lives, connection to one another and to the planet itself might be deepened by them.

Renowned psychotherapist and author Irvin Yalom (1980) distilled an essential set of four "existential givens" that seem to be a core part of our experience as human beings. These are death, freedom, isolation, and meaninglessness. Yalom (1980) sees these as universal themes that underlie many of the problems that bring people to psychotherapy. Within the Buddhist tradition, existence

DOI: 10.4324/9781003453598-16

is characterised by three "marks" that seem to pervade human experience – dukkha (commonly referred to as a sense of unsatisfactoriness or suffering); anicca or impermanence (nothing lasts, everything changes); and no (fixed or unchanging) self (anattā). The teaching of the Four Noble Truths along with these three "marks" of existence represent the Buddha's analysis of why human beings suffer (experience stress) to the extent we do and what we can do about it. These broader perspectives on the universal drivers of suffering underlie much of human experience and remain consistent over time.

A penetrative insight and core tenet of Buddhist wisdom is the recognition of impermanence. Nothing lasts, nothing stays the same, everything is constantly changing. By identifying impermanence as central to (human) existence, it simultaneously reveals one of the major drivers of human suffering – the tendency to relate to people and things as permanent, fixed and unchanging. Although we are surrounded by reminders of this (indeed the body itself is perhaps one of our most reliable reminders of change), it doesn't appear to diminish our desire for things to improve or, at the very least, continue and stay the same. Mindfulness can be especially helpful in remembering impermanence. In fact, one phrase that encapsulates the entire teaching on mindfulness has been summarised as *"Keep calmly knowing change"* (Anālayo, 2003, p. 267). This recognises both the inherent inevitability of change and the power that our reactions (i.e. when not "calmly") can have in compounding suffering. This advice, which on the surface may seem unduly pessimistic or defeatist, turns out to be compassionate and protective in the face of unnecessary or secondary suffering (earlier we looked at the Sallatha Sutta or "The Two Arrows" in Chapter 3).

THE ROLE OF CULTURE AND MEANING

The first existential conundrum we discuss here is that of meaninglessness. The existential position is that nothing has any inherent meaning. Rather, we are free to decide what any life circumstance, or indeed life itself, might mean. On the other hand, we appear to be meaning-making creatures and are "hardwired" to find patterns of meaning in the world (McGilchrist,

2019; Jung, 1968/2023). Whether we are facing a cancer diagnosis, a sudden death, or the timing of random events, we appear to default to want meaning. Even at a basic perceptual level, we infer shapes where we see dots on a page or clouds in the sky. The consequences of Nietzsche's (1883) famous dictum "God is dead" (uttered in recognition of humankind's increasing technological sophistication and anthropocentric worldview) is that we are thrown back upon *ourselves* to make sense of the world. As Nietzsche and others have outlined, it is "as if" we would be gods ourselves, a role too burdensome for us to carry individually.

One of the consequences of a growing secular orientation to the world is that traditional (not necessarily religious) ways of understanding need to be "re-made" by the individual her/himself each time an existential milestone is reached. Becker (1973) argued that a primary function of culture is to provide meaning in the context of awareness of death. To the extent to which we play a valued role in society, to that extent do we achieve a sense of self-esteem. For Becker and the authors of Terror Management Theory (Greenberg et al., 1986), self-esteem not only helps us to feel good about ourselves but also serves as a buffer against our anxiety about death.

Whatever the causes for the growth in a more secular and anthropocentric orientation to life in the modern West, fundamental questions regarding meaning remain. For all our technological sophistication, the reality of the various crises we are now facing bring the future survival of the planet and humanity into sharp focus. Perhaps the correct response is to find ourselves in a crisis of meaning. Authors such as Stephen Jenkinson, Daniel Schmachtenberger, Joanna Macy, and others encourage a thorough understanding of how things are before reaching for solutions. As Thomas Hardy (1902) wrote, "If a way to the better there be, it exacts a full look at the worst" (p. 447). To this end, we believe that mindfulness practice is vital to acknowledging the times we are living in.

FREEDOM AND RESPONSIBILITY

Linked to the question of meaning is the question of freedom. Depending on where we live in the world, we may be free to choose how to live and act and what values or principles to live by. However, even these are likely to be highly influenced by our upbringing, socio-cultural norms, and the context in which we live. There is an ethical foundation to mindfulness practice that makes profound practical sense, regardless of one's meaning or belief system. This ethical foundation rests on understanding that a mind that is dominated by thoughts or emotions that promote anger, aggression, jealousy, or hatred will inevitably be more unsettled. There is an intrinsic ethic that arises as a result of recognising the truth of this insight – do we want to live in a more-or-less constant state of agitation, irritation, and anxiety, or one characterised more by peace, ease, and calm? Our answer to this question can act as a guide as to how to live. For example, we can feel the physiological effects of living in a constant state of anger or jealousy. This might show up as muscular tension in the body, high blood pressure, or restlessness. It might show up in the mind as obsessive thinking, hypervigilance, and comparison. A mindful perspective might allow us to recognise the caustic mind–body effects of this way of living and instead cultivate qualities of acceptance and non-judgement. In doing so, we are likely to interrupt cycles of thinking and feeling that fuel stress reactivity.

Closely connected to the theme of freedom is that of responsibility. We are ultimately responsible for ourselves and for our actions in the world. How we are – how we think, feel and behave – has real consequences for ourselves, for others, and our world. We could feel burdened by this, or we could see the potential this offers us. We can choose to act in a way that aligns with our ethics and values. As mindfulness teacher and author Vidyamala Burch (n.d.) has insightfully identified, "the behavioural outcome of mindfulness is choice." The more we can see and be aware of, the more choice we have in how to act. When stressed or simply unaware, it can often feel as though we have no choice – we act habitually or on "autopilot." However, mindfulness reminds us we have a choice through offering a wider perspective. Instead of being confined to the same way of seeing or doing things, we might discover alternatives that had never occurred to us. Participants in MBSR discover this in a real way through the puzzle of the "9 dots." This puzzle requires us to join three rows of three evenly spaced dots with four straight lines – without removing pen from paper! MBSR participants discover that what initially seems unsolvable or impossible can be seen in a new light. The implications for MBSR programme participants are to bring qualities of not knowing, openness, and curiosity to the "stuck places" in their lives and see what happens. The willingness to see things in a new way requires us assuming a certain amount of responsibility for how we view them in the first instance.

LIVING THE EXISTENTIAL PARADOX OF DEATH AND DYING

Although we know intellectually that we will die and that death is certain, we do not know when we will die. For this reason, we tend to avoid or postpone thinking about death or assume that we will somehow magically go on living. We have a tremendous capacity to know we are mortal beings and yet not be paralysed by this. However, we cannot deny death forever – particularly when it visits us or those we love more directly. For precisely this reason, the First Foundation of Mindfulness (i.e. the body) traditionally includes instructions on contemplating the body in distinct stages of decay after death. Although this may seem morose or even traumatising, the wisdom inherent in this advice is like much of mindfulness practice – paradoxical. Like the traditional ecclesiastic greeting of "*memento mori*," to "remember dying," to that extent might we remember to live and not "miss" life. Considering the body in this way also allows us to begin to disentangle our identification with the body as "me" or "mine." If we are totally identified with the body and what it can or cannot do as who we are, we are likely to suffer more when the body begins to fail through illness or frailty. However, if we can relate to the body and physical sensations as just one aspect of experience (and not the totality of who we most fundamentally are), we are likely to suffer less. Language can also help us here. Speaking about "the body" instead of "my body" can be helpful here.

Remembering dying can paradoxically serve to inform and invigorate our connection to the present moment as something transient and precious. Mindfulness practice can also offer us a compassionate way to navigate dying that recognises the inherent limitations and mystery of life (i.e. that all living things must die). As in all aspects of life, we need only ever take things moment by moment, one step at a time. So too in death, we need only take dying one step at a time. This is not meant to imply that any of this is easy, but we do not need to go beyond what is happening in any given moment. The practice of mindfulness can offer a way to experience calm, manage difficult symptoms (such as pain), and deepen relationships at end-of-life (Shannon, 2021). When it comes to navigating dying, mindfulness can offer us a kindly way to support ourselves and see and respond to what is happening as a part of life.

Of course, the prospect of dying might be even more difficult to accept if, at the end of our lives, we realise we have not truly lived. In a wide-ranging interview with Oprah Winfrey (2017), Jon Kabat-Zinn (widely recognised as having introduced mindfulness into healthcare in the West) was asked whether he believed in life after death. He skilfully replied that he was more interested in life *before* death – specifically, on not missing out on living the life we have *before* we die. As mindfulness encourages us to "wake up" and cultivate qualities of mind and heart in relation to the present moment, it could be argued that mindfulness is synonymous with a life well-lived. This is a practice and attitudinal stance we can cultivate up to and including our final breath.

SELF-IDENTITY AND THE STORY OF "ME"

Another existential question revealed through the practice of mindfulness is that of identity – who we think we are. In the first part of our lives especially, we strive for independence and to establish ourselves in the world. Indeed, we develop our sense of self by finding our way in the world. As we enter mid-life, we may be especially identified with what we have achieved, our relationships, and our possessions. However, most of the world's wisdom traditions would agree that being solely identified with our various roles, acquisitions, or accomplishments is a seriously limited view of the self.

Through engagement with mindfulness practice, we begin to see how the self-narrative, the "story of me," is constructed and re-told from moment to moment. As we have seen, neuroscience has identified brain regions involved in the construction of self, which have become known as the default mode network or "narrative self" (e.g., Farb et al., 2007; Vago & Silbersweig, 2012). As mindfulness reveals to us, this inner dialogue is what we take to be "me." However, that which can be "seen" and "known" is not awareness itself. These are simply contents of awareness. Awareness is bigger. The essence of the Buddha's teaching has been summarised (Kabat-Zinn, 2005) by the phrase, "*Nothing is to be clung to as, I, me, or mine*" (p. 53). Similarly, the Stoic philosopher Epictetus' phrase "it is not things in themselves but our view of things that troubles us" (c. 55–c.135 AD) suggests that it is our tendency as human beings to identify with experience that often leads to greater suffering. The tendency to give more weight to certain thoughts/feelings over others (particularly those associated with self-identity and our sense of self, i.e., who we believe ourselves to be) is primarily a habit or default tendency. We ordinarily identify and take this to be who we are.

Integral philosopher Ken Wilber (1998) recommends deliberately practicing disidentifying with the contents of consciousness to reveal what might be considered our deepest or innermost self. This practice, adapted from Indian philosopher Sri Aurobindo, involves acknowledging that those parts of us which can be named and known are not self. This rests on the understanding that whatever can be known is not the Knower. Mindfulness practices, such as open awareness, allow us to let go of identifying with the contents of experience and instead rest in awareness itself. This can have the effect of freeing up the habitual tendency of the mind to grasp onto or identify with experience (as "me" or "not me" or "I like this/I don't like this") which underpins the narrative "false" self.

The practice of disidentification; *Ken Wilber's "The Witness" exercise* (1998, pp. 36–37).

Slowly begin to silently recite the following to yourself, trying to realise as vividly as possible the import of each statement (repeat several times):

- "I have a body, but I am not my body. I can see and feel my body, and what can be seen and felt is not the true Seer. My body may be tired or excited, sick or healthy, heavy or light, but that has nothing to do with my inward I. I have a body, but I am not my body."

- "I have desires, but I am not my desires. I can know my desires, and what can be known is not the true Knower. Desires come and go, floating through my awareness, but they do not affect my inward I. I have desires, but I am not desires."
- "I have emotions, but I am not my emotions. I can feel and sense my emotions, and what can be felt and sensed is not the true Feeler. Emotions pass through me, but they do not affect my inward I. I have emotions, but I am not emotions."
- "I have thoughts, but I am not my thoughts. I can know and intuit my thoughts, and what can be known is not the true Knower. Thoughts come to me and thoughts leave me, but they do not affect my inward I. I have thoughts, but I am not my thoughts."

Affirm as concretely as possible:

- "I am what remains, a pure centre of awareness, an unmoved witness of all these thoughts, emotions, feelings, and desires."

There appears to be a strong parallel between practices that reveal this kind of disidentification with experience and the dying process. Much of what we take to be our sense of self relies on the degree to which we can fulfil certain roles, responsibilities, and functions. We then take this to be "me." What the dying process reveals, however, is that we are more than what we can do or what functions we can perform. This stance is central to the modern hospice movement (Saunders, 1990). This realisation can be easily missed when the focus of healthcare is frequently oriented on a return to function (the implied equation being: your value = what you can do.) Indeed, as mentioned earlier, we derive our sense of self-esteem primarily from what we can do and not in relation to who we most fundamentally, intrinsically are. It appears that a strange reversal takes place as we age, as an infant's value has never relied on what it can do!

THE ROLE OF MINDFULNESS IN NAVIGATING DEATH, DYING, AND IDENTITY

Having looked separately at death, freedom, meaning, and identity, it seems timely to draw out some of the parallels between the more subtle aspects of mindfulness practice and the dying process. As the saying goes, "You have to be somebody before you can be nobody" (Engler, 2003). We need to develop and invest in our sense of self to go beyond the self. We have outlined in Chapter 3 how mindfulness practice itself can lead to a change in self-perspective (Hölzel et al., 2011b), up to and including self-transcendence (Vago & Silbersweig, 2012).

The inscription over the portal to the Greek monastery on Mount Athos encapsulates the potential of what Vago and Silbersweig (2012) term self-transcendence: *"If you die before you die, then when you die you won't die."* What could this riddle possibly mean? And what does it have to do with mindfulness? It is fascinating to think that one possible outcome of mindfulness practice is such a total disidentification with self that it could be interpreted as a moment-by-moment dying (and letting go of self-identification) to the fullness and potential of what American writer Henry David Thoreau (1817–1862) termed, *"the bloom of the present moment"* (Thoreau, 1854). From this perspective, one could see the practice of mindfulness as a gradual lessening of the bonds of identification with self. The ability to "die" at will (to the story of "me," the narrative self) to "I, me and mine" might ultimately prove to be the most profound and compassionate flowering of the practice.

This "dying before we die" might reveal a way of living that allows the fullness of what it means to be human to take our place, with right humility, in the world. Buddhist meditation teacher Rob Burbea (2014) has clearly outlined how different meditation practices, mostly based on mindfulness, can lead to decreased identification with self. Although there are some cautions in relation to these practices (Treleaven, 2018; Britton, 2019), when taken slowly and carefully, with supervision and guidance from someone familiar with them, they can be remarkably freeing.

The existential theme of isolation recognises the fact that we are ultimately alone in the world. We each inhabit a separate mind and body and for this reason, can never truly know the experience of another. No matter how capable we are of sharing and articulating our world with others, it is ultimately unknowable directly. There may be times in life when we experience this gap between ourselves and others more acutely. This can give rise to a sense of aloneness and self-isolation that we may seek to cover over, avoid, or deny. Feelings of isolation have been recognised as a key driver of suffering in illness (Cassell, 2001). Mindfulness offers us the possibility to meet the existential position of aloneness with warmth, compassion, and curiosity. This in turn can act as the basis from which to connect to others. To the extent to which isolation may be compounded by thoughts and feelings of separateness (the second "arrow"), mindfulness can help to simplify things by recognising unhelpful patterns and finding a more neutral focus of attention. We can also use feelings of isolation as a cue to meeting such moments with greater compassion. Mindfulness can help reduce feelings of isolation by actively cultivating a sense of common humanity and connection with others.

WHAT IT COULD MEAN TO BE HUMAN

Having considered a number of existential concerns, we now come full circle to the topic of human awareness itself. To be here and to know it is both terrifying and amazing. This is the existential plight of human beings – we are subject to both awe and dread (Kierkegaard, 1843; Solomon et al., 2015). Mindfulness can support us to appreciate moments of awe and to recognise and compassionately respond to moments of dread. It is perhaps our response to the limitations of what it means to be human that most defines who we are. Author Stephen Jenkinson (2015) concluded from his work in palliative care that it is especially when faced with endings that the fullness of our humanity can be expressed. In other words, rather than shrinking back, we have an opportunity to allow the deepest, wisest, and most compassionate parts of ourselves to show themselves.

The fact that we are often deepened by life experience – often unwanted or unsought – is a reminder that perhaps all the major turning points in life are given to us. Life itself, not us, is really in control. We advocate the practice of mindfulness as a compassionate way to meet the joys, challenges, limitations, and endings in life. By doing so with curiosity and kindness, we might recognise the calls of Mary Oliver's (2004) "Wild Geese," *"over and over announcing your place in the family of things."*

ENVISIONING A MINDFUL FUTURE: MINDFULNESS, SPIRITUALITY, AND NATURE CONNECTION

As the future unfolds, present moment by present moment, the need to bring mindful awareness to the crises of our times (see Chapter 11) becomes ever greater. What would the consequence(s) be of bringing qualities of open-heartedness, patience, and curiosity to the challenges of our time? These attitudes, infused with an understanding of impermanence and limits, might allow us to engage with ourselves, each other, and the planet in ways that reflect the best of what humanity has to offer. Mindfulness may lead to wise, compassionate action when called for and being with/allowing when further action is unclear or unskilful.

Iain McGilchrist (2023) has outlined how a world designed and dominated by left-hemisphere values, such as power and pleasure, utility and acquisition, lead to consequences such as feeling divorced from each other (loneliness), from the natural world, and from a relationship with the spiritual/sacred. These are all needed for greater meaning. Practices such as mindfulness and nature connection can help to shift the balance back to values more consistent with right-hemisphere ways of being and knowing. Here we can be nourished by practices that promote meaning making and live in a way that is aligned with our highest values.

The indigenous tribe of the Haudenosaunee in North America speak of our duty to our seventh-generation descendants. The realities of climate change make the legacy effects of how we live today discernible in their future. We too are living in the wake of what has happened and is happening now. Some consequences are clear, others not yet so clear. What is clear is that we have a duty of care to those who come after us. Groups such as The Mindfulness Initiative in the U.K., as well as the United Nations are helping to facilitate conversations where the effectiveness of mindfulness on the ground can inform policy and decision-making. This may also require a recognition of moving beyond conceptions of flourishing that rely on growth for its own sake. As climate change shows us, how we relate to the world matters. Our actions have an impact on everything around us – from what we consume to what we dispose of or waste. Bringing mindful awareness to our thoughts and actions in the world, especially how we view our relationship with the planet, will define life for future generations.

> What is one action you can take/have taken to support the planet? It may be something as simple as walking more when you can.

Ultimately, mindfulness practice reveals the beauty, fragility, and preciousness of life. As Canadian musician and one-time Zen practitioner Leonard Cohen (2001) so beautifully expressed, "we are so lightly here. It is in love that we are made, in love we disappear."

CHAPTER SUMMARY

- Mindfulness offers us a way to recognise the limits of what it means to be human.
- Most fundamentally, we are social beings who thrive on love and affection.
- The limits of the human condition also mean that we are finite, vulnerable, and prone to stress and suffering. Mindfulness offers us an evidence-based way to meet these limits.
- Rather than a shrinking away from the realities of life, mindfulness can support us in turning towards "the full catastrophe" of being human – with all this entails.
- Mindfulness or "heartfulness" offers us a way to recognise our responsibilities of caring to ourselves, one another, and the planet. May it be so.

CONCLUSION

As we arrive at the conclusion of *Mindfulness: The Basics*, it is worth reflecting on the journey this book has taken. From its foundational principles to its nuanced practices and broader societal implications, mindfulness has been revealed not just as a personal skill but also as a multifaceted phenomenon with the potential to address both individual and collective challenges. This concluding chapter synthesises the key insights from the preceding sections, offering final reflections on the enduring relevance of mindfulness in our complex and rapidly changing world.

REVISITING THE FOUNDATIONS OF MINDFULNESS

Section I laid the groundwork by addressing fundamental questions: "What is mindfulness?" "Where does it come from?" "How does it work?" and "Why practice it?" These chapters established mindfulness as a state of present-moment awareness, informed by both ancient wisdom traditions and contemporary science. Chapter 1 clarified that mindfulness is not merely a trend or a relaxation technique but an active, intentional practice that enhances awareness, reduces reactivity, and fosters greater emotional and psychological balance.

Chapter 2 explored mindfulness's roots in Buddhist teachings, revealing its rich history as a contemplative discipline. This historical context underscores that mindfulness is not a static concept but one that has evolved over centuries, adapting to diverse cultural and philosophical settings. Chapter 3 examined how mindfulness works, drawing on neuroscientific and psychological research to elucidate its mechanisms, from enhancing attention regulation to reducing the effects of stress on the brain and body. Chapter 4 then answered the critical question of *why* mindfulness is worth practising, highlighting its profound benefits for mental health, resilience, and interpersonal relationships.

These foundational chapters demonstrated that mindfulness is more than a cognitive process; it is a holistic way of being. By anchoring the practice in both its historical roots and modern applications, this section provided a lens through which to view mindfulness as both timeless and adaptable.

ENGAGING WITH MINDFULNESS PRACTICES

Building on this theoretical foundation, Section II shifted the focus to practical applications. Chapters 5–9 offered detailed guidance on integrating mindfulness into daily life. Chapter 5 emphasised the importance of clarifying intention and managing expectations when beginning or sustaining a mindfulness practice. It reminded readers that mindfulness is not about achieving a particular outcome but about cultivating a present-moment focus with curiosity and compassion.

Chapters 6–9 presented specific techniques, including the body scan, mindful movement, sitting practice, and short practices. These chapters acknowledged the diversity of mindfulness practices, making it accessible to individuals with different preferences, needs, and schedules. For instance, the body scan invites practitioners to develop a deeper connection with bodily sensations, fostering relaxation and awareness. Mindful movement integrates mindfulness with physical activity, while sitting practice focuses on cultivating stability and presence through connecting our awareness to a specific "anchor" such as the breath or soles of the feet. The chapter on short practices offered practical strategies for incorporating mindfulness into even the busiest of lives, reinforcing the idea that mindfulness is a state of mind and so is not to be confined to formal meditation sessions.

This section underscored the importance of practice in making mindfulness a lived experience. The techniques discussed not only provide tools for managing stress and enhancing well-being but also serve as entry points for deeper self-awareness and transformation. By offering step-by-step instructions and addressing common challenges, these chapters empowered readers to engage with mindfulness in ways that resonate with their unique circumstances.

MINDFULNESS IN BROADER CONTEXTS

In Section III, the focus expanded to consider the role of mindfulness in the wider world. Chapter 10 examined the mainstreaming of mindfulness, reflecting on its integration into fields such as healthcare, education, and corporate settings. While this chapter celebrated the widespread adoption of mindfulness as a valuable tool for enhancing well-being and productivity, it also critiqued the potential for commercialisation and superficial engagement. It posed important questions about how to maintain the integrity of mindfulness in its many applications, urging practitioners and advocates to honour its deeper purposes.

Chapter 11 explored the concept of the "meta-crisis," situating mindfulness within the context of global challenges such as climate change, social inequality, and technological disruption. This chapter argued that mindfulness is not only a tool for personal resilience but also a resource for collective transformation. By fostering clarity, compassion, and interconnectedness, mindfulness can contribute to the systemic changes needed to address these urgent crises.

The final chapter returned to the essence of mindfulness as a practice of embracing the full spectrum of human experience. It reflected on mindfulness as a way of cultivating authenticity, deepening relationships, and navigating the uncertainties of life with greater wisdom and equanimity. This chapter reminded readers that mindfulness is ultimately about living fully and meaningfully in the present moment, whatever circumstances may arise.

FINAL REFLECTIONS

The journey through this book has revealed that mindfulness is both profoundly simple and richly complex. At its core, it is about paying attention to the present moment with openness and acceptance. Yet, as the chapters have demonstrated, this simple act has far-reaching implications for individual well-being, social cohesion, and global sustainability.

One of the key insights from this exploration is that mindfulness is not a one-size-fits-all solution. Its practices can be tailored to meet diverse needs, from managing stress and enhancing focus to fostering compassion and addressing systemic issues. Whether practiced formally through meditation or informally in daily activities, mindfulness offers a pathway to greater awareness and balance in an increasingly fragmented world.

Another critical takeaway is the importance of intention. Mindfulness is not about achieving perfection or escaping challenges but about cultivating a deeper connection with oneself, others, and the world. This intentionality transforms mindfulness from a set of techniques into a way of being, grounded in values such as curiosity, compassion, and non-judgement.

As mindfulness continues to evolve and gain traction in various contexts, it is vital to approach it with a sense of respect and responsibility. This includes acknowledging its roots in contemplative traditions, engaging critically with its applications, and ensuring that its adoption serves meaningful purposes rather than superficial goals.

AN INVITATION TO PRACTICE

This conclusion is not an endpoint but an invitation to continue exploring mindfulness in your own life. Whether you are new to mindfulness or an experienced practitioner, the insights and practices in this book are meant to be lived and revisited. Mindfulness is a journey, not a destination – a continual process of returning to the present moment and rediscovering its richness.

As you move forward, consider how the principles of mindfulness can inform not only your personal well-being but also your interactions with others and your engagement with the world. In times of uncertainty and change, mindfulness offers a way to navigate life's challenges with greater clarity, compassion, and courage.

Ultimately, the practice of mindfulness is a celebration of what it means to be human: to experience joy and sorrow, certainty and doubt, connection and solitude, all within the unfolding of the present moment. This book has sought to illuminate this path, and the rest of the journey is yours to walk. May it be one of awareness, kindness, and growth.

GLOSSARY OF TERMS

A

Acceptance and commitment therapy (ACT) A therapeutic approach combining mindfulness with value-driven actions and acceptance of thoughts and emotions.

Aikido A modern Japanese martial art focusing on harmony and self-defence through joint locks, throws, and the redirection of an opponent's energy.

Alexander technique A method of improving posture, movement, and overall well-being by increasing awareness of physical habits.

Anapanasati A traditional Buddhist practice involving mindful awareness of the breath, often used as an anchor for present-moment focus.

Anchor A point of focus, such as the breath, used to return attention during mindfulness.

Attitudinal qualities of mindfulness Supportive attitudes such as patience, curiosity, and self-compassion, essential for sustaining mindfulness practice.

B

Being mode a state of mind where one is fully present in the current moment, accepting and observing experiences as they are without trying to change or judge them. It emphasises existing and experiencing rather than achieving or solving.

Body scan practice A mindfulness practice involving a detailed focus on different parts of the body to develop awareness and relaxation.

Buddha Literally "the awakened one," an Indian teacher who lived in the sixth century BCE and founded Buddhism.

C

Clear comprehension (Pali: Sampajañña) The awareness of one's actions, their purpose, and their impact on oneself and others, often linked to mindfulness practice.

Contemporary mindfulness The adaptation of traditional mindfulness concepts into modern psychological and therapeutic frameworks.

Chi Kung (Qi Gong) An ancient Chinese practice combining movement, breathing techniques, and meditation to cultivate energy (qi) and improve health.

Cognitive behavioural therapy (CBT) A form of psychotherapy that challenges and seeks to change cognitive distortions.

Cognitive flexibility The ability to adapt thought processes and behaviours to new or changing environments, supported by mindfulness practices.

Collective resilience Building community strength and adaptability through mindfulness.

Compassion and loving-kindness (Metta) Mindfulness practices aimed at fostering unconditional kindness and compassion for oneself and others.

D

Decentring The ability to observe one's personal experience from an objective, decentred standpoint.

Default mode network (DMN) Brain regions that remain active during rest and associated with daydreaming and mind wandering; responsible for the narrative self and reduced through mindfulness.

Dhyāna A Hindu practice of meditative consciousness aimed at stilling the mind.

Dialectical behaviour therapy (DBT) A therapy for conditions such as borderline personality disorder, incorporating mindfulness to enhance emotion regulation and interpersonal effectiveness.

Doing mode A state of mind characterised by goal-directed thinking and action. It focuses on solving problems, achieving outcomes, or addressing perceived discrepancies between how things are and how they should be.

Dorsolateral prefrontal cortex (DLPFC) The term given to a functional set of brain regions associated with so called "higher" or executive brain functions such as coordination, working memory, and inhibition.

E

Eco-anxiety Stress related to environmental issues, addressed through mindfulness.

Eightfold Path A central teaching in Buddhism, with "Right Mindfulness" as a core component, emphasising ethical and mental development.

Embodiment The experience and awareness of being present in one's physical body, often involving a connection between physical sensations and mental processes.

Emotional regulation Managing emotions and emotional reactivity (e.g. thoughts, behaviours) effectively through mindfulness.

Endorphins Hormones that act as natural pain relievers and enhance mood; they act in a similar manner to morphine but are naturally produced.

Equanimity (Pali: Upekkha) A state of mental balance where one remains composed and non-reactive in response to pleasant or unpleasant experiences.

Ethical mindfulness Mindfulness applied in alignment with ethical principles, often inspired by traditional Buddhist teachings or secular ethics.

Eudaimonia A state of human flourishing and well-being.

Everyday mindfulness Applying mindfulness in routine activities like eating or commuting.

Existential mindfulness Exploring deeper questions of human existence through mindfulness.

Expectation management Realistic understanding of what mindfulness can and cannot achieve.

Exposure The deliberate act of facing of feared thoughts/emotions/behaviour/environment in a gradual or controlled manner from a position of safety/security.

Extinction The weakening and gradual erasing of certain types of learned behaviour.

F

Feldenkrais A method of somatic education aimed at increasing self-awareness and improving physical function through gentle movement and mindfulness.

Four Foundations of Mindfulness The Buddha's systematic approach to establishing mindfulness/developing awareness through focusing on bodily sensations, feelings, the mind, and mental objects.

G

Guided meditations Pre-recorded or live audio instructions leading participants through mindfulness exercises, often used by beginners.

H

Haram Forbidden by Islamic Law.

Heartfulness Integrating qualities of kindness, compassion, and care into mindfulness.

Hypothalamic-pituitary-adrenal (HPA) axis A well-recognised pattern of physiological response to stress, involving activation of brain regions of the hypothalamus and pituitary gland, as well as the adrenal glands.

I

Impermanence (Pali: Anicca) A fundamental Buddhist concept emphasising that all phenomena, including thoughts and emotions, are transient and constantly changing.

Intention The purpose or motivation behind mindfulness practice.

Intention, attention, attitude (IAA) Three core axioms of mindfulness practices.

Interoception The sense of internal bodily signals, such as heartbeat, breathing, or hunger, providing awareness of the body's internal state.

K

Karate A Japanese martial art emphasising striking techniques, blocks, and discipline.

L

Li Po (Li Bai) (701–762) A Chinese poet acclaimed as one of the greatest and most important poets of the Tang dynasty.

Loving-kindness (Pali: Metta) A meditative practice and mindset that fosters compassion and goodwill toward oneself and others.

M

Mainstreaming Integration of mindfulness into healthcare, education, and workplaces.

Mental balance A state of equilibrium achieved through mindfulness, encompassing conative, cognitive, attentional, and affective balance.

Meta-cognitive awareness The ability to observe and understand one's thought processes, enhanced by mindfulness.

Meta-crisis Interconnected global challenges such as climate change and inequality.

Micro-practices Brief mindfulness exercises integrated into daily routines.

Mindful action (Pali: Samma Sati) The practice of applying mindfulness in daily life, particularly in ethical behaviour and speech, as part of the Buddhist Noble Eightfold Path.

Mindful Attention Awareness Scale (MAAS) A widely used tool to assess mindfulness levels, focusing on the frequency of present-moment attention and awareness.

Mindful pausing Stopping briefly to connect with the present moment.

Mindfulness Present-moment awareness characterised by kindness, curiosity, openness, and acceptance.

Mindfulness-Based Cognitive Therapy (MBCT) An evidence-based programme integrating mindfulness meditation with cognitive therapy techniques to prevent depressive relapse and address negative thought patterns.

Mindfulness-Based Interventions (MBIs) Therapeutic applications of mindfulness, including Mindfulness-Based Stress Reduction (MBSR) and Mindfulness-Based Cognitive Therapy (MBCT).

Mindfulness-based programs (MBPs) Structured interventions combining mindfulness with psychological insights.

Mindfulness-Based Relapse Prevention (MBRP) A mindfulness program designed to address addiction, helping individuals recognise triggers and prevent relapse through awareness and coping strategies.

Mindfulness-Based Stress Reduction (MBSR) A secular 8-week mindfulness programme developed by Jon Kabat-Zinn, combining mindfulness meditation, yoga, and group education to address stress, pain, and illness.

Mindfulness practices Formal techniques such as the body scan, sitting meditation, mindful movement, and mindful eating, alongside informal practices like mindfulness of daily activities.

Mindful loving-kindness (Metta) A practice of cultivating kindness, compassion, and goodwill towards oneself and others as an extension of mindfulness.

Mindful movement A practice of moving with attention and awareness, integrating mindfulness techniques to promote mental and physical health.

Mindful walking Walking with intentional focus on the sensations, rhythm, and experience of movement to cultivate mindfulness.

Muraqabah Islamic practice involving continuous awareness of Allah's presence.

N

Neuroplasticity The brain's ability to form new neural connections, enhanced by mindfulness.

NICE The National Institute for Health and Care Excellence (NICE) is an executive non-departmental public body of the UK Department of Health and Social Care. It is responsible for judging the cost-effectiveness of medicines and treatments, with its judgements informing decisions in Wales and Northern Ireland.

Noble Eightfold Path An early summary of Buddhist practice, consisting of right view, right resolve, right speech, right conduct, right livelihood, right effort, right mindfulness, and right samadhi ("meditative absorption or union").

Non-attachment Observing thoughts without identifying or clinging to them.

Non-judgemental awareness A key mindfulness component involving observation of one's thoughts, emotions, and sensations without attachment, aversion, or judgement.

Non-reactivity The ability to observe thoughts and emotions without immediate reaction, fostering emotional resilience and cognitive flexibility.

O

Operational definitions of mindfulness Specific definitions used in research to measure mindfulness, often tailored to the aspect being studied, such as attention, awareness, or acceptance.

P

Post-traumatic stress disorder (PTSD) A mental health condition triggered by experiencing or witnessing a traumatic event, characterised by symptoms such as flashbacks, hyperarousal, and emotional distress.

Posterior cingulate cortex (PCC) A highly connected midline brain region associated with memory, emotion and awareness; forms part of the brain's default mode network (DMN).

Present moment awareness The practice of maintaining attention on one's current experience rather than dwelling on the past or anticipating the future.

Prosociality Evolutionary perspective on ways in which human beings engage in behaviour that benefits others.

Q

Qualitative research methods The application of scientific research methods to the collection of non-numerical data; often in the fields of the human and social sciences.

R

Raja yoga Raja yoga is one of the four classical schools of yoga alongside Jnana (knowledge or self-study), Bhakti (devotion) and Karma (action), each offering a path to moksha (spiritual liberation) and self-realisation.

Reappraisal The reinterpretation of meaning in relation to emotionally charged stimuli.

Reconsolidation The access and integration of new learning into an existing framework.

Relational frame theory (RFT) A psychological framework underlying acceptance and commitment therapy (ACT), explaining the context and relationships between thoughts, emotions, and behaviours.

Reperceiving A shift in perspective that allows detachment from experiences, fostering clarity.

Resilience The capacity to recover from challenges, enhanced by mindfulness.

Right mindfulness (Pali: Samma Sati) A core element of the Buddhist Eightfold Path, emphasising mindful awareness in all aspects of life.

S

Samadhi A state of meditative absorption and unity.

Sati A Pali term for mindfulness, emphasising awareness and memory of the present moment.

Satipatthana sutta A discourse by the Buddha on establishing mindfulness. A key Buddhist text describing the Four Foundations of mindfulness, serving as a basis for many contemporary mindfulness practices.

Secular mindfulness Mindfulness practices adapted for non-religious contexts.

Self-compassion Being kind to oneself during challenging times, a component of mindfulness.

Self-regulation of attention The ability to maintain focus on present experiences, a key aspect of mindfulness practice.

Self-transcendence A broader, more expansive view of self beyond identification with immediate personal concerns; may be cultivated deliberately as part of a meditative or spiritual practice, or may arise spontaneously e.g., nature connection.

Sitting practice A formal meditation involving attention to breath, sensations, and thoughts.

Smriti A Sanskrit term meaning "remembering," related to mindfulness in the sense of staying present and aware of one's experiences.

Somatic awareness The conscious awareness of bodily sensations, movements, and internal physical states.

Stress response system Biological processes regulated by the hypothalamus-pituitary-adrenal (HPA) axis, often moderated by mindfulness practices.

T

Tai Chi A Chinese martial art and meditative practice characterised by slow, intentional movements that promote balance and relaxation.

Tango A social dance originating in Argentina, emphasising connection, rhythm, and fluid movements.

Trait mindfulness A stable, inherent capacity to maintain mindfulness consistently across situations.

Transitory nature of thoughts The understanding that thoughts and emotions are fleeting and constantly changing, central to mindfulness practice.

V

Vedanā An ancient Sanskrit term that refers to the immediate, present moment feeling tone of either pleasant, unpleasant or neutral

The Vedas A large body of religious texts originating in ancient India. Composed in Vedic Sanskrit, the texts constitute the oldest layer of Sanskrit literature and the oldest scriptures of Hinduism.

Vipassana A Buddhist meditation practice emphasising insight and awareness.

Y

Yoga (lit. "yoke" or "union") A group of physical, mental, and spiritual practices or disciplines that originated in ancient India, aimed at controlling body and mind to attain various salvation goals, as practised in the Hindu, Jain, and Buddhist traditions.

Yoga nidra A meditative practice also known as yogic sleep, combining deep relaxation with mindfulness and awareness.

Z

Zazen A term that refers to sitting meditation within the Zen Buddhist tradition.

Zen A school of Mahayana Buddhism popular in Vietnam, Korea, and Japan, emphasising direct experience and meditation.

BIBLIOGRAPHY

Adler-Neal, A. L., & Zeidan, F. (2017). Mindfulness meditation for Fibromyalgia: Mechanistic and clinical considerations. *Current Rheumatology Reports, 19*(9). https://doi.org/10.1007/s11926-017-0686-0

Alvear, D., Soler, J., & Cebolla, A. (2022). Meditators' non-academic definition of mindfulness. *Mindfulness, 13*, 1544–1554.

American Psychological Association. (2012). *Psychology dictionary.* APA.

Anālayo, B. (2003). *Satipaṭṭhāna: The direct path to realization.* Windhorse Publications.

Anālayo, B. (2019). *Mindfulness of breathing: A practice guide and translations.* Windhorse Publications.

Anālayo, B. (2020). Buddhist antecedents to the body scan meditation. *Mindfulness, 11*, 194–202.

Arch, J. J., & Craske, M. G. (2006). Mechanisms of mindfulness: Emotion regulation following a focused breathing induction. *Behaviour Research and Therapy, 44*(12), 1849–1858. https://doi.org/10.1016/j.brat.2005.12.007

Bach, P., & Hayes, S.C. (2002). The use of acceptance and commitment therapy to prevent the rehospitalization of psychotic patients: A randomized controlled trial. *Journal of Consulting and Clinical Psychology, 70*(5), 1129–1139. https://doi.org/10.1037//0022-006x.70.5.1129

Baer, R. A. (2003). Mindfulness training as a clinical intervention: A conceptual and empirical review. *Clinical Psychology: Science and Practice, 10*(2), 125–143.

Baer, R. A., Smith, G. T., Hopkins, J., Krietemeyer, J., & Toney, L. (2006). Using self-report assessment methods to explore facets of mindfulness. *Assessment, 13*(1), 27–45.

Baer, R. A., Smith, G. T., Lykins, E., Button, D., Krietemeyer, J., Sauer, S., Walsh, E., Duggan, D., & Williams, J. M. (2008). Construct validity of the five-facet mindfulness questionnaire in meditating and nonmeditating samples. *Assessment, 15*(3), 329–42. https://doi.org/10.1177/1073191107313003

Baijal, S., Jha, A., Kiyonaga, A., Singh, R., & Srinivasan, N. (2011). The influence of concentrative meditation training on the development of attention networks during early adolescence. *Frontiers in Psychology, 2*, 153. https://doi.org/10.3389/fpsyg.2011.00153

Barnes, S., Brown, K. W., Krusemark, E., Campbell, W. K., & Rogge, R. D. (2007). The role of mindfulness in romantic relationship satisfaction and responses to relationship stress. *Journal of Marital and Family Therapy, 33*(4), 482–500.

Barnes, S. M., Scott, M. S., Aupperle, R. L., Le, T. T., Larson, C. L., & June, J. D. (2019). The effects of mindfulness training on cognitive and physiological processes in traumatic brain injury: A pilot randomized controlled trial. *Mindfulness, 10*(3), 489–499.

Barrett, B., Grabow, M., Middlecamp, C., Mooney, M., Checovich, M. M., Converse, A. K., Gillespie, B., & Yates, J. (2016). Mindful climate action: Health and environmental co-benefits from mindfulness-based behavioral training. *Sustainability, 8*, 1040. https://doi.org/10.3390/su8101040,

Bartholomew, E., Chung, M., Yeroushalmi, S., Hakimi, M., Bhutani, T., & Liao, W. (2022). Mindfulness and meditation for psoriasis: A systematic review. *Dermatology Therapy, 12*(10), 2273–2283. https://doi.org/10.1007/s13555-022-00802-1

Bartley, T. (2011). *Mindfulness-based cognitive therapy for cancer.* Wiley-Blackwell.

Bartley, T. (2016). *Mindfulness: A kindly approach to being with cancer.* Wiley-Blackwell.

Bartley, T., & Griffith, G. (2022). *Teaching mindfulness-based groups: The inside out group model.* Pavilion.

Baumeister, R. F., & Vohs, K. D. (Eds.). (2007). *Encyclopedia of social psychology* (pp. 484–485). SAGE Publications, Inc. https://doi.org/10.4135/9781412956253

Bautista, G. T., Cash, A., Meyerhoefer, T., & Pipe, T. (2022). Equitable mindfulness: The practice of mindfulness for all. *Journal of Community Psychology, 50*(7), 3141–3155. https://doi.org/10.1002/jcop.22821

Bechara, A., & Damasio, A. R. (2005). The somatic marker hypothesis: A neural theory of economic decision. *Games and Economic Behavior, 52*(2), 336–372.

Beck, A. T. (1979). *Cognitive therapy and the emotional disorders.* Penguin.

Becker, E. (1997). *The denial of death.* New York: Free Press

Benson, H. (1975). *The relaxation response.* HarperTorch.

Benson, H., & Klipper, M. (2000). *The relaxation response.* William Morrow & company.

Bernal, E., Edgar, D., & Burnes, B. (2018). Building sustainability on deep values through mindfulness nurturing. *Ecological Economics, 146*, 645–657. https://doi.org/10.1016/j.ecolecon.2017.12.003

Biegel, G. M., Brown, K. W., Shapiro, S. L., & Schubert, C. M. (2009). Mindfulness-based stress reduction for the treatment of adolescent psychiatric outpatients: A randomized clinical trial. *Journal of Consulting and Clinical Psychology*, 77(5), 855–866. https://doi.org/10.1037/a0016241

Biggers, A., Spears, C. A., Sanders, K., Ong, J., Sharp, L. K., & Gerber, B. S. (2020). Promoting mindfulness in African American communities. *Mindfulness*, 11(10), 2274–2282. https://doi.org/10.1007/s12671-020-01480-w

Birdee, G. S., Yeh, G. Y., Wayne, P. M., Phillips, R. S., Davis, R. B., & Gardiner, P. (2016). Clinical applications of yoga for the pediatric population: A systematic review. *Academic Pediatrics*, 16(1), 3–9. https://doi.org/10.1016/j.acap.2015.07.010

Birk, M. (2020). *Make mindfulness a habit*. https://hbr.org/2020/11/make-mindfulness-a-habit

Birnie, K., Speca, M., & Carlson, L. E. (2010). Exploring self-compassion and empathy in the context of Mindfulness-Based Stress Reduction (MBSR). *Stress and Health*, 26(5), 359–371.

Birrer, D., & Morgan, G. (2010). Psychological skills training as a way to enhance an athlete's performance in high-intensity sports. *Scandinavian Journal Medical Science Sports*, 20(2), 78–87. https://doi.org/10.1111/j.1600-0838.2010.01188.x

Bishop, S. R., Lau, M., Shapiro, S., Carlson, L., Anderson, N. D., Carmody, J., Segal, Z. V., Abbey, S., Speca, M., Velting, D., & Devins, G. (2004), Mindfulness: A proposed operational definition. *Clinical Psychology: Science and Practice*, 11, 230–241.

Black, D. S., & Slavich, G. M. (2016). Mindfulness meditation and the immune system: A systematic review of randomized controlled trials. *Annals of the New York Academy of Sciences*, 1373(1), 13–24.

Bohlmeijer, E., Prenger, R., Taal, E., & Cuijpers, P. (2010). The effects of mindfulness-based stress reduction on mental health of adults with a chronic medical disease: A meta-analysis. *Journal of Psychosomatic Research*, 68(6), 539–544.

Bowen, S., & Marlatt, G. A. (2009a). *Mindfulness-based relapse prevention for substance use disorders: A clinician's guide*. The Guilford Press.

Bowen, S., Chawla, N., Collins, S.E., Witkiewitz, K., Hsu, S., Grow, J., Clifasefi, S., Garner, M., Douglass, A., Larimer, M. E., & Marlatt, A. (2009b). Mindfulness-based relapse prevention for substance use disorders: A pilot efficacy trial. *Substance Abuse*, 30(4), 295–305. https://doi.org/10.1080/08897070903250084

Bowen, S., Witkiewitz, K., Clifasefi, S. L., Grow, J., Chawla, N., Hsu, S. H., & Larimer, M. E. (2014). Relative efficacy of mindfulness-based relapse prevention, standard relapse prevention, and treatment as usual for substance use disorders: A randomized clinical trial. *JAMA Psychiatry*, *71*(5), 547–556.

Bowles, N. I. & Van Dam, N. T. (2025). Dose–response effects of reported meditation practice on mental-health and wellbeing: A prospective longitudinal study. *Applied Psychology: Health and Well-Being*, *17*, 1–27. https://doi.org/10.1111/aphw.70063

Boyce, B. (2011). *The mindfulness revolution*. Shambala.

Boyce, B. (2019, April 3). The mindful politician: Why Tim Ryan is promoting mindfulness in Washington. *Mindful*. https://www.mindful .org/the-mindful-politician-why-tim-ryan-is-promoting-mindfulness -in-washington/

Britton W. B. (2019). Can mindfulness be too much of a good thing? The value of a middle way. *Current Opinion in Psychology*, *28*, 159–165. https:// doi.org/10.1016/j.copsyc.2018.12.011

Brown, F. J., & Hooper, S. (2009). Acceptance and Commitment Therapy (ACT) with a learning disabled young person experiencing anxious and obsessive thoughts. *Journal of Intellectual Disability*, *13*(3), 195–201. https:// doi.org/10.1177/1744629509346173

Brown, K. W., & Ryan, R. M. (2003). The benefits of being present: Mindfulness and its role in psychological well-being. *Journal of Personality and Social Psychology*, *84*(4), 822–848.

Brown, K. W., Ryan, R. M., & Creswell, J. D. (2007). Mindfulness: Theoretical foundations and evidence for its salutary effects. *Psychological Inquiry*, *18*(4), 211–237.

Browning, C. R. (2018). The suffocation of democracy. *The New York Review*. https://www.nybooks.com/articles/2018/10/25/suffocation-of-democracy/

Buchanan, R. (2002). *Feldenkrais method: The evolution of consciousness through movement*. North Atlantic Books.

Buchheld, N., Grossman, P., & Walach, H. (2001). Measuring mindfulness in insight meditation (Vipassana) and meditation-based psychotherapy: The development of the Freiburg Mindfulness Inventory (FMI). *Journal for Meditation and Meditation Research*, *1*, 11–34.

Burbea, R. (2014). *Seeing that frees: Meditations on emptiness and dependent arising*. Hermes Amara Publications.

Burch, P. (n.d.). Five reasons why mindfulness can help with pain management. https://www.breathworks-mindfulness.org.uk/Blog/5 -reasons-why-mindfulness-can-help-with-pain-management

Burch, V., & Penman, D. (2013). *Mindfulness for health*. Piatkus.

Burton, A., Burgess, C., Dean, S., Koutsopoulou, G. Z., & Hugh-Jones, S. (2017). How effective are mindfulness-based interventions for reducing stress among healthcare professionals? A systematic review and meta-analysis. *Stress Health*, *33*(1), 3–13. https://doi.org/10.1002/smi.2673

Carlson, L. E., Speca, M., Patel, K. D., & Goodey, E. (2003). Mindfulness-based stress reduction in relation to quality of life, mood, symptoms of stress, and immune parameters in breast and prostate cancer outpatients. *Psychosomatic Medicine*, *65*(4), 571–581. https://doi.org/10.1097/01.psy.0000074003.35911.41

Carmody, J. (2008). *Mindfulness-Based Stress Reduction (MBSR) and health benefits*. Springer.

Carmody, J., & Baer, R. A. (2008). Relationships between mindfulness practice and levels of mindfulness, medical and psychological symptoms and well-being in a mindfulness-based stress reduction program. *Journal of Behavioral Medicine*, *31*(1), 23–33.

Carson, F., Kuiper, J., O'Connor, M., & Carson, F. (2017). Mindfulness-based interventions for improving cognition, academic achievement, behaviour, and socioemotional functioning of primary and secondary students. *Campbell Systematic Reviews*, *13*(1), 1–78.

Carson, J. W., & Carson, K. M. (2004). *Mindful couple: Enhancing sexual intimacy, communication, and understanding*. CreateSpace Independent Publishing Platform.

Carson, J. W., Carson, K. M., Gil, K. M., & Baucom, D. H. (2017). Mindfulness-based relationship enhancement. *Behaviour Therapy*, *48*(1), 1–13.

Cassell, E. J. (2001). *The nature of suffering and the goals of medicine*. Oxford University Press.

Catholic Herald. (2019). https://catholicherald.co.uk/zen-meditation-and-mindfulness-are-not-christian-prayer-spanish-bishops-warn/

Cebolla, A., Campos, D., Galiana, L., Oliver, A., Tomás, J. M., Feliu-Soler, A., Soler, J., García-Campayo, J., Demarzo, M., & Baños, R. M. (2017). Exploring relations among mindfulness facets and various meditation practices: Do they work in different ways? *Conscious Cognition*, *49*, 172–180. https://doi.org/10.1016/j.concog.2017.01.012

Chadwick, P., Hember, M., Symes, J., Peters, E., Kuipers, E., & Dagnan, D. (2008). Responding mindfully to unpleasant thoughts and images: Reliability and validity of the Southampton Mindfulness Questionnaire (SMQ). *British Journal of Clinical Psychology*, *47*(4), 451–455. https://doi.org/10.1348/014466508X314891

Chaix, R., Fagny, M., Cosín-Tomàs, M., Alvarez-López, M. J., Lemee, L., Regnault, B., Davidson, R. J., Lutz, A., & Kaliman, P. (2020). Differential DNA methylation in experienced meditators after an intensive day of mindfulness-based practice: Implications for immune-related pathways. *Brain Behavior and Immunity*, *84*, 36–44. https://doi.org/10.1016/j.bbi.2019.11.003

Chatzisarantis, N. L., & Hagger, M. S. (2007). Mindfulness and the intention-behavior relationship within the theory of planned behavior. *Personality and Social Psychology Bulletin*, *33*(5), 663–676.

Chiesa, A., & Malinowski, P. (2011), Mindfulness-based approaches: Are they all the same? *Journal of Clinical Psychology, 67*, 404–424.

Chiesa, A., & Serretti, A. (2009). Mindfulness-based stress reduction for stress management in healthy people: A review and meta-analysis. *Journal of Alternative and Complementary Medicine, 15*(5), 593–600. https://doi.org /10.1089/acm.2008.0495

Chiodelli, R., Mello, L. T. N. de, Jesus, S. N. de, Beneton, E. R., Russel, T., & Andretta, I. (2022). Mindfulness-based interventions in undergraduate students: A systematic review. *Journal of American College Health, 70*(3), 791–800.

Chodron, P. (2019). *Welcoming the unwelcome: Wholehearted living in a brokenhearted world.* Shambhala Publications.

Christian News Journal. (2020). https://mindfulness-alliance.org/2020/10 /30/is-mindfulness-christian/

Chu, L. C. (2010). The benefits of meditation vis-à-vis emotional intelligence, perceived stress and negative mental health. *Stress and Health, 26*, 169–180.

Clear, J. (2018). *Atomic habits.* Random House.

Cohen, L. (2001). Boogie street [Song]. On *Ten New Songs.* Sony Music.

Colzato, L. S., Ozturk, A., & Hommel, B. (2012). Meditate to create: The impact of focused-attention and open-monitoring training on convergent and divergent thinking. *Frontiers in Psychology, 3*, 116.

Condon, P., Desbordes, G., Miller, W. B., & DeSteno, D. (2013). Meditation increases compassionate responses to suffering. *Psychological Science, 24*(10), 2125–2127.

Cramer, H., Lauche, R., Haller, H., Steckhan, N., Michalsen, A., & Dobos, G. (2014). Effects of yoga on cardiovascular disease risk factors: A systematic review and meta-analysis. *International Journal of Cardiology, 173*(2), 170–183.

Crane, R. S. (2017). *Mindfulness-based cognitive therapy: Distinctive features.* Routledge.

Crane, R. S., Brewer, J., Feldman, C., Kabat-Zinn, J., Santorelli, S., Williams, J. M., & Kuyken, W. (2017). What defines mindfulness-based programs? The warp and the weft. *Psychological Medicine, 47*(6), 990–999. https://doi.org/10.1017/S0033291716003317

Crane, R. S., Callen-Davies, R., Francis, A., Francis, D., Gibbs, P., Mulligan, B., O'Neill, B., Pierce Williams, N.K., Waupoose, M., & Vallejo, Z. (2023). Mindfulness-based stress reduction for our time: A curriculum that is up to the task. *Global Advances in Integrative Medicine and Health, 12,* 27536130231162604. https://doi.org/10.1177/27536130231162604

Crane, R. S., Eames, C., Kuyken, W., Hastings, R. P., Williams, J. M., Bartley, T., Evans, A., Silverton, S., Soulsby, J. G., & Surawy, C. (2013).

Development and validation of the Mindfulness-Based Interventions - Teaching Assessment Criteria (MBI:TAC). *Assessment*, *20*(6), 681–688. https://doi.org/10.1177/1073191113490790

Crane, R. S., Karunavira, & Griffith, G. M. (Eds.). (2021). *Essential resources for mindfulness teachers*. Routledge.

Creswell, J. D. (2017). Mindfulness interventions. *Annual Review of Psychology*, *68*, 491–516.

Creswell, J. D., Way, B. M., Eisenberger, N. I., & Lieberman, M. D. (2007). Neural correlates of dispositional mindfulness during affect labelling. *Psychosomatic Medicine*, *69*(6), 560–565.

Dane, E. (2011). Paying attention to mindfulness and its effects on task performance in the workplace. *Journal of Management*, *37*(4), 997–1018.

David T. W. (1995). *Dialogues of the Buddha: Digha-Nikaya: v. 1 (Sacred Books of the Buddhists)*. Pali Text Society.

Davidson, R. J., Kabat-Zinn, J., Schumacher, J., Rosenkranz, M. A., Muller, D., Santorelli, S. F., Urbanowski, F., Harrington, A., Bonus, K., & Sheridan, J. F. (2003). Alterations in brain and immune function produced by mindfulness meditation. *Psychosomatic Medicine*, *65*, 564–570. https://doi.org/10.1097/01.PSY.0000077505.67574.E3

Davidson, R. J., Jackson, D. C., & Kalin, N. H. (2000). Emotion, plasticity, context, and regulation: Perspectives from affective neuroscience.*Psychological Bulletin*, *126*, 890–909. https://doi.org/10.1037//0033-2909.126.6.890

De Bruin, E. J., Meijer, A., & Bögels, S. M. (2020). The contribution of a body scan mindfulness meditation to effectiveness of Internet-delivered CBT for insomnia in adolescents. *Mindfulness*, *11*(4), 872–882.

de Kwant, J. (2019). Attention is the new gold. *Flow Magazine, 38*.

Ditto, B., Eclache, M., & Goldman, N. (2006). Short-term autonomic and cardiovascular effects of mindfulness body scan meditation. *Annals of Behavioral Medicine*, *32*(3), 227–234.

Dreeben, S. J., Mamberg, M. H., & Salmon, P. (2013a). Mindfulness, pain, and analgesia: The promise of mindfulness-based stress reduction. *Annals of Behavioral Medicine*, *46*(2), 159–160.

Dreeben, S. J., Mamberg, M. H., & Salmon, P. (2013b). The MBSR body scan in clinical practice. *Mindfulness*, *4*(4), 394–401.

Dunbar, R. I., Baron, R., Frangou, A., Pearce, E., van Leeuwen, E. J. C., Stow, J., Partridge, G., MacDonald, I., Barra, V., & van Vugt, M. (2012). Social laughter is correlated with an elevated pain threshold. *Proceedings of Biological Sciences*, *279*(1731), 1161–1167. https://doi.org/10.1098/rspb.2011.1373

Dunn, E. W., Aknin, L. B., & Norton, M. I. (2008). Spending money on others promotes happiness. *Science*, *319*(5870), 1687–1688.

Dydyk, J. (2020). *Living beyond chronic pain: A holistic approach to manage and mitigate chronic pain.* Independently Published.

Einstein, A. (1954). *The World as I see it.* Philosophical Library.

Engler, J. (2003). Being somebody and being nobody: A reexamination of the understanding of self in psychoanalysis and Buddhism. In J. D. Safran (Ed.), *Psychoanalysis and Buddhism* (pp. 15–100). Wisdom Publications.

Epel, E., Daubenmier, J., Moskowitz, J. T., Folkman, S., & Blackburn, E. (2009). Can meditation slow rate of cellular aging? Cognitive stress, mindfulness, and telomeres. *Annals of the New York Academy of Sciences, 1172,* 34–53. https://doi.org/10.1111/j.1749-6632.2009.04414.x

Epstein, B. (2019). *Living in the presence: A Jewish mindfulness guide for everyday life.* Urim.

Epstein, R. M. (1999). Mindful practice. *JAMA, 282*(9), 833–839. https://doi.org/10.1001/jama.282.9.833

Epstein, R. M. (2017). *Attending: Medicine, mindfulness, and humanity.* Scribner.

Erisman, S. M., & Roemer, L. (2010). A preliminary investigation of the effects of experimentally induced mindfulness on emotional responding to film clips. *Emotion, 10*(1), 72–82. https://doi.org/10.1037/a0017162

Farb, N. A., Segal, Z. V., Mayberg, H., Bean, J., McKeon, D., Fatima, Z., & Anderson, A. K. (2007). Attending to the present: Mindfulness meditation reveals distinct neural modes of self-reference. *Social Cognitive and Affective Neuroscience, 2*(4), 313–322. https://doi.org/10.1093/scan/nsm030

Farb, N., & Segal, Z. (2024). *Better in every sense.* Hodder & Stoughton.

Feiner, J. (2021). *Mindfulness: A Jewish approach.* Mosaica Press.

Feldman, G., Hayes, A., Kumar, S., Greeson, J., & Laurenceau, J.-P. (2007). Mindfulness and emotion regulation: The development and initial validation of the Cognitive and Affective Mindfulness Scale-Revised (CAMS-R). *Journal of Psychopathology and Behavioral Assessment, 29,* 177–190.

Feuerstein, G. (2012). *The Yoga tradition: Its history, literature, philosophy, and practice.* Hohm Press.

Fischer, D. (2017). *The mindful day: How to find focus, calm, and joy from morning to evening.* National Geographic.

Fischer, D., Messner, M., & Pollatos, O. (2017). Improvement of interoceptive processes after an 8-week body scan intervention. *Frontiers in Human Neuroscience, 11,* 452. https://doi.org/10.3389/fnhum.2017.00452

Fischer, D., Stanszus, L., Geiger, S., Grossman, P., & Schrader, U. (2017). Mindfulness and sustainable consumption: A systematic literature review of research approaches and findings. *Journal of Cleaner Production, 162,* 544–558.

Fisher, M. (2022). *The Chaos machine: The inside story of how social media rewired our minds and our World.* Littel Brown and Company.

Flook, L., Goldberg, S. B., Pinger, L., & Davidson, R. J. (2015). Promoting prosocial behaviour and self-regulatory skills in preschool children through a mindfulness-based kindness curriculum. *Developmental Psychology, 51*(1), 44–51.

Fox, K. C. R. (2016). Functional neuroanatomy of meditation: A review and meta-analysis of 78 functional neuroimaging investigations. *Neuroscience Biobehavior Review, 65,* 208–228.

Gallwey, T. (2024). *The inner game of tennis.* Macmillan.

Gan, R., Zhang, L., & Chen, S. (2022). The effects of body scan meditation: A systematic review and meta-analysis. *Applied Psychology of Health and Well Being, 14*(3), 1062–1080. https://doi.org/10.1111/aphw.12366

Gard, T., Noggle, J. J., Park, C. L., Vago, D. R., & Wilson, A. (2014). Potential self-regulatory mechanisms of yoga for psychological health. *Frontiers in Human Neuroscience, 8,* 770. https://doi.org/10.3389/fnhum.2014.00770

Gardner, F. L., & Moore, Z. E. (2007). *The psychology of enhancing human performance: The Mindfulness-Acceptance-Commitment (MAC) approach.* Springer Publishing Company.

Gerritsen, J. (2018). *Mindfulness in positive psychology: The science of meditation and wellbeing.* Routledge.

Gethin, R. (1998). *The foundations of Buddhism.* Oxford University Press.

Gibson, J. (2019). Mindfulness, interoception, and the body: A contemporary perspective. *Frontiers in Psychology, 10,* 2012. https://doi.org/10.3389/fpsyg.2019.02012

Gilbert, P. (2010). *The compassionate mind.* Constable.

Gilbert, P., & Simos, G. (2022). *Compassion focused therapy: Clinical practice and applications.* Routledge.

Gilbert, P., Catarino, F., Duarte, C., Matos, M., Kolts, R., Stubbs, J., Ceresatto, L., Duarte, J., Pinto-Gouveia, J., & Basran, J. (2017). The development of compassionate engagement and action scales for self and others. *Journal of Compassionate Health Care, 4,* 4. https://doi.org/10.1186/s40639-017-0033-3

Giuntella, O., McManus, S., Mujcic, R., Oswald, A. J., Powdthavee, N., & Tohamy, A. (2023). The midlife crisis. *Economica, 90,* 65–110. https://doi.org/10.1111/ecca.12452

Goldberg, S. B., Knoeppel, C., Davidson, R. J., & Flook, L. (2020). Does practice quality mediate the relationship between practice time and outcome in mindfulness-based stress reduction? *Journal of Counseling Psychology, 67*(1), 115–122. https://doi.org/10.1037/cou0000369

Goldberg, S. B., Riordan, K. M., Sun, S., & Davidson, R. J. (2022). The empirical status of mindfulness-based interventions: A systematic review of 44 meta-analyses of randomized controlled trials. *Perspectives on Psychological Science, 17*(1), 108–130.

Goldberg, S. B., Tucker, R. P., Greene, P. A., Davidson, R. J., Wampold, B. E., Kearney, D. J., & Simpson, T. L. (2018). Mindfulness-based interventions for psychiatric disorders: A systematic review and meta-analysis. *Clinical Psychology Review, 59*, 52–60. https://doi.org/10.1016/j.cpr.2017.10.011

Goldin, P., & Gross, J. (2010). Effect of mindfulness meditation training on the neural bases of emotion regulation in social anxiety disorder. *Emotion, 10*(1), 83–84.

Goleman, D., & Davidson, R. J. (2017). *Altered traits: Science reveals how meditation changes your mind, brain, and body*. Avery.

Gotink, R. A., Meijboom, R., Vernooij, M. W., Smits, M., & Hunink, M. G. (2016). 8-week mindfulness based stress reduction induces brain changes similar to traditional long-term meditation practice - A systematic review. *Brain and Cognition, 108*, 32–41. https://doi.org/10.1016/j.bandc.2016.07.001

Goyal, M., Singh, S., Sibinga, E. M., Gould, N. F., Rowland-Seymour, A., Sharma, R., Berger, Z., Sleicher, D., Maron, D. D., Shihab, H. M., Ranasinghe, P. D., Linn, S., Saha, S., Bass, E. B., & Haythornthwaite, J. A. (2014). Meditation programs for psychological stress and well-being: A systematic review and meta-analysis. *JAMA Internal Medicine, 174*(3), 357–368. https://doi.org/10.1001/jamainternmed.2013.13018

Graham, B. (1991). *In the Dukkha magnet zone: An interview with Jon Kabat-Zinn*. Tricycle.

Graham, L. (2018). *Resilience: Powerful practices for bouncing back from disappointment, difficulty, and even disaster*. New World Library.

Greenberg, J., Pyszczynski, T., & Solomon, S. (1986). The causes and consequences of a need for self-esteem: A terror management theory. In R. F. Baumeister (Ed.), *Public self and private self* (pp. 189–212). New York: Springer.

Gregg, J. A., Callaghan, G. M., Hayes, S. C., & Glenn-Lawson, J. L. (2007). Improving diabetes self-management through acceptance, mindfulness, and values: A randomized controlled trial. *Journal of Consulting and Clinical Psychology, 75*(2), 336–843. https://doi.org/10.1037/0022-006X.75.2.336

Grossman, P. (2008). On measuring mindfulness in psychosomatic and psychological research. *Journal of Psychosomatic Research, 64*, 405–408.

Grossman, P., Niemann, L., Schmidt, S., & Walach, H. (2004). Mindfulness-based stress reduction and health benefits: A meta-analysis. *Journal of Psychosomatic Research, 57*(1), 35–43.

Gu, J., Strauss, C., Bond, R., & Cavanagh, K. (2015). How do mindfulness-based cognitive therapy and mindfulness-based stress reduction improve mental health and wellbeing? A systematic review and meta-analysis of meditation studies. *Clinical Psychology Review, 37*, 1–12.

Gunaratana, H. (2012). *The four foundations of mindfulness in plain English.* Simon and Schuster.

Hanh, T. N. (1991). *The miracle of mindfulness.* Rider.

Hanh, T. N. (1993) *Interbeing.* Parallax.

Halladay, J. E., Dawdy, J. L., & McNamara, B. (2015). Strengths-based mindfulness approaches: Viewing clients as active agents in the therapy process. *Journal of Humanistic Psychology, 56*(4), 411–432. https://doi.org/10.1177/0022167815594713

Hamilton, N. A., Kitzman, H., & Guyotte, S. (2006). Enhancing health and emotion: Mindfulness as a missing link between cognitive therapy and positive psychology. *Journal of Cognitive Psychotherapy, 20*(2), 123–134. https://doi.org/10.1891/jcop.20.2.123

Hardy, T. (1902). *De Profundis II.* Poems, past and present. MacMillan and Co. Ltd.

Hari, J. (2023). *Stolen focus.* Bloomsbury.

Harper, D. (2023). *A to Z of mindfulness for Christians.* Circle.

Harrington, A., & Dunne, J. D. (2015). When mindfulness is therapy: Ethical qualms, historical perspectives. *The American Psychologist, 70*(7), 621–631.

Hayes, S. C. (1991). A relational control theory of stimulus equivalence. In L. J. Hayes & P. N. Chase (Eds.), *Dialogues on verbal behavior* (pp. 19–40). Context Press.

Hayes, S. C., Barnes-Holmes, D., & Roche, B. (Eds.). (2001). *Relational frame theory: A Post-Skinnerian account of human language and cognition.* Plenum Press.

Hayes, S. C., & Smith, S. (2005). *Get out of your mind and into your life: The new acceptance and commitment therapy.* New Harbinger.

Helderman, I. (2019). *Prescribing the dharma: Psychotherapists, Buddhist traditions, and defining religion.* UNC Press Books.

Herrmann, T., Marchand, W. R., Yabko, B., Lackner, R., Beckstrom, J., & Parker, A. (2020). Veterans' interests, perceptions, and use of mindfulness. *SAGE Open Medicine, 31*, 2050312120938226. https://doi.org/10.1177/2050312120938226

Hilton, L., Hempel, S., Ewing, B. A., Apaydin, E., Xenakis, L., Newberry, S., & Maglione, M. A. (2017). Mindfulness meditation for chronic pain: Systematic review and meta-analysis. *Annals of Behavioral Medicine, 51*(2), 199–213.

Himelstein, S., Saul, S., Garcia-Romeu, A., & Pinedo, D. (2019). Mindfulness training in criminal justice settings: Recent findings and future directions. *Journal of Criminal Justice, 61*, 76–84.

Hinduism Today. (2019). https://www.hinduismtoday.com/magazine/oct-nov-dec-2019/publishers-desk-a-hindu-view-of-mindfulness/

Hoare, J. (2022). *Laughter Yoga for joy*. Independently Published.

Hodgins, H. S., & Adair, K. C. (2010). Attentional processes and meditation. *Consciousness and Cognition*, *19*(4), 872–878. https://doi.org/10.1016/j.concog.2010.04.002

Hölzel, B. K., Carmody, J., Vangel, M., Congleton, C., Yerramsetti, S. M., Gard, T., & Lazar, S. W. (2011a). Mindfulness practice leads to increases in regional brain gray matter density. *Psychiatry Research: Neuroimaging*, *191*(1), 36–43.

Hölzel, B. K., Lazar, S. W., Gard, T., Schuman-Olivier, Z., Vago, D. R., & Ott, U. (2011b). How does mindfulness meditation work? Proposing mechanisms of action from a conceptual and neural perspective. *Perspectives on Psychological Science: A Journal of the Association for Psychological Science*, *6*(6), 537–559. https://doi.org/10.1177/1745691611419671

Huang, T., Ding, D., Sallis, J. F., Foster, C., & Mavoa, S. (2020). Mindful movement in physical activity interventions: A systematic review. *BMC Public Health*, *20*, 145. https://doi.org/10.1186/s12889-020-8247-4

Hughes, J. W., Fresco, D. M., Myerscough, R., van Dulmen, M. H., Carlson, L. E., & Josephson, R. (2013). Randomized controlled trial of mindfulness-based stress reduction for prehypertension. *Psychosomatic Medicine*, *75*(8), 721–728.

Huppert, F. A., & Johnson, D. M. (2010). A controlled trial of mindfulness training in schools: The importance of practice for an impact on well-being. *The Journal of Positive Psychology*, *5*(4), 264–274.

Institute for Economics and Peace. (2023). *Global peace index 2023*. https://www.economicsandpeace.org/wp-content/uploads/2023/09/GPI-2023-Web.pdf

Internal Displacement Monitoring Centre. (2023). *2023 Global report on internal displacement*. https://www.internal-displacement.org/global-report/grid2023/

Irving, J. A., Dobkin, P. L., & Park, J. (2009). Cultivating mindfulness in health care professionals: A review of empirical studies of Mindfulness-Based Stress Reduction (MBSR). *Complementary Therapies in Clinical Practice*, *15*(2), 61–66.

ITV. (2023). https://www.itv.com/news/2023-11-06/brianna-gheys-mother-calls-for-mindfulness-in-schools-in-memory-of-daughter

James, W. (1890). *The principles of psychology* (Vol. 1). Henry Holt and Co. https://doi.org/10.1037/10538-000

Jahnke, R., Larkey, L., Rogers, C., Etnier, J., & Lin, F. (2010). A comprehensive review of health benefits of Qigong and Tai Chi. *American Journal of Health Promotion*, *24*(6), e1–e25.

Jain, S., Shapiro, S. L., Swanick, S., Roesch, S. C., Mills, P. J., Bell, I., & Schwartz, G. E. (2007). A randomized controlled trial of mindfulness meditation versus relaxation training: Effects on distress, positive states of mind, rumination, and distraction. *Annals of Behavioral Medicine, 33*(1), 11–21. https://doi.org/10.1207/s15324796abm3301_2

Jazaieri, H., Lee, I. A., McGonigal, K., Jinpa, T., Doty, J. R., Gross, J. J., & Goldin, P. R. (2016). A wandering mind is a less caring mind: Daily experience sampling during compassion meditation training. *Journal of Positive Psychology, 11*(1), 37–50. https://doi.org/10.1080/17439760.2015.1025418

Jennings, P. A., & Frank, J. L. (2013). Enhancing teachers' social and emotional competence: A randomized controlled trial of the CARE for Teachers program. *Developmental Psychology, 49*(3), 340–351.

Jenkinson, S. (2015). *Die Wise: A manifesto for sanity and soul.* North Atlantic Books.

Jha, A. P. (2021). *Peak mind.* Piatkus.

Jha, A. P., Krompinger, J., & Baime, M.J. (2007). Mindfulness training modifies subsystems of attention. *Cognitive Affective & Behavioral Neuroscience, 7*(2), 109–119. https://doi.org/10.3758/cabn.7.2.109

Jha, A. P., Rogers, S. L., & Morrison, A. B. (2014). Mindfulness training in high stress professions. In R. B. Baer (Ed.), *Mindfulness-based treatment approaches: Clinician's guide to evidence base and applications* (pp. 347–366). Academic Press Inc. https://doi.org/10.1016/B978-0-12-416031-6.00015-3

Jha, A. P., Stanley, E. A., Kiyonaga, A., Wong, L., & Gelfand, L. (2010). Examining the protective effects of mindfulness training on working memory capacity and affective experience. *Emotion, 10*(1), 54–64. https://doi.org/10.1037/a0018438

Johnson, D. C., Thom, N. J., Stanley, E. A., Haase, L., Simmons, A. N., Shih, P. A., & Paulus, M. P. (2016). Modifying resilience mechanisms in at-risk individuals: A controlled study of mindfulness training in Marines preparing for deployment. *American Journal of Psychiatry, 173*(9), 961–968.

Jones, F. (1998). *Freedom to change: The development and science of the Alexander technique.* Mouritz.

Joyce, J. (1914). *Dubliners.* Grant Richards Ltd.

Jung, C. J. (1968/2023). *Man and his symbols.* Bantam.

Kabat-Zinn, J. (1982). An outpatient program in behavioral medicine for chronic pain patients based on the practice of mindfulness meditation: Theoretical considerations and preliminary results. *General Hospital Psychiatry, 4*(1), 33–47.

Kabat-Zinn, J. (1992). *Further reflections on the clinical use of mindfulness meditation in the treatment of stress-related disorders. Psychological Inquiry, 3*(4), 267–274.

Kabat-Zinn, J. (1990). *Full catastrophe living: Using the wisdom of your body and mind to face stress, pain and illness.* Delacorte.

Kabat-Zinn, J. (1994). *Wherever you go, there you are: Mindfulness meditation in everyday life.* Hyperion.

Kabat-Zinn, J. (2003). Mindfulness-based interventions in context: Past, present, and future. *Clinical Psychology: Science and Practice, 10*(2), 144–156.

Kabat-Zinn, J. (2005). *Coming to our senses: Healing ourselves and the World through mindfulness.* Hachette.

Kabat-Zinn, J. (2006). *Mindfulness for beginners.* Sounds True.

Kabat-Zinn, J. (2009). *Wherever you go, there you are: Mindfulness meditation in everyday life.* Hachette Books.

Kabat-Zinn, J. (2011). Some reflections on the origins of MBSR, skillful means, and the trouble with maps. *Contemporary Buddhism, 12*(1), 281–306.

Kabat-Zinn, J. (2013). *Full catastrophe living, revised edition: How to cope with stress, pain and illness using mindfulness meditation.* Hachette.

Kabat-Zinn, J. (2018a). *The healing power of mindfulness: A new way of being.* Piatkus.

Kabat-Zinn, J. (2018b). *Falling awake.* Piatkus.

Kabat-Zinn, J. (2019). Foreword: Seeds of a necessary global renaissance in the making: The refining of psychology's understanding of the nature of mind, self, and embodiment through the lens of mindfulness and its origins at a key inflection point for the species. *Current Opinion in Psychology, 28*, xi–xvii.

Kabat-Zinn, J., Lipworth, L., & Burney, R. (1985). The clinical use of mindfulness meditation for the self-regulation of chronic pain. *Journal of Behavioral Medicine, 8*(2), 163–190.

Kabat-Zinn, J., Massion, A.O., Kristeller, J., Peterson, L., Fletcher, K., Pbert, L., Lenderking, W., & Santorelli, S. (1992). Effectiveness of a meditation-based stress reduction program in the treatment of anxiety disorders. *The American journal of psychiatry, 149*, 936–943. https://doi.org/10.1176/ajp.149.7.936

Kabat-Zinn, J., Wheeler, E., Light, T., Skillings, A., Scharf, M. J., Cropley, T. G., Hosmer, D., & Bernhard, J. D. (1998). Influence of a mindfulness meditation-based stress reduction intervention on rates of skin clearing in patients with moderate to severe psoriasis undergoing phototherapy (UVB) and photochemotherapy (PUVA). *Psychosomatic Medicine, 60*(5), 625–632. https://doi.org/10.1097/00006842-199809000-00020

Kang, Y., Gray, J. R., & Dovidio, J. F. (2013). The non-discriminating heart: Loving kindness meditation training decreases implicit intergroup bias. *Journal of Experimental Psychology: General, 142*(3), 1081–1086.

Karelse, C.-M. (2023). *Disrupting white mindfulness: Race and racism in the wellbeing industry.* Manchester University Press. https://doi.org/10.7765/9781526162069

Karunavira. (2021). Working the 'hard' and 'softer edges' in Chi Kung based mindful movement – practice. https://www.youtube.com/watch?v =QZKmNRQUy5g

Kastner, C. T. (2024). A lighthearted approach to mindfulness: Development and evaluation of a humor-enriched mindfulness-based program in a randomized trial. *Frontiers in Psychology, 14*, 1324329. https://doi.org/10 .3389/fpsyg.2023.1324329

Kearney, D. J., McDermott, K., Malte, C., Martinez, M., & Simpson, T. L. (2013). Association of participation in a mindfulness program with measures of PTSD, depression and quality of life in a veteran sample. *Journal of Clinical Psychology, 69*(1), 14–27.

Kemper, K. J., Mo, X., & Khayat, R. (2015). Are mindfulness and self-compassion associated with sleep and resilience in health professionals? *Journal of Alternative and Complementary Medicine, 21*(8), 496–503. https:// doi.org/10.1089/acm.2014.0281

Keng, S. L., Smoski, M. J., & Robins, C. J. (2011). Effects of mindfulness on psychological health: A review of empirical studies. *Clinical Psychology Review, 31*(6), 1041–1056. https://doi.org/10.1016/j.cpr.2011.04.006

Kessler, R. C., Aguilar-Gaxiola, S., Alonso, J., Benjet, C., Bromet, E. J., Cardoso, G., Degenhardt, L., de Girolamo, G., Dinolova, R. V., Ferry, F., Florescu, S., Gureje, O., Haro, J. M., Huang, Y., Karam, E. G., Kawakami, N., Lee, S., Lepine, J. P., Levinson, D., Navarro-Mateu, F., … Koenen, K. C. (2017). Trauma and PTSD in the WHO World Mental Health surveys. *European Journal of Psychotraumatology, 8*(Sup5), 1353383. https://doi.org/10.1080/20008198.2017.1353383

Khoury, B., Lecomte, T., Fortin, G., Masse, M., Therien, P., Bouchard, V., & Hofmann, S. G. (2013). Mindfulness-based therapy: A comprehensive meta-analysis. *Clinical Psychology Review, 33*(6), 763–771.

Kierkegaard, S. (1843/2014). *Fear and trembling.* Martino Fine Books.

Killingsworth, M., & Gilbert, D. (2010). A wandering mind is an unhappy mind. *Science, 330*, 932.

Kincade, S. (2023). https://www.mindandlife.org/media/the-global -refugee-crisis-how-can-mindfulness-compassion-training-help/

Klayman, J. (1995). Varieties of confirmation bias. *Psychology of Learning and Motivation, 32*, 385418.

Kraegel, I. (2020). *The mindful Christian.* Fortress Press.

Kral, T. R. A., Davis, K., Korponay, C., Hirshberg, M. J., Hoel, R., Tello, L. Y., Goldman, R. I., Rosenkranz, M. A., Lutz, A., & Davidson, R. J. (2022). Absence of structural brain changes from mindfulness-based stress reduction: Two combined randomized controlled trials. *Science Advances, 8*(20), eabk3316. https://doi.org/10.1126/sciadv.abk3316

Kral, T. R. A., Imhoff-Smith, T., Dean, D. C., Grupe, D., Adluru, N., Patsenko, E., Mumford, J. A., Goldman, R., Rosenkranz, M. A., & Davidson, R. J. (2019). Mindfulness-based stress reduction-related changes in posterior cingulate resting brain connectivity. *Social Cognitive and Affective Neuroscience, 14*(7), 777–787.

Kral, T. R. A., Schuyler, B. S., Mumford, J. A., Rosenkranz, M. A., Lutz, A., & Davidson, R. J. (2018). Impact of short- and long-term mindfulness meditation training on amygdala reactivity to emotional stimuli. *NeuroImage, 181,* 301–313. https://doi.org/10.1016/j.neuroimage.2018.07.013

Krasner, M. (2024). https://mindfulpracticeinmedicine.com/resources/

Kristeller, J. L., & Johnson, T. (2005). Cultivating loving kindness: A two-stage model of the effects of meditation on empathy, compassion and altruism. *Zygon, 40,* 391–408.

Kuyken, W., Ball, S., Crane, C., Ganguli, P., Jones, B., Montero-Marin, J., Nuthall, E., Raja, A., Taylor, L., Tudor, K., Viner, R. M., Allwood, M., Aukland, L., Dunning, D., Casey, T., Dalrymple, N., De Wilde, K., Farley, E.-R., Harper, J., … Williams, J. M. G. (2022). Effectiveness and cost-effectiveness of universal school-based mindfulness training compared with normal school provision in reducing risk of mental health problems and promoting well-being in adolescence: The MYRIAD cluster randomised controlled trial. *BMJ Mental Health, 25,* 99–109.

Kuyken, W., Warren, F. C., Taylor, R. S., Whalley, B., Crane, C., Bondolfi, G., Hayes, R., Huijbers, M., Ma, H., Schweizer, S., Segal, Z., Speckens, A., Teasdale, J. D., Van Heeringen, K., Williams, M., Byford, S., Byng, R., & Dalgleish, T. (2016). Efficacy of mindfulness-based cognitive therapy in prevention of depressive relapse: An individual patient data meta-analysis from randomized trials. *JAMA Psychiatry, 73*(6), 565–574. https://doi.org/10.1001/jamapsychiatry.2016.0076

Kuyken, W. (2024). *Mindfulness for life.* Guilford Press.

Langer, E. J. (1989). *Mindfulness.* Da Capo Press.

Langer, E. J., Bashner, R., & Chanowitz, B. (2014). Decreasing authoritarianism by increasing awareness of inconsistency. *Journal of Personality and Social Psychology, 12*(3), 218–222.

Lau, M. A., Bishop, S. R., Segal, Z. V., Buis, T., Anderson, N. D., Carlson, L., Shapiro, S., Carmody, J., Abbey, S., & Devins, G. (2006). The Toronto mindfulness scale: Development and validation. *Journal of Clinical Psychology, 62*(12), 1445–1467. https://doi.org/10.1002/jclp.20326

Lawrence, B. (1999). *Practice of presence of God.* Revell.

Lazar, S. W., Kerr, C. E., Wasserman, R. H., Gray, J. R., Greve, D. N., Treadway, M. T., McGarvey, M., Quinn, B. T., Dusek, J. A., Benson, H.,

Rauch, S. L., Moore, C. I., & Fischl, B. (2005). Meditation experience is associated with increased cortical thickness. *Neuroreport, 16*(17), 1893–1897. https://doi.org/10.1097/01.wnr.0000186598.66243.19

Legge, J. (2018). *Tao te ching.* Simon and Brown.

Leiberg, S., Klimecki, O., & Singer, T. (2011). Short-term compassion training increases prosocial behaviour in a newly developed prosocial game. *PLoS One, 6*(3), e17798.

Lengacher, C. A., Johnson-Mallard, V., Post-White, J., Moscoso, M. S., Jacobsen, P. B., Klein, T. W., Widen, R. H., Fitzgerald, S. G., Shelton, M. M., Barta, M., Goodman, M., Cox, C. E., & Kip, K. E.. (2009). Randomized controlled trial of Mindfulness-Based Stress Reduction (MBSR) for survivors of breast cancer. *Psycho-Oncology, 18*(12), 1261–1272.

Lengacher, C. A., Reich, R. R., Paterson, C. L., Ramesar, S., Park, J. Y., Alinat, C., & Johnson-Mallard, V. (2019) Examination of broad symptom improvement resulting from mindfulness-based stress reduction in breast cancer survivors: A randomized controlled trial. *Journal of Clinical Oncology, 37*(35), 3272–3282.

Linehan, M. (1993). *DBT skills training manual.* Guilford Press.

Linehan, M. (2014). *DBT skills training manual* (2nd ed.). Guilford Press.

Low, C. A., Stanton, A. L., & Bower, J. E. (2008). Effects of acceptance-oriented versus evaluative emotional processing on heart rate recovery and habituation. *Emotion, 8*(3), 419–24. https://doi.org/10.1037/1528-3542.8.3.419

Lu, H., & Telles, S. (2016). Interventions for improving performance on the Stroop test in normal subjects, and brain damaged patients. *Journal of Bodywork and Movement Therapies, 20*(4), 789–796. https://doi.org/10.1016/j.jbmt.2016.06.005

Lueke, A., & Gibson, B. (2014). Mindfulness meditation reduces implicit age and race bias: The role of reduced automaticity of responding. *Social Psycho-Logical and Personality Science, 5*(5), 522–530.

Magee, R. V. (2019). *The inner work of racial justice: Healing ourselves and transforming our communities through mindfulness.* TarcherPerigee.

Malarkey, W. B., Jarjoura, D., & Klatt, M. (2013). Workplace based mindfulness practice and inflammation: A randomized trial. *Brain, Behavior, and Immunity, 27*, 145–154.

Malhotra, R., & Viswanathan, V. (2022). *Snakes in the Ganga.* Occam BluOne Ink.

Mani, M., Kavanagh, D. J., Hides, L., & Stoyanov, S. R. (2015). Review and evaluation of mindfulness-based iPhone apps. *JMIR mHealth and uHealth, 3*(3), e82.

Marlatt, G. A., & Gordon, J. R. (1985). *Relapse prevention: Maintenance strategies in the treatment of addictive behaviors.* Guilford Press.

Mayer, J. D., & Salovey, P. (1997). What is emotional intelligence? In P. Salovey & D. J. Sluyter (Eds.), *Emotional development and emotional intelligence: Educational implications* (pp. 3–34). Basic Books.

McGilchrist, I. (2018). *Ways of attending: How our divided brain constructs the World*. Routledge.

McGilchrist, I. (2019). *The master and his emissary: The divided brain and the making of the western World*. Yale University Press.

McGilchrist, I. (2023). *The matter with things: Our brains, our delusions and the unmaking of the world*. Perspectiva.

McGonigal, K. (2015). *The upside of stress: Why stress is good for you and how to get good at it*. Vermilion.

Mehta, R., Sharma, K., Potters, L., Wernicke, A. G., & Parashar, B. (2019). Evidence for the role of mindfulness in cancer: Benefits and techniques. *Cureus, 11*(5), 1–13. https://doi.org/10.7759/cureus.4629

Menon, V. (2023). 20 years of the default mode network: A review and synthesis. *Neuron, 111*(16), 2469–2487.

Mirams, L., Poliakoff, E., Brown, R. J., & Lloyd, D. M. (2013). Brief body-scan meditation practice improves somatosensory perceptual decision making. *Consciousness and Cognition, 22*(1), 348–359.

Mishra, J. (2023). *Mindfulness and the climate crisis*. Mind & Life Institute. https://www.mindandlife.org/insight/mindfulness-and-the-climate-crisis/

Montero-Marin, J., Allwood, M., Ball, S., Crane, C., De Wilde, K., Hinze, V., Jones, B., Lord, L., Nuthall, E., Raja, A., Taylor, L., Tudor, K., MYRIAD Team, Blakemore, S. J., Byford, S., Dalgleish, T., Ford, T., Greenberg, M. T., Ukoumunne, O. C., Williams, J. M. G., … Kuyken, W. (2022). School-based mindfulness training in early adolescence: What works, for whom and how in the MYRIAD trial?. *Evidence-Based Mental Health, 25*(3), 117–124. Advance online publication. https://doi.org/10.1136/ebmental-2022-300439

Moore, A., & Malinowski, P. (2009). Meditation, mindfulness and cognitive flexibility. *Conscious Cognition, 18*(1), 176–186. https://doi.org/10.1016/j.concog.2008.12.008

Morrison, I., Björnsdotter, M., & Olausson, H. (2016). Vicarious responses to social touch in posterior insular cortex are tuned to pleasant caressing speeds. *Journal of Neuroscience, 36*(11), 2695–2701. https://doi.org/10.1523/JNEUROSCI.4171-15.2016

Moyers, B. [Producer/Director]. (1993). *Healing and the mind: Healing from within* [Film]. BillMoyers.com. https://billmoyers.com/content/healing-from-within/

Mumford, G. (2016). *The mindful athlete*. Parallax.

My, G. C. H. (2020). What are the origins of mindfulness? https://community.thriveglobal.com/what-are-the-origins-of-mindfulness/

Nakamura, T. (2013). *The way of Aikido: Life lessons from an American Sensei.* Kodansha International.

Nanthakwang, N., Siviroj, P., Matanasarawoot, A., Sapbamrer, R., Lerttrakarnnon, P., & Awiphan, R. (2020). Effectiveness of deep breathing and body scan meditation combined with music to improve sleep quality and quality of life in older adults. *The Open Public Health Journal, 13*(1), 232–239.

Neff, K. D., & Germer, C. K. (2013). A pilot study and randomized controlled trial of the mindful self-compassion program. *Journal of Clinical Psychology, 69*(1), 28–44.

Neff, K., & Germer, C. (2018). *The mindful self-compassion workbook: The proven way to accept yourself, build inner strength and thrive.* Guilford Press.

Ngomane, N. (2019). *Everyday Ubuntu.* Bantam Press.

Nice Guidance. (2022). https://www.nice.org.uk/guidance/ng222/chapter/recommendations#table-1)

Nielsen, L., & Kaszniak, A. W. (2006). Awareness of subtle emotional feelings: A comparison of long-term meditators and nonmeditators. *Emotion, 6*(3), 392–405.

Nietzsche, F. (1883). *Also sprach Zarathustra: ein buch fuer Alle und Keinen.* Ernst Schmeitzner.

Nisbet, M. C. (2017). The mindfulness movement: How a Buddhist practice evolved into a scientific approach to life. *Skeptical Inquirer, 41*(3), 24–26.

Nyanaponika, T. (1962). *The heart of Buddhist meditation.* Rider & Co.

Oliver, M. (1986). *Dream work.* Grove/Atlantic.

Oliver, M. (2004). *Wild Geese: Selected poems.* Bloodaxe Books.

Osincup, P. (2024). https://themighty.com/topic/chronic-illness/using-humor-coping-strategy-health

Parrish, D., & Maull, F. (2017). Research in brain science that indicates the efficacy of evidenced based mindfulness training as the basis of a future model for treatment in corrections. http://dx.doi.org/10.2139/ssrn.2904743

Parsons, C. E., Crane, C., Parsons, L. J., Fjorback, L. O., & Kuyken, W. (2017). Home practice in mindfulness-based cognitive therapy and mindfulness-based stress reduction: A systematic review and meta-analysis of participants' mindfulness practice and its association with outcomes. *Behaviour Research and Therapy, 95*, 29–41. https://doi.org/10.1016/j.brat.2017.05.004

Pellegrini, A. (2016). *Tango lessons: Movement, sound, image, and text in contemporary practice.* Oxford University Press.

Pilkington, K., Kirkwood, G., Rampes, H., & Richardson, J. (2005). Yoga for depression: The research evidence. *Journal of Affective Disorders, 89*(1–3), 13–24. https://doi.org/10.1016/j.jad.2005.08.013

Po, L. (1998). *The selected poems of Li Po* (D. Hinton, Trans.). Anvil Press Poetry.

Purser, R. (2019). *McMindfulness: How mindfulness became the new capitalist spirituality.* Repeater Books.

Raichle, M. E., MacLeod, A. M., Snyder, A. Z., Powers, W. J., Gusnard, D. A., & Shulman, G. L. (2001). A default mode of brain function. *Proceedings of the National Academy of Sciences of the United States of America, 98*(2), 676–682. https://doi.org/10.1073/pnas.98.2.676

Rilke, R. M. (1903/2012). *Letters to a young poet.* Penguin Classics.

Roemer, L., Williston, S. K., & Rollins, L. G. (2015). Mindfulness and acceptance-based behavioural therapies for anxiety disorders. In B. D. Ostafin, B. P. Meier, & M. D. Robinson (Editor), *Handbook of mindfulness and self-regulation* (pp. 283–302). Springer.

Roeser, R. W., Schonert-Reichl, K. A., Jha, A., Cullen, M., Wallace, L., Wilensky, R., Oberle, E., Thomson, K., Taylor, C., & Harrison, J. (2013). Mindfulness training and reductions in teacher stress and burnout: Results from two randomized, waitlist-control field trials. *Journal of Educational Psychology, 105*(3), 787–804.

Rogers, H., & Maytan, M. (2019). *Mindfulness for the next generation: Helping emerging adults manage stress and lead healthier lives* (2nd ed.). Oxford University Press.

Rosenkranz, M. A., Dunne, J. D., & Davidson, R. J. (2019). The next generation of mindfulness-based intervention research: What have we learned and where are we headed? *Current Opinion in Psychology, 28*, 179–183. https://doi.org/10.1016/j.codoipsyc.2018.12.022

Rusch, H. L., Rosario, M., Levison, L. M., Olivera, A., Livingston, W. S., Wu, T., & Gill, J. M. (2019). The effect of mindfulness meditation on sleep quality: A systematic review and meta-analysis of randomized controlled trials. *Annals of the New York Academy of Sciences, 1445*(1), 5–16. https://doi.org/10.1111/nyas.13996

Saad, L. F. (2020). *Me and white supremacy: Combat racism, change the world, and become a good ancestor.* Sourcebooks.

Samuelson, M., Carmody, J., Kabat-Zinn, J., & Bratt, M. (2017). Mindfulness-based stress reduction in Massachusetts correctional facilities. *The Prison Journal, 97*(3), 325–343.

Santorelli, S., & Kabat-Zinn, J. (2013). *Mindfulness-based stress reduction professional education and training.* Center for Mindfulness in Medicine, Health Care, and Society, University of Massachusetts Medical School.

Santorelli, S. F., Kabat-Zinn, J., Blacker, M., Meleo-Meyer, F., & Koerbel, L. (2017). *Mindfulness-Based Stress Reduction (MBSR) authorized curriculum guide.* Center for mindfulness in medicine, health care, and society (CFM). University of Massachusetts Medical School.

Saper, R. B., Lemaster, C., Delitto, A., Sherman, K. J., Herman, P. M., Sadikova, E., Stevans, J., Keosaian, J. E., Cerrada, C. J., Femia, A. L., Roseen, E. J., Gardiner, P., Gergen Barnett, K., Faulkner, C., & Weinberg, J. (2017). Yoga, physical therapy, or education for chronic low back pain: A randomized noninferiority trial. *Annals of Internal Medicine*, *167*(2), 85–94. https://doi.org/10.7326/M16-2579

Saunders, C. (1990). *Hospice and palliative care: An interdisciplinary approach*. Hodder Arnold.

Schmachtenberger, D. (2023, September 20). *Daniel Schmachtenberger: An introduction to the metacrisis* [Video]. Youtube. https://www.youtube.com/watch?v=4kBoLVvoqVY&t=1244s

Schultchen, D. (2019). *Mindfulness-based stress reduction for teens*. New Harbinger Publications.

Schultchen, D., Messner, M., Karabatsiakis, A., Schillings, C., & Pollatos, O. (2019a). Effects of an 8-week body scan intervention on individually perceived psychological stress and related steroid hormones in hair. *Mindfulness*, *10*(12), 2532–2543. https://doi.org/10.1007/s12671-019-01222-7

Schultchen, D., Reichenberger, J., Mittl, T., Weh, T. R. M., Smyth, J. M., Blechert, J., & Pollatos, O. (2019b). Bidirectional relationship of stress and affect with physical activity and healthy eating. *British Journal of Health Psychology*, *24*(2), 315–333. https://doi.org/10.1111/bjhp.12355

Sec. Movement Science Volume 14 - 2023.

Segal, Z. V., Williams, J. M. G., & Teasdale, J. D. (2002). *Mindfulness-based cognitive therapy for depression: A new approach to preventing relapse*. The Guilford Press.

Segal, Z. V., Williams, J. M. G., & Teasdale, J. D. (2013). *Mindfulness-based cognitive therapy for depression* (2nd ed.). The Guilford Press.

Shannon, D. (2021). *"Eternity in an hour ...": Exploring the role of mindfulness with patients receiving palliative care: An interpretative phenomenological analysis* (Doctoral thesis). London Metropolitan University.

Shapiro, S. L., Brown, K. W., & Biegel, G. M. (2007). Teaching self-care to caregivers: Effects of mindfulness-based stress reduction on the mental health of therapists in training. *Training and Education in Professional Psychology*, *1*(2), 105–115.

Shapiro, S. L., Carlson, L. E., Astin, J. A., & Freedman, B. (2006). Mechanisms of mindfulness. *Journal of Clinical Psychology*, *62*(3), 373–386. https://doi.org/10.1002/jclp.20237

Shapiro, P., Lebeau, R., & Tobia, A. (2019). Mindfulness meditation for medical students: A student-led initiative to expose medical students to mindfulness practices. *Medical Science Educator*, *29*(2), 439–451. https://doi.org/10.1007/s40670-019-00708-2

Siegel, D. (2010). *The mindful therapist: A clinician's guide to mindsight and neural integration.* W. W. Norton & Company.

Simon, H. (1971). Designing organizations for an information rich world. In M. Greenberger (Ed.), *Computers, communications and the public interest.* The Johns Hopkins Press.

Singleton, M. (2010). *Yoga body: The origins of modern posture practice.* Oxford University Press

Skipper, C. (2018). https://www.gq.com/story/yuval-noah-harari-tech-future-survival

Slagter, H. A., Lutz, A., Greischar, L. L., Francis, A. D., Nieuwenhuis, S., Davis, J. M., & Davidson, R. J. (2007). Mental training affects distribution of limited brain resources. *PLoS Biology, 5*(6), e138. https://doi.org/10.1371/journal.pbio.0050138

Smith, B. W., Ortiz, J. A., Steffen, L. E., Tooley, E. M., Wiggins, K. T., Yeater, E. A., & Bernard, M. L. (2011). Mindfulness is associated with fewer PTSD symptoms, depressive symptoms, physical symptoms, and alcohol problems in urban firefighters. *Journal of Consulting and Clinical Psychology, 79*(5), 613–617.

Solberg, E. E., Berglund, K. A., Engen, O., Ekeberg, Ø., & Loeb, M. (2019). Mindfulness-Based Stress Reduction (MBSR) in elite athletes: A controlled pilot study. *Cognitive Behaviour Therapy, 48*(3), 226–234.

Solomon, S., Greenberg, J., & Pyszczynski, T. (2015). *The worm at the core: On the role of death in life.* Random House.

Spaccapanico Proietti, S., Chiavarini, M., Iorio, F., Buratta, L., Pocetta, G., Carestia, R., Gobbetti, C., Lupi, C., Cosenza, A., Sorci, G., Mazzeschi, C., Biscarini, A., & de Waure, C. (2024). The role of a mindful movement-based program (Movimento Biologico) in health promotion: Results of a pre-post intervention study. *Frontiers in Public Health, 11*(12), 1372660. https://doi.org/10.3389/fpubh.2024.1372660

Stahl, B., & Goldstein, E. (2010). *A mindfulness based stress reduction workbook.* New Harbinger Publications.

Stanley, S. (2012). Mindfulness: Towards a critical relational perspective. *Social and Personality Psychology Compass, 6*, 631–641.

Stanley, S., Barker, M., Edwards, V., & McEwen, E. (2015). Swimming against the Stream?: Mindfulness as a psychosocial research methodology. *Qualitative Research in Psychology, 12*(1), 61–76.

Stanley, T. (2021). *Radiant rest.* Shambala Publications.

Sundquist, J., Lilja, Å., Palmér, K., Memon, A. A., Wang, X., Johansson, L. M., & Sundquist, K. (2015). Mindfulness group therapy in primary care patients with depression, anxiety and stress and adjustment disorders: Randomised controlled trial. *British Journal of Psychiatry, 206*(2), 128–135. https://doi.org/10.1192/bjp.bp.114.150243

Tan, C.-M. (2013) *Search inside yourself.* Harpercollins.

Tang, Y. Y., Tang, R., & Posner, M. I. (2015). Mindfulness meditation improves emotion regulation and reduces drug abuse. *Drug and Alcohol Dependence, 163,* S13–S18.

Taren, A. A., Gianaros, P. J., Greco, C. M., Lindsay, E. K., Fairgrieve, A., Brown, K. W., Rosen, R. K., Ferris, J. L., Julson, E., Marsland, A. L., Bursley, J. K., Ramsburg, J., & Creswell, J. D. (2015). Mindfulness meditation training alters stress-related amygdala resting state functional connectivity: A randomized controlled trial. *Social Cognitive and Affective Neuroscience, 10*(12), 1758–1768. https://doi.org/10.1093/scan/nsv066

Tassi, P., López-Gajardo, M. A., Leo, F. M., Díaz-García, J., & García-Calvo, T. (2023). An intervention program based on team building during tactical training tasks to improve team functioning. *Frontiers in Psychology, 14,* 1065323. https://doi.org/10.3389/fpsyg.2023.1065323

Teasdale, J. D. (2022). *What happens in mindfulness: Inner awakening and embodied cognition.* The Guilford Press.

Teasdale, J. D., & Barnard, P. J. (1993). *Affect, cognition, and change: Re-modelling depressive thought.* Lawrence Erlbaum Associates.

Teasdale, J. D., & Chaskalson, M. (2013a). How does mindfulness transform suffering? I: The nature and origins of dukkha. In J. M. Williams & J. Kabat-Zinn (Editor), *Mindfulness: Diverse perspectives on its meaning, origins and applications* (pp. 89–102). Routledge.

Teasdale, J. D., & Chaskalson, M. (2013b). How does mindfulness transform suffering? II: The transformation of dukkha. In J. M. Williams & J. Kabat-Zinn (Editor), *Mindfulness: Diverse perspectives on its meaning, origins and applications* (pp. 103–124). Routledge.

Teasdale, J. D., Segal, Z. V., Williams, J. M., Ridgeway, V. A., Soulsby, J. M., & Lau, M. A. (2000). Prevention of relapse/recurrence in major depression by mindfulness-based cognitive therapy. *Journal of Consulting and Clinical Psychology, 68*(4), 615–623. https://doi.org/10.1037//0022-006x.68.4.615

Teasdale, J. D., Williams, J. M., & Segal, Z. V. (2014). *The mindful way workbook.* The Guilford Press.

Telch, C. F., Agras, W. S., & Linehan, M. M. (2001). Dialectical behavior therapy for binge eating disorder. *Journal of Consulting and Clinical Psychology, 69*(6), 1061.

Thanissaro, B. (1994). Kalama Sutta: To the Kalamas. https://www.accesstoinsight.org/tipitaka/an/an03/an03.065.than.html

Thanissaro, B. (1997). Sallatha Sutta: The Arrow. https://www.accesstoinsight.org/ati/tipitaka/sn/sn36/sn36.006.than.html

The Guardian. (2017). https://www.theguardian.com/lifeandstyle/2017/oct/22/mindfulness-jon-kabat-zinn-depression-trump-grenfell?CMP=share_btn_fb

Thera, N., & Bodhi, B. (Trans.). (2010). *Anguttara nikaya: Discourses of the Buddha, an anthology, part I*. Buddhist Publication Society.

Thoreau, H. D. (1854). Walden; or, Life in the woods [In *Sounds, Para. 2*]. Ticknor and Fields.

Tippett, K. (Host). (2008, February 28). John O'Donohue: The inner landscape of beauty. In *On Being with Krista Tippett*. On Being. https://onbeing.org/programs/john-odonohue-the-inner-landscape-of-beauty

Treleaven, D. A. (2018). *Trauma-sensitive mindfulness: Practices for safe and transformative healing*. W. W. Norton & Company.

Trousselard, M., Steiler, D., Claverie, D., & Canini, F. (2014). L'histoire de la Mindfulness à l'épreuve des données actuelles de la littérature: questions en suspens [The history of Mindfulness put to the test of current scientific data: Unresolved questions]. *Encephale, 40*(6), 474–480. https://doi.org/10.1016/j.encep.2014.08.006

Tuckman, B. (1965). Development sequences in small groups. *Psychol Bulletin, 63*, 384–399.

U Ba Khin, S. (1997). *The essentials of Buddha-Dhamma in meditative practice*. Pariyatti.

Ussher, J. (2014). *Mindfulness-based cognitive therapy for chronic pain*. Wiley.

Ussher, M., Cropley, M., Playle, S., Mohidin, R., & West, R. (2009). Effect of isometric exercise and body scanning on cigarette cravings and withdrawal symptoms. *Addiction, 104*, 1251–1257.

Ussher, M., Spatz, A., Copland, C., Nicolaou, A., Cargill, A., Amini-Tabrizi, N., & McCracken, L. M. (2014). Immediate effects of a brief mindfulness-based body scan on patients with chronic pain. *Journal of Behavioral Medicine, 37*(1), 127–134. https://doi.org/10.1007/s10865-012-9466-5

Vago, D. R., & Silbersweig, D. A. (2012). Self-awareness, self-regulation, and self-transcendence (S-ART): A framework for understanding the neurobiological mechanisms of mindfulness. *Frontiers in Human Neuroscience, 6*, 296. https://doi.org/10.3389/fnhum.2012.00296

Van Dam, N. T., van Vugt, M. K., Vago, D. R., Schmalzl, L., Saron, C. D., Olendzki, A., Meissner, T., Lazar, S. W., Kerr, C. E., Gorchov, J., Fox, K. C. R., Field, B. A., Britton, W. B., Brefczynski-Lewis, J. A., & Meyer, D. E. (2018). Mind the hype: A critical evaluation and prescriptive agenda for research on mindfulness and meditation. *Perspectives in Psychological Science, 13*(1), 36–61. https://doi.org/10.1177/1745691617709589

Van den Hurk, P. A., Giommi, F., Gielen, S. C., Speckens, A. E., & Barendregt, H. P. (2010). Greater efficiency in attentional processing related to mindfulness meditation. *Quarterly Journal of Experimental Psychology, 63*(6), 1168–1180. https://doi.org/10.1080/17470210903249365

Van der Kolk, B. (2014). *The body keeps the score*. Allen Lane.

Van Gordon, W., Shonin, E., Griffiths, M. D., & Singh, N. N. (2015). There is only one mindfulness: Why science and Buddhism need to work together. *Mindfulness, 6*(1), 49–56.

Veehof, M. M., Trompetter, H. R., Bohlmeijer, E. T., & Schreurs, K. M. G. (2016). Acceptance- and mindfulness-based interventions for the treatment of chronic pain: A meta-analytic review. *Cognitive Behaviour Therapy, 45*(1), 5–31. https://doi.org/10.1080/16506073.2015.1098724

Vipassana Research Institute. (n.d.). Sagyagyi U Ba Khin. Retrieved November 18, 2021.

Vox. (2023). https://www.vox.com/the-gray-area/23999825/mindfulness-meditation-jon-kabat-zinn-the-gray-area

Wachs, K., & Cordova, J. V. (2007). Mindful relating: Exploring mindfulness and emotion repertoires in intimate relationships. *Journal of Marital and Family Therapy, 33*(4), 464–481.

Wallace, B. A. (2002). The Spectrum of Buddhist practice in the west. In C. S. Prebish & M. Baumann (Eds.), *Westward Dharma: Buddhism beyond Asia* (pp. 34–50). University of California Press.

Wallace, B. A., & Shapiro, S. L. (2006). Mental balance and well-being: Building bridges between Buddhism and Western psychology. *American Psychologist, 61*(7), 690–701. https://doi.org/10.1037/0003-066X.61.7.690

Wason, P. (1960). On the failure to eliminate hypotheses in a conceptual task. *Quarterly Journal of Experimental Psychology, 12*, 129–140.

Webb, C. A., Hirshberg, M. J., Gonzalez, O., Davidson, R. J., & Goldberg, S. B. (2024). Revealing subgroup-specific mechanisms of change via moderated mediation: A meditation intervention example. *Journal of Consulting and Clinical Psychology, 92*(1), 44–53. https://doi.org/10.1037/ccp0000842

Wilber, K. (1991). *Grace and grit: Spirituality and healing in the life and death of Treya Killam Wilber.* Shambhala.

Wilber, K. (1998). *The essential Ken Wilber.* Shambhala.

Williams, J. M. (2010). Mindfulness and psychological process. *Emotion, 10*(1), 1–7. https://doi.org/10.1037/a0018360

Williams, J. M. G., & Kabat-Zinn, J. (Eds.). (2011). Mindfulness: Diverse perspectives on its meaning, origins, and multiple applications at the intersection of science and dharma. *Contemporary Buddhism, 12*(1), 1–18.

Williams, M., & Penman, D. (2011). *Mindfulness: A practical guide to finding peace in a frantic World.* Piatkus.

Williams, M., & Penman, D. (2023). *Deeper mindfulness.* Piatkus.

Williams, M., Teasdale, J., Segal, Z., & Kabat-Zinn, J. (2024). *The mindful way through depression, freeing yourself from chronic unhappiness* (2nd ed.). Guilford Press.

Wilson, J. (2014). *Mindful America: Meditation and the mutual transformation of Buddhism and American culture.* Oxford University Press.

Winfry, O. (2017). *How mindfulness can be a gateway to joy.* OWN. https://www.oprah.com/own-super-soul-sunday/oprah-and-jon-kabat-zinn-how-mindfulness-can-be-a-gateway-to-joy

Witkiewitz, K., & Bowen, S. (2010). Depression, craving, and substance use following a randomized trial of mindfulness-based relapse prevention. *Journal of Consulting and Clinical Psychology, 78*(3), 362–374.

Wongtongkam, N., Krivokapic-Skoko, B., Duncan, R., & Bellio, M. (2017). The influence of a mindfulness-based intervention on job satisfaction and work-related stress and anxiety. *International Journal of Mental Health Promotion, 19*(3), 134–143.

Wood, A. M., Froh, J. J., & Geraghty, A. W. (2010). Gratitude and well-being: A review and theoretical integration. *Clinical Psychology Review, 30*(7), 890–905.

Yalom, I. D. (1980). *Existential psychotherapy.* Basic Books.

Zanesco, A. (2018). *The science of meditation: How to change your brain, mind and body.* Norton & Company.

Zanesco, A. P., King, B. G., MacLean, K. A., & Saron, C. D. (2018). Cognitive aging and long-term maintenance of attentional improvements following meditation training. *Journal of Cognitive Enhancement, 2*(3), 259–275. https://doi.org/10.1007/s41465-018-0068-1

Zeidan, F., Grant, J. A., Brown, C. A., McHaffie, J. G., & Coghill, R. C. (2012). Mindfulness meditation-related pain relief: Evidence for unique brain mechanisms in the regulation of pain. *Neuroscience Letters, 520*(2), 165–173.

Zenner, C., Herrnleben-Kurz, S., & Walach, H. (2014). Mindfulness-based interventions in schools—a systematic review and meta-analysis. *Frontiers in Psychology, 5,* 603.

Zoogman, S., Goldberg, S. B., Hoyt, W. T., & Miller, L. (2015). Mindfulness interventions with youth: A meta-analysis. *Mindfulness, 6*(2), 290–302.

Zou, L., Sasaki, J. E., Wei, G. X., Huang, T., Yeung, A. S., Neto, O. B., & Hui, S. S. (2018). Effects of mind–body exercises (Tai Chi/Yoga) on heart rate variability parameters and perceived stress: A systematic review with meta-analysis of randomized controlled trials. *Journal of Clinical Medicine, 7*(11), 404. https://doi.org/10.3390/jcm7110404

INDEX

For Product Safety Concerns and Information please contact our EU
representative GPSR@taylorandfrancis.com
Taylor & Francis Verlag GmbH, Kaufingerstraße 24, 80331 München, Germany